WITHDRAWN

TOUR
of
DUTY

John
Dos Passos

DECORATIONS BY HOWARD BAER

TOUR

of

DUTY

GREENWOOD PRESS, PUBLISHERS
WESTPORT, CONNECTICUT

Library of Congress Cataloging in Publication Data

Dos Passos, John, 1896-1970.
  Tour of duty.

  Reprint of the ed. published by Houghton Mifflin,
Boston.
  1. World War, 1939-1945--Personal narratives,
American. 2. Dos Passos, John, 1896-1970. 3. World
War, 1939-1945--Pacific Ocean. 4. Germany--History--
Allied occupation, 1945-   I. Title.
D811.5.D64 1974   940.54'26'0924 [B]   73-17919
ISBN 0-8371-7279-9

Acknowledgments

Grateful acknowledgment is made to *Life Magazine* for permission to reprint seven articles and to *The New Leader* for the use of some of the additional material included in this book.

Originally published in 1946 by Houghton Mifflin Company, Boston

Reprinted with the permission of Mrs. John Dos Passos

Reprinted in 1974 by Greenwood Press, a division of Williamhouse-Regency Inc.

Library of Congress Catalog Card Number 73-17919

ISBN 0-8371-7279-9

Printed in the United States of America

Contents

PART ONE

The Atolls and the Ships

1

The Islands

Waikiki

THE SUN HAD SET. Among the broadleaved trees that overhung the beach in front of my room, a bunch of myna birds kept up an impudent cackling and whistling. In the coconut palms overhead doves were gloomily cooing. From the bungalow in back came a sound of young men's and young women's voices and the clink of ice in a shaker. Looking down into the lighted window I could make out groups of legs in suntans, light dresses, and a corner of a Christmas tree.

While I was finishing packing, my phone rang. A serious youthful voice told me my flight was delayed. My transportation would call for me at twenty-thirty instead of eighteen-thirty.

The voices in the bungalow began to sing 'Holy Night.' Outside, the sky was swelling huge with the last dusk. A light blinked from the bridge of a destroyer escort proceeding in indigo silhouette along the edge of the indigo ocean beyond the pale fringe of reef. It was lonesome waiting in the narrow room full of the muffled whistles of the birds settling into their roosts and the voices of people I didn't know singing Christmas songs under the Southern sky.

Walking up and down, I was remembering the takeoff from San Francisco two weeks before. It had been an unusually warm afternoon for December. There had been a wait in a stuffy office in the Federal Building under a clock that kept up a loud portentous ticking. The secrecy about the time of departure, the getting into uniform, the drop into the groove of military routine, had given me the feeling of sinking back through the intervening quarter of a century into the earlier war. The years between had begun to seem misty and dreamlike. I was picking up a thread dropped that July afternoon of wan French sunlight when I walked out of headquarters in Tours with my discharge in my pocket.

Everything I looked at on the long bus trip over to Oakland had taken on the etched significance of scenes remembered from childhood: the empty and listlessly youthful face of the sailor at the wheel, the groups of small black ducks that dove and stood up to flap their wings just at the edge of the fog on the oily surface of the bay, the intent stance of a Mexican Boy Scout in a white Sam Browne belt who was marshaling a group of school-children at an intersection, the sappy father look on the red countenance beaded with sweat of the fat cop who lifted his arm to stop the traffic and let the children pass, the houses of Oakland swimming past vague in the sunny haze as if already far away.

The mist hardened into blocks of square gray warehouses that glowed a little on the side toward the sun. We crossed sedgy salt flats, a golf course crowded with gulls, the tumbled débris of a city dump. Then with dramatic suddenness we had come rumbling out onto the great flat expanses between ranked planes of the airport.

Our flight had been postponed from hour to hour. The passengers sat drowsing in easy-chairs in the wardroom upstairs in the passenger terminal. Beside me two young naval officers talked low over their pipes.

'It's the size of it,' one said in a whisper creaky with earnestness. 'It's all wet. It's all ours. But now what?'

'We finish up the Nips and then we hold the island bases. We gotta do that,' the other said. He had a plausible lecturer's voice.

'I know, but now what?'

'We take Hirohito to pieces to see what makes him tick.'

'Sure we will. But now what?'

'Then we all go home and marry the pinup girl.'

'Okay, we're home . . . Now what?' the man's voice rose.

Then they had noticed I was listening. I let my eyelids drop back over my eyes, but too late. Their mouths closed like traps. A lighter clicked as one of them relit his pipe. Across the room somebody snored on the windowseat.

When at last we had settled into our seats on the plane, almost immediately the roar of four motors became the cushion of sleep. Morning came fast. The Pacific Ocean showed wrinkled and dark and boundaryless under a white dapple of clouds. The sun shone on us as we rode across billows and billows of bright cotton. Then scud overhead and a cold oyster-colored floor below. Then streaks of tinfoil sea melting into immense sunny ocean with the blue bloom of a plum on it. To the west a white cloud range topped by tossing plumes of cumulus barring the way. The plane plunged into it with a hiss of rain against metal. The clouds pressed tight against the windows. The plane bucked, shaking in the choppy air currents, to bore through into a pale still sunless world of frozen cloud shapes.

Then half a day later a cloud to the southwest had taken on the outlines of an island. On the shining saucer of faintly ruffled ocean beneath us we had seen tiny toylike shapes of tankers, cargo ships, a string of destroyers. As we circled, fuzzy green land rose to block the sky. About us spun deep valleys brimmed with cloud, and sawtooth mountains hemming in an amphitheater of white and cream and reddish houses. Those silvery streaks between tangled gray masses of ships, clamped together with wharves, docks, warehouses, barrack buildings, had turned out to be Pearl Harbor. More planes than anyone had ever seen had whizzed by parked in ranks on a smooth coral floor. A sunburned officer with round glasses had stuck his head in the door and announced, 'Welcome to Honolulu.'

Recollections were dropping through my head like the pictures in an oldfashioned stereopticon; shuffled in among them were memories of other lonesome waits, of the days piling scrapiron at Gièvres, of the time I had to wash all those windows at the camp in Allentown. All the times of waiting and vacuum and lonesomeness, when one kind of existence had come to an end and a new kind hadn't quite begun, were merging together in my head and becoming one time.

Down in the bungalow they had started in on 'I Saw Three Ships Go Sailing By.' It was dark. The birds were quiet. Better go out to get something to eat.

It was after seven, so all the restaurants along the broad main street of Waikiki were closed. At every corner queues of soldiers and sailors bound home to their quarters were waiting for busses. The only place I could find open was a dingy softdrink parlor with a lunchcounter. A mongrel yellow boy in a damp aloha shirt was sponging off the oilcloth. Further down stood a blankeyed woman of Japanese extraction in a white apron. Yes, she chirped out in crisp English, she had steak.

A sallowfaced young sawedoff marine sitting on the next stool tilted his head my way.

'Which way you bound, Mister?'

I mumbled something about forward areas.

'Ain't you kind of old for that?'

I answered stiffly that correspondents came all ages.

We asked each other where our homes were. When I said Cape Cod, he showed all his uneven teeth in a laugh. He came from Pawtucket. Sure he knew the Cape.

'I stole a car in Buzzard's Bay wonct,' he cried out in happy reminiscence. 'Gawd I used to have fun.'

He added that he'd been out twenty-two months. He hardly looked as if he'd shaved yet, so I said he must have started his life of crime pretty early.

'That don't mean nutten,' he answered cheerfully. 'I got my stripes now.'

Our plates had come. We started eating. Did I see any snow before I left home, he asked with his mouth full of fried potatoes. I said it had been cold as blazes the night I left New York. It had been snowing in Omaha. The Sierras had been covered with snow.

'Tell all about it,' he said. 'Honest to Gawd if I got in a good snowstorm I'd take off my clothes and roll in it. Out there it's all pretty scenery . . . too goddam pretty. I hate pretty scenery. I can't look at it without smellin' dead Japs.'

He let his voice drop to a whisper as he noticed the little Japanese-looking woman coming toward us back of the counter. He winked at me as he turned to say something sweet to her.

'After twenty-two months they all look white,' he whispered hoarsely.

I paid my bill and slipped off my stool.

'Well, good luck, Mister. Take it easy. Me, I'm back for the rest cure.' As I walked out he dropped me another large wink.

When my transportation finally came, it turned out to be a station wagon in which I was the only passenger. The night was chilly enough to make you shiver a little. It was after curfew. The streets of Honolulu were empty as stage scenery. There wasn't a car on the broad truckworn highway that leads through the swamps to Pearl Harbor. Out at John Rogers Airport the rows of planes, some silvery, some olive drab, swam in the moonlight beside the white coral runways like sleeping whales.

In the passenger terminal there was a Christmas tree. Three drowsy-eyed Red Cross ladies presided over doughnuts and coffee and bowls of sliced pineapple at the free-lunch counter. The only other passenger on my flight was a medical officer. He was a tall rawboned man with a lined face who walked up and down and up and down as if he were walking the deck of a ship. He was cursing quietly under his breath. I joined him and asked him what the trouble was. He spread out his arms a little and made a gesture with both thumbs down. Flight late. He'd miss his connection at Kwajalein for Majuro. He had to get there in time to make an eleven-thirty plane next day. He made a gesture with both thumbs up. Down in Majuro were two cases of whiskey and a bunch of right guys, Christmas Eve party. He made an O with his thumb and forefinger and all the creases in his face ran together in a grin.

A polite NATS lieutenant came up and said that if we liked he'd put us on our plane. Flight was scheduled for twenty-four hundred, but might get off a little early. The moon seemed brighter than ever as we walked out over acres of smooth white coral among the great ships shiny and dun, mediumsized, large, and immense. Here and there from across the runway came the roar of motors from a plane warming up. We heaved in our own gear and with a good-bye and a Merry Christmas climbed up the little ladder and settled down into the two padded seats, of the type known all over the Pacific as MacArthur seats, to the rear of the carefully corded pile of cargo. After a few minutes the plane taxied out through the milky moonlight, the motors roared, and we were craning our necks to look out through the grimed plexiglass at dark mountains and flickering strings of light. Rapidly the plane climbed into the empty sky where even the moon began to look small and lonely. The air grew cold. The flight orderly came back with a couple of blankets for us.

He crouched beside us for a moment to pass the time of day. He was a lean, hairy, sunburned young man with no hips, a carpenter by profession. He lived along the highway about ten miles out from Phoenix, Arizona. He'd just had word that his younger brother, who was the baby of the family, had been killed in France. That would be tough on the old people. He brought out a picture of a pretty wife and two little kids on a lawn beside a neat little white house he'd built himself, a typical carpenter's house. . . . He cleared his throat as he put it away in his wallet with the short snorter we'd just been signing. He was crazy about this duty, he said, smiling, he felt he was seeing the world. He left us to go to sleep.

The change in the sound of the motors from a steady beat to a singsong woke us. We were circling for a landing on Johnston Island. The orderly came back to tell us we'd have time for breakfast. Up forward the co-pilot was squinting out through the window with a flashlight. One motor was backfiring. We might be held over. That gave the medical officer a fit of the twitches. He just had to get into Kwaj in time to make that plane for Majuro or he'd miss his Christmas.

From the runway the place looked like any small airfield out in the Middle West except that back of the low buildings everywhere was the ocean. You couldn't see it, but you could hear the surf very close. From somewhere on the beach came a continued moaning, like the sound of a buoy in a fog. 'Gives me the creeps,' said the medical officer, thrusting down his thumbs; 'it's gulls.' In the cleanswept messhall we sat at a long table eating bacon and eggs while the big unshaded electric-light bulbs stung our sleepy eyes. Back in the plane it turned out there was nothing wrong with that motor after all. The medical officer made an enthusiastic O with his thumb and forefinger and snuggled back into his blanket to sleep.

When day broke we were very high over a pearly ocean of clouds. We dozed and read through eight hundred long miles of morning until the pilot came back to get us to look at something up forward. Through a threadbare place in the clouds we barely could make out a faint irregular ring, whitish outside, dark inside, that went out of sight and appeared again like a germ under a badly focused microscope.

'Ailuk . . . atoll . . . Marshall Islands,' the pilot's lips formed the unfamiliar words against my ear. Then he tried to get us to make out another atoll fifty miles to the left, Wotje. There still were Japs there.

As we worked our way down through the cloud floor, the sky cleared. We could see the blue Pacific strewn with little spits of foam. Then we were low enough to make out flying fish taking off and diving from the long swells, and then, as the plane banked, a surf-bordered strip of island slid past the plexiglass unexpectedly clear. The orderly was crawling through the cabin with his insect-control bomb fizzling in his hand, leaving a fresh-smelling trail of pyrethrum mist. We went back to our seats and fastened our safety belts for the landing.

Christmas Across the Date Line

When you climb out of the plane at Kwajalein into the dazzle of leveled coral of the airfield, the densely packed tents and Quonset huts round the edges of the strip have the look of an Arizona mining village or of one of those rattletrap boom towns that spring up round new oilwells. Here and there a shriveled coconut palm, or the big skeleton of a blasted breadfruit that managed to stand up through the bombing and shelling at the time of our landing and the subsequent leveling off of the island by the bulldozers, juts out in the middle of a row of tents. Everything looks gray and grimed from the driving coral dust. The sun is hot, but the northeast trade blows steady, bringing a taste of surf and of endless miles of ocean.

After we have dragged our baggage into the operations hut, we find ourselves facing a big blue map of the Marshall Islands. Beside it is a calendar. The medical officer, who has just been cheered by the news that he can get a plane to Majuro in half an hour, stands staring at it with sagging jaw.

'What's the trouble?'

'It's the goddam dateline. We've skipped Christmas Eve.'

'Yes, sir, this is Christmas Day. Kwajalein was the first spot in the civilized world to have church services this Christmas,' says the young man in torn khaki shorts behind the desk with a note of pride in his voice.

'They sure will have drunk up that whiskey,' groans the medical officer. He lets himself drop on a bench and sits there limp as a rag. To kid him we all wish him a Merry Christmas.

Meanwhile the public relations lieutenant from a marine air group has arrived with an invitation to dinner from the general in command. He's from Milwaukee. He used to work on a paper there. He has black hair and olive skin bronzed as an Indian's from the sun. His people were Polish. He's been three years in the marines. He's keen about his work and his outfit and his commanding officer. He makes no secret of the fact that he's convinced that a marine is about the finest thing the sun ever shines on. His name is Louis Olszyk. He says there's time to show me the island before dinner.

The part of Kwajalein our troops have occupied is a narrow strip of trampled coral barely above sea level between the roaring surf on the reef and the immense lagoon that gives this atoll the reputation of being the largest in the world. Everywhere, as we grind slowly along in our jeep, we pass cheerful chow lines of sweating bronzed men in khaki pants and shorts waiting in the sun outside of festooned messhalls. A smell of roast turkey and stuffing comes from the galleys. About every tent has something rigged up in the middle of it to look like a Christmas tree. There are a great many signs, painted in red and green, reading 'Season's Greetings' or 'Merry Christmas.' Phonographs and radios blare out Christmas music. As the island is all of two miles long, it doesn't take very long to drive from the landing wharf of rusty pontons with gray navy picket boats tied up alongside, and the inevitable Liberty ship anchored far out in the blue lagoon, to the far end where the bulldozers are making land by pushing out over the reef the dumped fibrous roots of coconut palms and twisted bits of Jap guns and tanks, and tin cans, and crumpled planes, and broken concrete from Jap pillboxes, and waterlogged cartons, and splintered packing-cases.

'Cleaning up after the ballgame,' said Louis; 'it's quite a problem. Even now we can't even dig a new latrine without turning up a dead Jap or two.'

Wherever we stop we are offered cold beer. In one outfit we find a Japanese staff car. It has lost its doors and has been plentifully ventilated by flying shell splinters. Somebody has patched it up and managed to make it run. A big sweating redhead, crimson all over from the dinner and the heat and the beer, tells us it's a Jap admiral's car and offers to take us for a ride in it. We haven't gone far when an angry young man in his drawers comes running after us.

'Hey, where are you goin' with that car? I'm responsible for that car. That's the best souvenir on the damned island.'

'Hell,' says the redhead as we all pile out . . . 'I wasn't goin' to stop till I hit Chicago.'

At the end of each row of tents a small windmill spins merrily in the unfailing tradewind. The windmills are as much a feature of the landscape of Kwajalein as they are of Holland. They are made of all kinds of wood and metal débris patched together. Many of them are made of aluminum parts from wrecked Jap planes. Louis stopped his jeep abreast of one and I was just about to ask what the devil it was when a deeply tanned marine in very fragmentary shorts came out of a tent carrying a bucket of soiled clothes. He stirred up some washing powder, set the plunger in the bucket, attached it to a roughly made wooden cam and started the windmill spinning. The plunger worked the clothes up and down and the suds began to rise in the bucket. He looked up at us and grinned. 'It's a mechanical war, ain't it,' he said and slouched back into his tent.

'It's a mechanical war,' said the freckled sergeant who was caring for the big stills that distilled fresh water from sea water to the tune of about eleven gallons of fresh water to a gallon of fuel oil. 'It's a mechanical war,' said the blue-eyed lieutenant who showed off the mechanical cow, an intricate contraption of stainless steel that mixed up dried milk and butterfat to produce something more nearly the equivalent of fresh milk than what came out of a can. 'It's a mechanical war,' said the man in blue dungarees who opened up the great square refrigerator safe and showed us how the ice machine worked. 'It's a mechanical war,' we both echoed as we drove back toward the headquarters tents of the Marine Air Group, along a row of grumbling B29's just flown in that filled the dispersal areas. The roaring of their great motors as the mechanics tuned them up shook the island.

Back at 'Kwaj Lodge,' the visitors' tent, there was time for a swim in bluegreen water full of splinters of sunlight before Louis took me over to meet General Wood. The General was a stocky young-looking man with blue eyes and a cheerful direct manner. Under the paleblue silk parachute that was draped as a ceiling for his tent he set us up to some Christmas drinks. In a corner with a couple of correspondents he talked for a moment about the work of his command. The Marshalls and Gilberts were a bypassed area all right, he said, a little ruefully, but they were still important as stepping-stones and as bases for his planes that had the job of a blocking tackle on a football team. His business was to keep raiding aircraft and submarines from getting through to bother our train of ships moving forward to the fighting fronts. His night-fighters must knock down any stray plane that got through and his fighter-bombers must keep the Japs isolated and miserable on the atolls we hadn't considered it worth

while to take. They had to be kept from building boats, re-
pairing airstrips, and receiving reinforcements. It was a
patrol that covered a patch of ocean ten times the area of the
State of Texas. It was dull routine work for flyers, who
would much rather be up in the forward areas. But he was
getting results. In the last six weeks only one Jap plane had
gotten through. As a training area, too, it was magnificent.
His boys could train with live bait. 'Well,' he ended up with
a quick smile, 'now that I've made my little sales talk, we
might as well go eat our turkey.'

After dinner Louis Olszyk and I roamed around the island
talking to the soldiers. Whenever we stepped out of the
breeze behind a hut or a tent, the afternoon heat wrapped
itself about us like a wet steamy blanket. At the beer garden,
where there was more beer than garden, everybody seemed to
have a Christmas cigar. When men heard you were fresh from
the mainland, they would look at you with searching eyes as
if they expected to see a picture of home in your face, and ask
in a worried tone, 'What's it like back home? Are the States-
side folks really back of us? Are they putting everything into
it?'

Nothing you answered seemed quite to satisfy them. They
had mail and Christmas boxes and fruitcake and candy. They
had the mimeographed daily news-sheets, the movies they sat
through with a desperate kind of attention every night, but it
wasn't enough. Too many thousands of miles of ocean lay
between. Every man was listening for the word that would
call up the picture of home just like it was when he left.

There was a bunch of seabees at one end of the beer garden
celebrating a baseball game with a team from Majuro. A
middleaged man with white hair who looked the mechanic to
his blunt fingertips brought up a rangy young fellow whom he

introduced as the sweetest goddam third baseman in the Marshall Islands. 'Hell,' he said, 'I'd trade four seabees for him.'

'Ain't he the atoll Connie Mack!' piped up a kidding voice.

The middleaged man took us across the island to see his outfit's repair truck. 'We could just about rebuild a battleship with it,' he boasted proudly.

When we went back to the beer garden, we found a sweaty youth sitting on an oil drum and bitching in a singsong voice about what a hell of a miserable goddam thing it was to spend Christmas away from home on a lonely island with ten thousand miles of water all around you.

'Lonely?' a voice yelled. 'Kwaj is about as lonely as Times Square on election night.'

We looked around at the crowds of marines and seabees and navy men milling about in every direction among the close-packed tents and the Dallas huts and the Quonset huts, and the trucks and the reefers and the rattling distillators, and the slambanging repair shops and the ranks of fighter planes at the end of every vista, and laughed.

'Son,' said our friend the mechanic, 'you don't need to talk. You young fellers don't need to talk who ain't even married yet. You don't know what it's like for us old guys.' His voice dropped gruffly. 'You don't know what it is to have home cookin'.'

In the radio station that night they were playing over a recording they had made the Sunday before of Marshallese singing. It was men and women singing in parts. The voices were low and sweet. The announcer, a mild-mannered man with thinning red hair who had worked in a radio station in Los Angeles, whispered that it sounded like Bach. 'That was the Lutheran influence . . . German missionaries were in here for fifteen years.'

'Sounds more like Moody and Sankey,' said somebody else.

'That was the Boston Mission. It was Hiram Bingham and his New England missionaries who converted all these people to Christianity.'

A slender dark brown man in khaki pants and undershirt was standing just inside the swath of light of the doorway. He had high cheekbones and lustrous brown eyes in bluish eyeballs deepset under a broad low forehead. 'Come in, Jim,' said the youthful captain with the teddybear haircut.

The man in the doorway gave a little giggle and showed his irregular yellow teeth in a grin. He made a stiff little bow.

'Quit that Jap stuff and come in and sit down,' said the captain in a cordial middlewestern tone of voice.

The brown man let out a long ripple of laughter and walked in with a supple stride and sat down in the empty chair.

'He didn't want to come because he hasn't had a bath,' explained the sergeant. 'He's a foreman in this Marshallese work battalion we have here. He knows more English than you would think . . . Meet Jim Milne, sir.'

The brown man sat quiet, casting a slow look of inquiry at the circle of sweating white faces around him. A resigned bashful look came over his face and he leaned forward attentively with his long arms hanging over his knees waiting to be asked a question.

I asked him if his people remembered the Boston missionaries. He didn't answer for a moment, but sat there as if letting the question sink in. Then he answered seriously in precise rather fragmentary English that the American missionaries were good people and had always been very kind to the natives.

'You are no more natives than we are . . . We're all natives of some place,' said the captain.

'But we are savages,' said Jim Milne in his low modest voice.

'Who isn't?' said the sergeant.

'Missionaries teach us everything,' he said, smiling.

'They sure are Christians,' said the sergeant. 'Your people are all right, Jim.'

Jim went on in his slow low fragmentary speech to say that his grandfather was an Englishman. I asked him if his people remembered the days before the missionaries came.

'Then we all time fight war . . . worshiped the ancients,' he said, pronouncing the word slowly and correctly as if dragging it out of some deep recess of his memory.

We asked him if his people liked working with the Americans.

He laughed. 'Very good,' he said.

Was the work hard?

He laughed again. 'No work,' he said. 'Machine do all work.'

On our way back to our area, Louis and I stopped for a second to see a movie. There was a little covered balcony to the projection booth where the officers sat. The men sat on coconut logs, or on packingboxes or folding chairs they had brought from their tents, or on the bare coral. We'd hardly seen enough of the picture to recognize Laurel and Hardy when a sudden squall came up. Nobody moved. A few men stuck their heads into ponchos or drew raincoats up around them. Some pulled off their shirts to keep them dry, but most of them went on sitting there in the stinging rain looking at the screen with intent faces.

We ducked into the nearest shelter. It turned out to be the dispensary. A doctor with round glasses and a round sallow face was sitting at his field desk writing a letter. We asked him what kind of a Christmas he'd had.

'Lousy,' he said. Then he added scornfully: 'What a question to ask a man on Kwajalein.'

The doctor and Louis had both landed on D5. We got to talking about the process by which a palmfringed island occupied by a few brown natives and some Jap battalions with plenty of ammunition dug into pillboxes of reinforced concrete became in a few days or weeks a farflung scrap of America. First we sprayed them with explosives and metal from the ships and the planes. Then we landed the tanks and the bulldozers and started pushing the Japs and their débris off the end of the island. The trees went, the undergrowth went, the bulldozers dug the dead Japs under and leveled the coral off on top of them. The levelers and the sheepfoot scrapers and the rollers came and we began to have an airstrip.

As we talked, the doctor's manner lost its listlessness.

'Once the Japs are dead, sanitation becomes the major problem,' he said. 'We bury the filth and the stinking corpses. We dig heads and screen 'em. From now on flies are enemy number one. We screen the mess tents and the galleys and all refuse containers. We bring distillators ashore for fresh water. We fight the rats. We oil all standing water against mosquitoes. The way to fight flies and rats is to starve 'em out.'

Did they use DDT?

Never needed it, he answered proudly. Of course, he admitted, Kwajalein was a simple problem because on this island when we came ashore there wasn't a damn thing left, not a tree, not a native hut. Make a clean sweep and start over, that was the best way he said.

'I haven't heard anybody talking about sickness here,' I began.

The doctor puffed out his chest and glared at me through his glasses. 'Sickness,' he snapped. 'This, sir, is the healthiest damned island in the Pacific.'

Stevenson's South Seas

A thin line of sharp yellow was just beginning to pierce the cloudy indigo of the eastern horizon when we drove up to the plane. The pilot, a plump redheaded boy from southern Illinois, was heaving a box of canned goods into the cabin, under his arm he had a bundle of white sheets and some colored print material. 'Lava-lava for the gouks,' he said. By the time he had warmed up his motors, the sky had cleared and it was day. The takeoff was smooth as cream. As he banked to set his course, we got a last glimpse of the gray ranks of fighter-bombers and the palms bunching together like grass and the yellow bench of the reef spuming with surf between the green lagoon and the blue ocean. The atoll shrank to the size of a broken piece of pretzel and became a vague blur on the horizon.

Soon far to the left another atoll appeared. That was Mille, the navigator said. Still Japs there. Machinegun fire. We gave it a wide berth. For a while there was nothing in sight but the ocean steaming with white and lilac-shaded clouds. Then under a whiter patch of cloud a streak of land rose up and sprouted palms as we drew near.

That was Makin, a halfmoon-shaped piece of jungle set in puttycolored banks of coral mud. A rank steamy latrine smell rose up from it. The tide was dead low. High and dry on the edges of the lagoon a couple of Jap hulks quietly rusted red in a patch of sunlight. A black schooner was at the wharf. You could still make out the streaks and wallows,

like muskrat paths through a marsh back home, that showed
where our landing craft had gone ashore when we hit the
beach there. We skimmed thatched roofs of huts, a white
church bombed to pieces and then the airstrip. Ours was the
only plane. When we climbed down, we crossed the puddles
left by the recent rain and walked over to a little shack
marked 'Operations.' Under the tent flap that served for a
porch, we found a hawknosed army lieutenant with a little
truck on his collar.

'Nothing left here,' he said belligerently, talking out of the
corner of his mouth without moving his lips. We explained
that we were just making a short call on the way to Tarawa.
He looked a little less blank and muttered that he was just
here to tidy up the odds and ends. 'Housecleaning after the
party,' he said with a dry little laugh. He had damn little
transportation left, but he guessed he could show us around.
We piled into his jeep and set off down the edge of the airstrip.
'Built it in fifteen days,' he said, puffing out his chest as if he'd
done it all himself.

On Makin there were still palm trees, but they were moth-
eaten from their spraying with shrapnel. Where the marines
had camped, the thinnedout jungle had the look of a vast
picnic ground on Monday morning. There were signs and
rutted roads going off at right angles into the trampled empty
wilderness like in a Florida realestate development that has
failed.

The rain began again. We drove through a village of dripping thatched huts. On the platforms of the houses brown
people wearing odds and ends of army issue, scraps of printed
stuff and occasionally grass skirts, were lolling in every conceivable posture of ease. As we passed, they raised bare arms
in greeting, and smiled.

'They are nice people. There's no getting around it,' said
the lieutenant thoughtfully. 'A lot of those girls have quite
nice dresses, and they are very clean. Not in a sanitary way,
but no B.O. and all that. You ought to see them at parties,
and that's every night between Christmas and New Year's. I
guess that's enough village. They are all alike.'

He spun the jeep around and drove us back to his headquarters. He took us into a building made out of several
Dallas huts fitted together. 'Here I reside in solitary glory,'
he said.

He went to the icebox and brought out some cans of beer.
'Damned unusual thing,' he said, as he opened them and
handed them around, 'for me to fetch my own beer. I just
clap my hands and one of the gouks gets it . . . I don't know
where the hell they've all gone today. I've got two little
boys wait on me all the time. They are twins, so I can't tell
which is which. Faithful as dogs. When I want a coconut
they shinny up a tree and get one for me. These folks seem to
like to wait on people . . .' He sprawled out on his cot, pouring the beer out of the can into his mouth. 'Now don't get
me wrong about those dances,' he said a little later, raising
himself on one elbow. 'They ain't orgies or anything like
that . . . No rolling in the hay. The old folks all come and
all the kids, and they watch their daughters just like people
back home do. The only trouble is you can't get away from
'em. The girls ask the fellers to dance and the dances go on for
hours. "You Are My Sunshine," that's their favorite tune.
They'll play it a thousand times. When they get too sleepy,
they lie down and go to sleep right there on the dance floor
. . . it's mats, you know . . . and then they wake up and
start dancing again. Quite a life for mother's darling boy.
Might be a whole lot worse, I guess. Since the doctors

cleaned this place up, it's the healthiest damned island in the Pacific.'

We began to thread our way through rainclouds southward. The next atoll was Abeiang where Hiram Bingham first planted his mission and started putting Mother Hubbards on the heathen way back in the forties of the last century, and imbued the Micronesians of these islands forevermore with a faint shadow of a New England conscience. We flew low over Abeiang. It was like a coral island in a dream. Round the shallow lagoon, pitted and scarred like the face of the moon, in various tints of green deepening to emerald and to a clear blue in the deeper places, ran a necklace of green islets. Fishtraps made a series of spearhead designs over the marl in the shallow channels between. The villages looked very neat from the air, each with a long communal hall in the middle of rows of thatched houses. There were two gleaming white churches and mission buildings with broad porches amid tufts of breadfruit trees and masses of orange and red flowers. Every house had a straight walk leading to a little thatched privy over the lagoon. Outrigger canoes were drawn up on the beach or scudded under triangular white sails through the shallows. As we flew over, thousands of snowy terns rose and fluttered above the glittering ranks of palms.

Tarawa is like Gettysburg. Betio, the fortified island at the end of one of the legs of the V-shaped atoll, seems hardly larger than a baseball field. On the edge of the airstrip are squares of white crosses, little plots with signs reading, '150 Japanese dead,' '200 Japanese dead.' On the Japanese pill-boxes and strongpoints are carefully lettered explanations of the phases of the battle. Men from the various services staging through walk reverently around with their hats in their hands spelling out the story of that hotly contested landing. You can walk around the emplacement of reinforced concrete and rotting coconut logs and look with awe at the Vickers guns and the trenches and the great square command centers that rim the airfield, crowded today with ranks of shiny new Liberators staging westward. At the end of the island somebody has put up a sign with a white arrow pointing northeast that reads, '9137 miles to NAUGATUCK, CONN.'

In a neatly thatched group of huts, with a frozen smile on his too youthful face, sits the commissioner who represents His Britannic Majesty in the Crown Colony of the Gilbert Islands, serving tea in the afternoon as imperturbably as if he were looking out on the green lanes of England instead of on a green lagoon spotted with ugly-looking Liberty ships.

That night a Pittsburgh lawyer, still somewhat dazed to find himself in suntans on a coral island, six thousand miles from anywhere, invited me out of the glaring moonlight of the airfield, where the propellers of Liberators about to take off churned up great clouds of coral dust, into his brightly lit hut to drink a spot of Old Grand Dad with him. He couldn't get over the fact that he'd been elected to sweat out the war on this particular postage stamp on the ocean. He'd kind of expected that with his background and training he would end up in Military Government. But here he was. It was monotonous, but it was a healthy life. 'This, Sir,' he said, setting down his glass to emphasize the statement, 'is the healthiest damned island in the Pacific.'

'We don't have any proper weather reports in these latitudes,' said the pilot cheerfully as we settled down to our course the next morning. 'There always seems to be a front of bad weather just north of the Equator, but we never know where it is till we hit it.'

Sure enough, soon we were threading our uneven way through tunnels of cumulus. Now and then patches of hissing rain blanked everything out. Then we would nose out into the sunlight again and dive into changing golden or bluish or greenish landscapes of cloud, strange set tableaux that reminded you of the pasteboard scenery you used to come out on winding through the dark passages of the Old Mill in amusement parks years ago. The plane bucked and pitched until suddenly we broke through into a curious serene region of dense blue against which little porcelain clouds stood out in cameo like the pattern on a Wedgwood teapot. A half-hour further south the sky was clear again and the oval atoll of Apamama began to sharpen into focus dead ahead.

When the plane came to rest on the runway, there was absolute silence. We climbed down onto the empty airfield beside the still palms. The sweet hot air ran down our faces like molasses.

We walked slowly down the edge of the clearing toward the palegreen glare of the lagoon. There was no one in sight. Far out an outrigger canoe with a white sail sliced fast over the water in the light wind. Then we began to hear the sound of a motor far away up the curving beach. 'I reckon the Britisher heard us,' said the pilot. 'I sure buzzed him plenty . . . You gentlemen go with the commissioner and we'll walk over to Titty City to do our tradin' with the gouks.'

Already a pair of bare brown men wearing GI helmets had appeared at the edge of the road and stood watching us smiling as if waiting for us to speak first.

After a while a jeep came in sight driven by a yellow man.

The Australian captain who was British commissioner sat beside him. Yes, he could drive us around if we didn't want to go too far, he said. This jeep was all the transportation he had. He didn't like to drive it too far. No spare parts.

He drove us slowly along a narrow shady road arched with gleaming palm fronds. The road followed the edge of the lagoon that shone behind the graywhite palm trunks in every brilliance of ultramarine and sapphire and milky jadegreen. Here and there we passed rows of thatched huts along the water's edge. On their raised platforms the brown people lolled and watched us go by, smiling their indolent smile. Everybody had on his best pink and green and blue-flowered lava-lava for the holiday. In the deep shade of the long community shelters, people sat in family groups round piles of fruit or bowls of food.

This was Stevenson's Apamama, the South Sea Islands as young Presbyterians in the last century dreamed of them in Bible class.

'They are waiting for noon to start dancing,' said the captain. 'From Christmas to New Year's, there's no work done . . . Soon somebody will come around to get permission to start dancing.'

To pass from one islet to the other, we had to cross shallow channels where the jeep slipped and floundered over coral rocks worn smooth by the tide. Pretty little speckled snipe ran ahead of us pecking at the sea snails. At each lurch the captain shook his head mournfully over the wear and tear on his jeep. 'When this breaks down,' he said, 'it'll be shank's mare for me.'

We stopped beside some ruined concrete walls at the edge of a deeper inlet of murky jade water. 'This was the Burns

Philps Station,' said the captain. 'Copra traders. The Japs made their headquarters here.'

'Over there' — he gave us a reproachful look as he pointed through the pallid trunks of the palms — 'is the village you bombed by mistake. The natives hadn't run away because they saw American markings on the planes and thought they were friends. They killed the native pastor, didn't they?'

'Yes, sir,' spoke up Domingo, the yellow driver. 'He wake up in the night . . . thirsty . . . tell his wife go get him drink of water . . . and when she come back house all gone, he dead.'

Mumbling our national apologies, we walked over to the inlet. The marly banks were crawling with small red crabs.

'You see we landed on the next island,' the captain was saying . . . 'I came out from Oahu in the submarine. We were packed in like sardines, twenty-nine of us besides the crew. The Japs had only a small force. Your planes bombed them a bit and then we landed. They had some machineguns here. But in the end the beggars turned out rather considerate. They pulled off their shoes and shot themselves under the chin with their rifles . . . pulled the trigger with their toes . . . about fifteen of them right here in this trench, so all we had to do was to pile the earth back on top of them.'

Driving along the winding track between sunken gardens of bananas and taro, I asked the captain if it wasn't rather lonely here now that the American troops had pulled out. He had been telling us that he had no radio, that his only contact with the Empire was a schooner every three months, but that so far no supplies had come. He was still living on GI canned goods.

'We've been too busy clearing up after you to feel lonely. You make rather a mess, you know . . . I've had fifteen

years of this. After I'd had three years of Ocean Island, my
wife and I got married. I thought it was up to me to take her
back to Melbourne. We stood it for a few months and then
one fine day I said, "Dear, suppose we go back." She said
"Rather," and here we've been ever since . . . She's waiting
in Suva now . . . As soon as you fellows push a bit further
west, I hope to get her up here . . . We could never live in
suburbia after this.'

At the Catholic mission on the next island, the Sisters
brought out their best cups and a pot of tea and a fruitcake for
us. The three of them were Australians. Their names were
Sister Gregory, Sister Dolores, and Sister Raphael. Sister
Dolores, the thin-faced one with glasses who taught school
for the natives, was the most talkative.

'How had it been when the Japs were here?' we were asking.

'Horrid,' she said. 'They were horrid little people. . . .
They never came in by the path. They'd always pop out of
the bushes somewhere and frighten you to death. They were
always searching for radio sets, they'd be after every scrap of
paper. We had a time hiding poor Father Mell's wine.
They'd steal anything to eat. We'd have starved to death if
it hadn't been for the natives. They managed to bring us
something now and then. They weren't supposed to come in
the church. Their officers were dreadfully strict with them
. . . always boxing them on the ears. I should think they
would all be deaf. The soldier would just stand there and bow
each time the officer hit him. Poor downtrodden wretches.
It was a nightmare the way they infiltrated in through the
shrubbery . . . I gave a couple of them a fright one day myself.
They'd been in the church touching things and throwing
stones at the statues, and they came over to the door and

stood there looking at me and grinning. I was so angry I ran right up to them and poked my fingers in their faces like this' . . . She screwed up her mouth and made aggressive poking gestures with two fingers of each hand out of her long white sleeves . . . '"Taboo, taboo," I said and they understood that. One of them pointed to the other one as if to say: "He did it, not me," but I just kept poking my fingers at them and saying, "Taboo" till their knees began to shake and they ran away.'

We all sat primly in the nuns' narrow little white-walled parlor drinking tea and eating fruitcake. Outside the steamy sunlight poured down on the fine green grass and the flowering hibiscus and the thatched huts of the mission compound. When we had finished our tea, Sister Dolores got up and collected our cups on a little lacquer tray. Her white robe quite filled the small room as she bustled about. She opened a cupboard in the corner and brought down a bottle of wine and four tiny glasses.

'I have a favor to ask of you,' she said, smiling, as she squinted in our faces through her glasses. 'It's that you'll go and drink a glass of wine for the New Year with Father Mell . . . The poor dear soul is so ill . . . It'll do him good.'

We asked what was the matter.

'Oh, it's the fever and the weakness, and it's all we've been through . . . it's preyed on his mind, the poor man. It's the weakness.'

One of us asked if they were all quite well themselves after being prisoners and everything.

'Oh, we're quite strong,' they all piped together.

'Now you go over and have a drink of wine with Father Mell . . . just for the New Year,' said Sister Dolores briskly. 'It'll do him good.'

She led the way across the grassy garden with her fast short steps to a whitewashed hut under the shade of some big trees. The sunlight when you came out of the shade was like a hot stroke of velvet on your face.

Father Mell was a stocky little Alsatian with a soft round face and a blunt black beard. He lay on a tumbled cot in the bare white room. When he raised himself on one elbow to shake hands, the sweat started out along the line of dark hair on his forehead. His hand was cold and wet.

'I am always cold,' he said.

Sister Dolores stood on the porch and set the tray and glasses on the windowsill and poured out the wine. Meanwhile an old whitehaired man with a sunbeaten face gnarled and knobby as the root of a briar had come up out of the garden.

'He's Brother Miller,' the Sister whispered. 'He's eighty-five years old and he's been here too long.'

He stood with his head cocked to one side, and the sun beating on his tangled white hair and beard, looking into the hut through the window. His face was screwed into an attitude of deepest puzzlement. As he stared, his old twisted fingers plucked at a tear in the knee of his worn khaki trousers.

We took in the tray and stood around Father Mell's bed and handed him his glass and wished him a Happy New Year. He drank off the tiny glass of wine and lay with his head on his elbow looking up at us with moist eyes and smiling vaguely, 'Ah, the New Year,' he said, as if trying to remember something. His eyes closed and his head fell back gently on the pillow.

Bypassed Area

When the picket boat drew up to the landing, made of rusty pontons linked together, that juts out from the crescent beach at Laura Village, we were met by a very tall native and a very short native who shook hands exuberantly. Everywhere we went along the dusty street between hedges of a shrub with waxy pink and green and yellow variegated leaves, people came out of their houses and shook hands and said, 'How do you do, sir? I am very well, thank you.'

This was a village of frame houses with porches painted white that had a faintly early-American look. We walked to the end of the village between rich tangled thickets of breadfruit and papaya and flowering hibiscus with rank patches of the elephant-ear leaves of taro sprouting out of the damper spots. At the end of the village was the church. It was a big bare building with a definitely evangelical cast. The little sawedoff schoolteacher pointed up proudly at the elaborate structure that supported the roof and explained that they had rebuilt every bit of it all by themselves when it had been blown down in a storm ten years ago. Beyond that was the thatch and bamboo house of the interpreter.

The interpreter's name was Mike Madison. He was a large-boned brown man with an aquiline nose and a subtly Roman cast of countenance. He spoke in low tones in a clipped English that had a faintly Australian twang to it. He had a little of the Britisher's offhand manner. He explained that he hadn't been able to come to meet us because he had a bad leg. While we talked to him, his wife and daughters, who wore American-type cotton dresses, beamed sweetly at us from the corners of the hut.

'Yes,' said Mike Madison, 'in the old days it was all copra.

I was in the business a bit myself. Everybody dried and collected copra. The stuff shrinks.' He made a twisted smile.
'My word, the stuff shrinks and loses weight when you ship
it. Now the ladies make baskets and shellwork for the Americans. You know the cowrie shell.'

'We can dispose of all you can make,' said the Military
Government man. 'Our service men are in the market for
souvenirs in a big way.'

'Tell them if they don't hurry up and make us a lot of handi-
craft,' said one of the doctors, 'the seabees'll take the market
away from them.'

When we started to leave Mike Madison's house, his wife
and daughters, laughing and giggling, brought us each out a
shell basket as a present. 'You can't refuse,' whispered the
Military Government officer, 'they'd be offended.'

As we walked back to the landing, he asked me if I'd heard
about the seabee who used to get himself up in a grass skirt
and paddle an outrigger canoe out to the transports staging
through. He did a tremendous business in native handicrafts.
He made them all himself. The seabees can make anything.

On the way back to the end of the atoll where the camps
were, the doctor read off the names of the islands. While the
landing operation was being planned they all had to have
American names. There was Laura where the native village
was, and then across the lagoon began Victoria, Tresa, Toot-
sie, Simone, Sherry, Sara, Sheila, Salome, Ruth, Ruby, Rosa-
lie, and Rita. 'That kept us from getting tangled up with the
native names.'

The tradewind was blowing briskly and kicking up a
choppy sea so that the spray soon drove us below. Sitting
sweating in the little cabin of the picket boat, we listened to
the Military Government officer tell the story of how the

natives on the ungarrisoned atoll of Aur had captured three Japanese who had come over from their island of Maleolap to forage for food. 'They sure had 'em tied up . . . They got their arms away from them . . . The natives think the Japs are licked already. They are filtering over to our atolls. We have two of the kings of Maleolap with us now. They claim that the Japanese have threatened to behead the whole native population. They say there isn't enough food to go around. We dropped a message on the Japs offering to evacuate the native population and take care of them. The affirmative was to be the showing of a panel on the airfield. No panel ever appeared, so we gather that they don't want to co-operate.'

That evening we ate dinner with Captain Grow, the atoll commander, in his neatly finished plywood bungalow at the edge of the reef. On the wall at the end of the room there hung a portrait of a tiny stately old dame whose arms were tattooed in such a fine pattern that it looked as if she wore black lace sleeves.

'That's my sweetheart,' said Captain Grow. 'As fine a lady as I've ever met. She is eighty-four years old.' The painter was the tall Filipino boy who was waiting on table. 'You see we don't neglect the arts here,' said the captain, smiling.

We got to talking about the attitude of the natives toward our forces in the Pacific. The atoll commander said that so far as he knew only on Bougainville had our forces met anything like hostility. Everywhere else the people had welcomed us as friends and given us all the information and help they could. Our record in the islands was pretty fair, even though the crews of our whaling ships in the early days had been a pretty bad lot. Our missionaries made up for it.

'I wonder if it doesn't come from Hawaii,' said a tall man with blue glasses at the end of the table. 'It always seemed to me there was something specially tolerant and decent about the relations between the races in Hawaii . . . The early settlers intermarried some into the chiefly families. Of course the sugar planters did import coolie labor, first Chinese, and then Okinawans and Japs, but they got a break . . . You can't deny that they got a break.'

I put in that I'd been amazed to find the university at Honolulu full of Jap students. I'd gone to a barn dance in the student union and the boys and girls were all Japs, one hundred per cent American Japs.

'Sure,' said the man with blue glasses. 'In the territorial elections last fall one of the candidates published an advertisement in the paper explaining that he wasn't anti-Japanese . . . Quite different from California . . . the Chinese have gotten rich and are the backbone of the business community. The descendants of the Okinawan coolies go to school and college and get to be dentists and doctors and lawyers. The oldtime palefaces grumble about not being able to get any labor, but they are pretty tolerant too.'

'Where the devil are the Hawaiians?' asked a lieutenant. 'I swear you see more Hawaiians on Times Square than you do in Honolulu.'

'They've just been absorbed, melted away . . . The Hawaiians were a people who never had to struggle for existence like the peoples of Europe and Asia; of course, they had their wars and the chiefly caste sitting on their necks, but there wasn't the daily scamper after food and shelter and money that made ravening wolves out of most of the peoples of the world. The Hawaiians have gone, but their easygoing ways have lived on in the present population. Sometimes I think that if we could keep that Hawaiian atmosphere in our conquests through the Pacific, we'd accomplish something worth while.'

'It's a responsibility,' said Captain Grow seriously. 'Discounting all the nonsense that's been written about the South Seas there's a sort of a sweetness about these people.'

'When we've cleaned up the yaws and taught them to screen their latrines and bury their garbage, they'll be a whole lot sweeter,' growled the doctor.

The atoll commander went on to tell about how last Thanksgiving he had explained to the people of Majuro that we celebrated that day every November to commemorate our thanks for the first harvest at a time when we were a very small nation indeed, numbering about as many as the people of Majuro; and they had answered that they would institute a Thanksgiving day, too, to commemorate the day the Americans landed. Either they really liked us or else they were showing exquisite tact.

The phone rang in the outside room and the atoll commander was called to it. He came back frowning, but picked up the conversation where he had left it.

'No,' he said, 'I think they are sincerely for us. Of course, they've been subject to various governments, German and Japanese, within the last generation and they've learned to be pretty smooth. The more I see of them the more I think the early missionaries did a good job . . . They were the first white men who tried to help these people. They made pretty good Christians of them. They are not far out of the polished stone age, but they certainly aren't stupid and they appreciate it.'

There was a pause. The men along the table were looking at the atoll commander's frowning face.

'Bad news,' he said shortly. 'A plane down . . . operational . . . near Arno . . . the next atoll.'

We got up from the table a little clumsily. Nobody had anything to say.

The colonel in command of the landbased planes was making arrangements to send me out with the Dumbos in the strike against Mille, one of the Jap-held atolls, that was planned for next day. Down at the operations hut on the airstrip, we asked for news of the ditched plane.

The thin towheaded boy on the teletype showed us his entries.

'The search plane reported an oil slick, sir,' he said. 'The atoll commander has sent out a DV.' When the colonel walked up to the other end of the Quonset hut, the towheaded boy said to me confidentially: 'The only time we get any excitement any more is when somebody's in trouble. Makes you feel kind of bad to find yourself enjoying it.'

The next morning we were up long before daybreak, but a lieutenant came to the door, while we were bolting our breakfast, to say that the strike had been postponed until noon on account of unfavorable weather conditions over the target.

At breakfast the atoll commander had a radio message from one of the search planes cruising near Arno that they had seen a group of natives on the reef pointed at something in the water that might be the wreckage of the plane. 'Well, maybe they got ashore,' we all began to say. The atoll commander said nothing.

The tide was low on the reef that morning. I wandered around looking at the hermit crabs and the variously striped fish in the diamond-clear pools in the rock and the speckled snipelike birds that hopped, always a little ahead of you, over the wide coral bench, and talked to the shell collectors. All along the reef men were wading around in shorts looking for cowrie shells. Then I visited the tent of a man who had caught two big greeen lizards of a type that he said he thought the Japs had introduced from some other island to catch rats. We saw one of them catch a small striped local lizard and eat it up in two bites. Then we went on to Majuro University, a couple of big Quonsets which the personnel officer had fixed up as classrooms for men who wanted to take school and college extension courses. Afterwards we made a call on the enlisted men who got up the local mimeographed daily news-sheet, *The Marshall Air*.

There's something pleasant about Majuro. The narrow strip of gray coral between the reef and the lagoon is covered by ranks of undamaged coconut palms that rustle and gleam in the tradewind. The snowy terns swoop and flutter above them. In their shade are neat rows of tents and Quonset huts. There's a look of cheerful organization about the place. The little chapel and the recreation buildings were built out of palm-thatch by the islanders who come over to work in gangs for Uncle Sam. There are baseball fields and picnic grounds and beer gardens. Some of the boys have built themselves sailboats and catamarans out of discarded fuel tanks off planes. The great mania is collecting shells. When you ask men how they like it, they say it's deadly dull; that they'd get the hell out if they could, but they admit that after all there are worse places to sweat out the war in than Majuro. At least it's healthy. Their faces brighten and they add: 'It's the healthiest damned island in the Pacific.'

At the airstrip after lunch before we took off in the Dumbo for the strike, they told us that Joint Air Command had a message from the search planes: 'Found plane, too late to help.' As we climbed aboard the Dumbo, the colonel said, with an eager youthful look of hope on his face, 'Well, those boys still might be alive . . . We never give anybody up around here.'

This was an amphibian plane that had seen a lot of service. The colonel apologized for its untidy look. 'We are always in the air, never get time to police up,' he said. Its function as a Dumbo was to follow after the fighters and bombers and circle around out of range ready to give assistance if a plane should ditch or if somebody should have to bail out. If the sea was smooth enough, the Dumbos came down to pick up the survivors. If not, they kept their location spotted for the crash boats.

Our place was in the big bulging blisters in the rear. During the takeoff, I sat on the little seat beside the machinegun looking down into the great canvas sheet anchors and the pile of gear, half marine and half aerial, that filled up the tail. At my feet was a blue volume of *Best American Short Stories* that the gunner had evidently been reading. We raced past ranks of the gray fighter-bombers with their backs to the surf and immediately we were off the island and purring across the limitless unchanging ocean. After half an hour the fighter-bombers passed us on the way to the target, a formation of tiny crosses high overhead.

The atoll, when we reached it, looked much like other atolls, a ragged necklace of islands around a green lagoon at the edge of the immense foamlaced blue dish of the Pacific. As we circled near waiting for the attacking planes to peel off and do their stuff, I began to understand what the word 'neutralized' meant in relation to the atolls the Japs still held. A rusty freighter sunk in the lagoon looked like a toy boat somebody had stepped on. There was a strange dusty desolation about the main islet. The few palms still standing had been shredded by fragmentation bombs. The airstrip was pitted and scarred by direct hits. Beside the mangled pier there was a trace of something that had once been a boat.

After circling the place, the Dumbo lumbered back out over the ocean to give the attackers air room.

We saw the dense puttycolored smoke curling up out of the island before we saw the planes. Then we saw them, small midges speeding across the target and out over the lagoon and away. A few bombs made geysers in the water beside the pier. The Dumbo swooped low. When next I could see the island out of my blister, dust and smoke hid the target. The red-faced gunner, who looked more like a truckdriver than an aviator, tried to make me see the figure of a man running along the barbed wire on the beach. There were some bursts from a machinegun that he said were aimed at us. 'They're got a pillbox,' he shouted into my ear.

Then we were out over the ocean again and the colonel had made his way aft and was standing beside me and saying, a little breathlessly, 'We can't show you our stuff today, thank God. Looks like everybody was all right . . . You'll have to take it from me that these boys do a mighty good job when it comes to air-sea rescue work.'

Two last planes were making a run over the target.

'They are out of formation, must have had trouble getting their bombs loose,' grumbled the colonel, wrinkling his brows. We circled the island once more, well out of range of the machineguns. The smoke had blown off and it looked empty and gray and desolate as before, more like a sample photograph of a target than a real island where living men of flesh and blood were eking out an existence in burrows underground. The Dumbo took a couple of turns outside the reef to make sure every plane had gone home and set off on a straight course over the ocean for Majuro.

Back at the airfield, Operations told us that the boys who had crashed the day before were both dead. Bodies had been taken ashore by the natives. An LCI was on its way to bring them back. When we drove up in the jeep to the door of the atoll commander's bungalow, he met us at the door carrying a sheet of paper. Without saying anything he placed it in my hand and strode into his bedroom.

It was the report in stiff Ņavy English from the commander of the patrol boat. He had landed on Arno and interrogated the natives with the help of an interpreter. The natives had seen the plane crash in the shallow water at the edge of the reef and gone out in canoes and brought back the bodies. They had tried artificial respiration for twenty minutes, but both men were dead. Then they had gone back to the wreck and rescued as much gear as possible. All the articles had been carefully itemized on a sheet of paper by the native scribe. They had further made coffins for the two men and piled flowers over them and held a funeral service in the Marshallese language, the account of which was enclosed.

Attached was a sheet of lined schoolroom paper covered with unfamiliar words written in a fine Spencerian hand.

The atoll commander stood looking at us severely from his bedroom door.

'I must get that translated . . . Touching, isn't it?' he said.

Majuro, January 7, 1945

2

Way Station

THE AIR that had been hissing in cool through the unplugged ports of the C47 began to come hot and steamy again. The passengers were sweating under their Mae Wests. The pilot had asked me forward to get a good look at the shipping in the anchorage as we came in, so I began to climb over the roped-down cargo of frayed cartons and octagonal wooden boxes and bulky shapes wrapped in burlap. Stripped to the waist, a skinny young member of the crew sat perched in the middle of it reading a large blue book, entitled *Christianity and Philosophy*, with a small happy smile on his face. I slipped past the navigator's desk and stood beside the flight orderly, a curly-haired youth with a heavyweight's heavy neck and shoulders and a hula girl in green and red tattooed on the big muscle of his arm, and looked out between the intent tranquil heads of the pilot and co-pilot.

Again the long dim streak of an atoll began to take shape at the horizon's edge. Beyond the reefs, marbled with foam, the water in the huge lagoon showed palest green and bright blue against the darker, grayer, purpler, blue of the ocean. Once again the plane was circling for a landing above a roadstead, with its rows of ships, gray and green and mottled with

scruffed paint, and the pilot boats and gigs and landing craft
that zigzagged among them trailing furrows of foam. Once
again the narrow land checkered with rows of tents sped by
under the plane and the wormeaten palms and the ranks of
gray fighter-planes, and the dullgreen transports poised like
dryflies, and the gleaming four-motor bombers, and the Quonset huts, and the thatched roofs, and the long sheds, and the
wharves of linked pontons, and the rusty landing craft bow-on
to the beach. Once again we were scudding along an island
airstrip taxiing after the 'Follow Me' jeep through a gray
swirl of coral dust. As soon as the plane stopped, the heat
rose about us breathless.

After I had dumped my gear in the transient tent, and pulled
off my wet shirt and rubbed down with a towel, and put on
dry things, I walked over to the Island Command to find the
man who had been described to me as the man who really understood logistics. He was a big bruiser of a man with a
broad brow and heavy lines from the flanges of the nose to the
corners of his mouth. He had an intermittent epigrammatic
way of talking like a machinegun trying for the range. It
happened that he was just out of a conference and could take a
few minutes to cool off. There were big rings of sweat under
the armpits of his navy grays. He had sweated through his
trousers at the knees. We walked slowly over to the officers'
club past the ships' store where somebody had put up a sign:
'It's a Privilege to Trade at Enewetok,' into the comparative
coolness under the highpitched thatched roof of the officers'
club. The bar wasn't open yet. We stood irresolutely staring
at the murals around the walls. Then we went and sat in two
deck chairs in the breezy corner of the porch. We sat for a
moment in silence staring at the water, transparent blue as an
alcohol flame in the oblong of shade under the landing built of
coconut logs out from the shelly beach.

'What we are doing,' he said suddenly, puffing on his cigarette, 'is licking a geometrical progression.' He thought for a moment, then he added: 'This damn thing doubles every six months. Six months ago we thought we were stretched like a rubber band, but look at us now.' He paused. 'Here's the whole story,' he burst out again; 'for each man we landed in the Gilberts, five tons of material had to be put on the beach . . . I'm speaking in terms of thirty-day maintenance . . . In the Marshalls it took seven and two-tenths tons, in the Marianas it took about ten tons. I don't know the figures for Leyte, because that's out of my sphere, but I'm sure they are a whole lot bigger.' He threw his cigarette out in the water and lit another. 'When it takes seventy-two days steaming to get a load out to the firing line, you can't make any mistakes about what makes up that load. Supply has to be dreamed up six months ahead, that's when we have to look in the crystal ball. If you think of the whole operation as a continuous train of ships or a pipeline, you'll see that every new island we take causes a leak in the pipeline. Each one makes new demands on logistics. So now we are spread like a branching elm tree. At the end of each branch is a base. What we have to fight for is to keep the trunk large as far out as possible.' He closed his mouth up tight. You could tell at once he wasn't going to say any more.

The tall man from Minnesota who joined us has sat listening silently. 'Well,' he says, after a long pause, 'I don't know the general picture, but I do know my own little operation. It's a naval aviation supply depot. We do anything that has to be done in the way of maintenance, repairs, supply. I've been out here six months, ever since the depot was set up, and today is the first day I've been able to take a couple of hours off. I guess it's that we're getting to be a bypassed

area, and the word is we'll soon be a thing of the past. Here
I've been working seventeen hours a day and my men have
been working seventeen hours a day, damn heavy work for
men who weren't reared up to it. I've got lawyers and a
college professor and printers and truck gardeners and they
work their heads off. But what I want you to explain to me
is why we tolerate these strikes back home. My men get all
hot and bothered so that they can't do their work; whenever
they get a hometown paper or a letter in the mail they just
about blow their top. And then we get these merchant marine boys . . . can't do this and can't do that because the union
won't let them. Looks like the only thing the union would
let them do is sit on their ass and get paid. There have been
cases when marines have been taken out of action when there
weren't enough ablebodied men left to defend the perimeter
because our gallant merchant seamen refused to unload the
ships . . . Christ!'

'That reminds me,' said the man who knew about logistics,
getting gradually to his feet, 'things will be piling up in the
office. I must be back in Pearl Harbor tomorrow. The de-
mand on supply doubles every six months . . . that's our
problem. How long can we keep it up?'

He turned on his heel and walked in through the deep
shadow of the club.

'Now you've just come out from the States,' insisted the
man from Minnesota. 'Maybe you can tell me. Can we keep
on doubling our effort if most people are in the state of mind
of the merchant marine and the war workers?'

'But on the whole we haven't got that state of mind among
war workers or in the merchant marine. It's just isolated
instances,' I said.

'You just explain to me in words of one syllable what kind

of a country we've got,' said the man from Minnesota.

That night the men who sat drinking whiskey round a rickety cardtable in the bungalow on the beach, spreading their bare shoulders to the barely perceptible freshness that came in through the screened window with each lunge of the breakers along the level coral, got to asking the same question: What kind of a country have we got?

Two of them were Annapolis men, a sandyhaired squadron leader from naval aviation, and the redheaded skipper of a destroyer in the harbor. Then there was a doctor and a tall gangling man with deepset eyes under dark brows they introduced as their candidate for President. I had been roaming along the edge of the beach when they saw me through the screen and invited me in. The argument seemed to have been going on for a long time.

The squadron leader was insisting that a naval officer had no business to stick his head into policy. He took an oath to support the Constitution and that was as far as it went. The men whose business it was decided on policies in Washington and instructed the War and Navy Departments, and they put out the orders and it was an officer's business to carry the orders out.

'You're a citizen, brother, before you're a naval officer,' drawled the destroyer skipper. He was from Georgia and spoke in a deep drowsy voice. 'As a citizen it's your bounden duty to take a proper interest in public affairs instead of sittin' here an' bellyachin' about strikes an' the bunch of stupids we've got in Congress. We're gettin' the government we deserve because none of us won't do nothin' about it.'

'I took an oath to support the Constitution of the United States,' said the squadron leader with drunken solemnity.

'But how can you know what you're supporting unless you

give it some thought and study?' asked the man they said they were going to run for President.

'What kind of a country have we got, Mister?' asked the destroyer skipper. 'We're puttin' out a certain amount of effort out here, but what I want to know from you is, is the country worth it?'

They all looked angrily at me as the man most recently arrived from the States. Before I could pull myself together to answer, the doctor had started to talk.

'It looks to me as if our country was made up of a lot of people who were busy selling it out,' he said in a rasping voice. 'All these groups, pressure groups they call 'em, they'll sell us downriver, the Catholics for the Vatican, the Jews for Zion, the Communists and Liberals for the Soviet Union. The politicians will sell us out just to keep their lousy jobs . . . Labor'll sell us out for the checkoff and the fat union dues. Capital'll sell us out for profits . . . We've got a hundred per cent everything except Americans.'

'What kind of a goddam government is that?' asked the destroyer skipper. 'I tell you people like us have got to put our minds on how this country works or we won't have any country.'

'The long and the short of it is that the country is the people,' said the man they said they were going to run for President. 'If the people are no account, the country'll be no account.' The table danced when he brought his fist down hard in the middle of it.

'My kids on that old can out there, they are part of this country,' said the redheaded skipper. 'They are swell and so are the seabees, and the marines, and the goddamned sloggin' infantry . . . We're fightin' a pretty good war . . . because we git together on it. . . . Why can't we all git together stateside, back home?'

'Now you tell what kind of a country we've got,' they asked me again. Before I could answer, everybody got to talking at once. 'Quiet, quiet,' said the squadron leader, spreading his hands out over the cardtable. Then he wagged his finger at us: 'I took an oath,' he said, 'to support the Constitution of the United States.'

Enewetok, January 9, 1945

3

The American Marianas

The Chamorros

WHEN YOU CLIMB DOWN from the plane at Guam, the first
thing you see is the new passenger terminal at the airport.
You have to scramble over piles of broken coral rock to get to
it, but there it stands brandnew, a rakish oblong of glowing
white concrete. In the waitingroom inside there are murals
of bare Chamorritas against blue seascapes. Behind a counter
there's a brandnew shining coffee urn, and beside it wait, to
the frank amazement of a group of soldiers and sailors who
haven't seen anything like that since they left Pearl Harbor,
two brandnew Red Cross girls. The boys are pinching themselves to see if they are dreaming.

We rumble in a command car through rutted tracks across
abandoned cornfields and come out on a broad new four-lane
highway where streams of trucks and jeeps jostle through the
coral dust. Where once was cultivated land the bulldozers
and graders are leveling-off landing strips. Concrete mixers
churn and rattle. Dump trucks fill in the wrecked jungle with
crushed coral. On fresh cement foundations seabees in blue
pants are assembling Quonset huts. Their sweating backs

shine red in the searing sunlight. We slither out into the deep mud of a cutting where mechanical shovels are chewing away a hill and climb steeply through the clay up to a row of tents on a muddy tableland fringed with trees that overlooks the blue bay and the big headlands along the coast.

'The seabees sure are takin' this island to pieces and puttin' it together different,' said the boy from Texas who drove us up to the Island Command. 'That officers' club is Nob Hill,' he added, pointing out a palm-thatched building that topped the fringy thicket of a hill overlooking the bay. 'So they're callin' where you fellers are goin' to be Snob Hill.' He made a gesture with his head toward the crowd of new Quonsets on the summit of the highest hill beyond. The fresh red gash of a new road curved up the flank of it. 'They shot four Japs back of that hill last night,' he said, and burst out laughing.

From the steps of the long drab tent marked 'Correspondents,' you can look out, over the crowded roads that cut through the flattened ruins of the poor little old Spanish town of Agaña directly below and across the green bay hemmed in from the blue by the lacy-white curve of spume of the reef, toward the great purple headlands where there still are Japs in hiding. A rusty landing craft is just threading the tiny gap in the reef. Behind the black chimney of the ruined power-plant you can see a row of them nosing into the beach. Inland, clouds of dust hang above the construction work on new airfields and a pillar of black smoke spirals up from the asphalt plant. The rumble and hum of motors rising from the plain mingles with the muffled roar of nine superfortresses crossing in formation overhead.

Inside the correspondents' tent typewriters chirp like dryflies in a drouth. Sitting on your cot at a table improvised out of raw boards, you find yourself looking out under the flaps at some stonyfaced Japanese prisoners who are cutting down the weeds under the direction of a marine sergeant and managing to give a very good imitation of the slow motion of an old-fashioned WPA gang. Under the burlap screen round the showers you can see the white feet and legs of the bathers hopping about on the wet planks. Birds are singing in the thickets that fringe the hilltops. In a lull in the roar of the motors from the plain and the sky comes the contemplative voice of a man in his underdrawers shaving in the shade of a lightgreen feathery tree at the edge of the cliff: 'The flowers are in bloom all over the island . . . Just like spring on the mainland. Do you know that? Smell just like the old lilocks.'

Down among the ruins on the waterfront it's sticky and hot. The broken walls are full of morning-glories. The sweat prickles on your back as you stumble across crumbling stonework and mashed galvanized iron roofing. Here and there a piece of ancient Spanish masonry stands up with grim dignity amid the burnedout buildings. Wherever half a house is standing or a few pieces of iron can be propped to- gether to make a shelter from the rain, people have moved back into the sites of their homes. Round brown and yellow faces look out smiling at an American uniform when you pass. The odds and ends of clothing they have managed to salvage from the trash heaps their city has been reduced to are clean and freshly washed. They have nice teeth. There's a shy, smiling dignity about these Chamorros of Guam that is as refreshing as a glass of cold water in their island's steamy heat.

Our Military Government people are set up in tents in the central plaza, across from the jaunty little tin bandstand that somehow escaped damage, where now a loudspeaker dins out dance music from the radio station to cheer up the inhabitants. I find myself sitting on a bench talking to a lieutenant. He's a young man who talks in bursts. He's full of enthusiasm for his work. In the first place he likes this part of the world. He tells how, when he was working his way through an agricultural college in California, he started to hone for the Far East. He wangled a trip to Manila one summer as a workaway on a freighter and got himself a job with an export firm. He'd stayed in those parts ever since. He met an English girl from out there whom he later married. Her people were in business in Singapore. He slipped out of Singapore a jump ahead of the Japs and came home to the States. She had gone to Australia. For a long time they thought they had lost each other. Then one day he suddenly got her on the phone and induced her to come to New York and get married. Now he is in the Navy. His job is to revive farming on Guam.

He's got his work cut out for him. He says that our military and naval installations are already taking up most of the good farming land on the island. He no sooner gets a piece of land laid out for a farm than somebody comes around with a blueprint and takes it away from him to build a repair shop or a warehouse on it. He's afraid the people here will forget about farming altogether. Even before the war the Chamorros had preferred to work for the Navy than for themselves. The agricultural school had to shut down because all the boys wanted to go to the Navy mess attendants' school. They had the reputation of making the best stewards ever. They were clean, polite, thoughtful. Admirals fought to get them. There must be about a thousand of them in the Navy right now. Serving in the Navy was considered work of social distinction. The parish priest's brother was a chief steward. Work on the military and naval installations was taking more hands every day. There were only about twenty-one thousand people on the island. That meant a working population of six thousand at most. The way people lived here before the war was that every family had a house in one of the towns and a little patch of land with a shack on it, that they called their 'loncho,' where they grew their crops. There had been few rich people and no poor. It had been a pleasant wellbalanced life in the old days. He didn't see why that couldn't be restored. To be sure, livestock was ninety per cent down, but new stock was on order from the States. He wanted to introduce a fishing industry, too. He didn't see why Guam shouldn't be made one of the most prosperous spots in the Pacific. He liked the people. He didn't see why this shouldn't be a model island.

We threaded our way between heaps of old squared stones to find the parish priest. He was a softspoken oliveskinned young man with a small subtle smile that only occupied the center of his mouth. When he laughed, he laughed very softly. We found him sitting on an army cot in his tiny room in the back of the chapel which the people, with the help of some seabees, had built out of coconut matting to replace the ruined cathedral. First he had taken us out to see the tiny doll-like Virgin with ivory hands that was the patroness of the island. She had been miraculously saved when the cathedral roof fell in. Then we went back and sat on his cot and talked about his people. He had just come back from his ordination at the Jesuit college in Manila when war broke out. Immediately he had found himself in the hands of the Japanese. It had been very difficult for so young a priest, especially when they beheaded Father Dueñas, whom they suspected of helping hide a radio station, and left him the only priest on the island.

'We Chamorros are a happy people, we don't worry much,' he said, 'but of recent years we have had to learn patience, patience like Job. We have learned to be cheerful and humble under adversity,' he said. His voice became very serious. 'God has called our people to a position in the world where it is impossible for them to govern themselves, so we have to be patient and humble and carry out as well as we can the orders of those who are called to govern us.'

When we got up to go, he said a little wearily as if he'd said it a great many times before: 'You must not forget that our people like to think of themselves as Americans. Before the war we sent a delegation to Congress to ask to be treated as American nationals . . . Politics we do not care for, but we are a very loyal people. Many people tell me they are happy to have houses destroyed if it means that the United States will come back. They are willing to make the sacrifice. During the shelling when we were hiding in the hills, a man came to me and said he had two houses and he was sorry neither had been hit yet. He had his wish.' Father Calvo smiled his small smile. 'We are ruined,' he went on, 'but we managed to raise two hundred and eleven thousand dollars for the Sixth War Loan . . . I made campaign all over the island.'

We went back to the Military Government tents to see the man who had been the native judge for many years under the United States Naval Government. Judge Manibusan is a stocky man, well along in years, with closecropped gray hair. His brown skin and high cheekbones give him a slightly more South Sea Island look than many of the Chamorros. When he's asked a question, he pauses for a moment before answering. There's a slyly humorous look about his mouth when he speaks. Like all his people he has a low voice. His English is rapid and clipped. When the Japanese came, he was determined he would not collaborate, he said. He decided to be very old and sick. He dressed in rags and put sandals made of old automobile tires on his feet that made him limp, and stumbled along with a cane. It was easy to look like a beggar because soon the Chamorros were all very poor. Any business he sent his son to do. The Japanese wanted to make him part of their government, but he sent his son. He stayed out at his loncho in the country and waited for the Americans to come back. He smiled. And now he wasn't sick at all. He began to laugh gently.

We asked him what kind of cases he had since his court had reopened. 'Very simple cases,' he said. 'Everything in Guam is simple. The other day I give the judgment of Solomon. Two families are quarreling about a pig. I say, "Kill the pig and eat it together." Everybody had good meal together and go away friends.' He was still laughing when we shook hands to say goodbye.

It was Sunday when we drove around in a jeep to make a tour of the island. In a space back from the roaring road beyond the beaten-up cemetery a couple of miles out of town, Father Calvo was saying Mass in a tiny open chapel. Soldiers and sailors and townspeople in odds and ends of GI clothing stood or kneeled in a semicircle in the open field in front of it. The older women wore the puffed gauze sleeves in cream and chocolate and caramel and white of the oldfashioned Filipino costume. This was the first time this pilgrimage had been celebrated since the Japs had come, they told us smiling.

Further on was a great quarry of coral. Trucks were unloading huge white hunks to dump at the end of the new breakwater. Night and day they never stopped. Meanwhile finger piers grew out into the green water inside the harbor. Liberty ships, LCI's, LST's banked up against temporary rows of floating pontons to unload. We drove past the old white-and-red-tiled Pan-American terminal that looked tiny and forlorn, almost like a prehistoric ruin amid the widespaced airy new buildings of the naval base, and out to the beach where our first troops had landed hardly six months ago. Agat, the second town on the island, used to stretch along that beach among gardens and groves of coconuts, but hardly a trace of it remained. Instead, rows of temporary thatched huts had been put up around the low graypainted building of a dispensary. A few wrecks of tanks and ruined amphibians rusted quietly in the shallow green water a little out from the white sand. To get a view along the coast we clambered up an outcropping of coral rock under a tuft of bushes which the Japanese had dug out to form a machinegun nest. We found ourselves stepping on something that gave. It was the dried husk of the leg of a very small man. It was wrapped in a scrap of Japanese uniform and it wore a boot.

Our own graveyard is on the slope of the hill back of the town. The rows of white crosses stand very neat in the green meadow that lies in a hollow below the ridges where the heaviest fighting was. Somebody has put up an old bronze ship's bell on a white arch of two-by-fours. The grass is clipped short. On many of the crosses friends have tacked metal plaques made from a piece of shellcasing or the bottom of a messkit. On them are engraved the last messages from the outfit. 'In memory of a grand guy,' 'A Good Scout,' 'He Served Us Well.' Under one heartshaped piece of plexiglass is a clipping from a hometown paper with the picture of a tanned young man smiling out from under an overseas cap set at an angle.

In front of the dispensary we met Doctor Minema. Long-necked and lanky in his blue denims he stood looking at us blinking his redrimmed eyes in the lashing glare of the sun off the rutted sand of the beach. He held out his hand. 'You see I'm back,' he said. 'Here is where I landed on D plus four.'

Talking we walked back and forth on the road back of the temporary village. The doctor began to tell us how it was. He'd no sooner hit the beach, he said, than he'd had to dig a foxhole. He'd been there huddling in the sand for hours. The Japs had us pinned down. He'd felt pretty bad until a marine had come running past his hole with a Jap rifle that he wanted to sell for fifty dollars.

'That made me feel the marines had the situation in hand,' the doctor said, screwing up his face. 'After that we were all so busy we didn't have time to be scared. We were still up to the neck in our own wounded when about a week after the landing, the natives, these Chamorros, began to come in.'

He pointed at a green fold in the hills about halfway up the flank of the mountain above the cemetery we had just come down from. They came through there, only two hundred at first, men, women, and children, but a couple of days later it was two thousand. 'Do you remember the old billboard poster advertising *The Birth of a Nation*? Well, that's how they came, like a crowd on a billboard. We were two doctors and five corpsmen. By the first of August we were taking care of eighty-five hundred people . . . four or five babies born a day, malnutrition, wounds, pneumonia, exposure, people Jap soldiers had hacked at trying to behead them. We didn't lose a wounded patient, but we had many deaths from malnutrition. I was paying natives Japanese yen to move medical equipment up from the beach. Before long we'd connived some canvas off a ship and built a hundred-bed hospital.'

The people themselves were very helpful. They had a high

IQ anyway. He had native boys working for him now in his T.B. hospital. All this island needed to be a very healthy place was a few doctors who meant it. When the time came for him to go home to his general practice in Winnetka, and to his wife and baby he might add, he was going to take a couple of these young Chamorros with him to see if he couldn't get them through medical school. He was sure they had what it took to make firstclass doctors.

Our slow walk had brought us back to the door of the dispensary. A smell of frizzling meat came from the tent beyond. 'How about chow?' asked the doctor. 'I don't know what they've got, but I wish you'd stay.'

We explained that we had a lot of miles to cover and climbed into our jeep that was hot as a cookstove from standing in the noon sun. We rode sizzling back to the naval base beside the harbor. There, after scraping some of the mask of dust off our faces, we lunched in a cool messhall at a table with a cloth beside some large pale men who represented the moving-picture industry. They asked us how the GI's liked the sort of pictures they were seeing. Remembering the boys sitting huddled in the rain to see the pictures through in front of every screen set up in every natural amphitheater on the island, we said sure they liked the pictures. Afterwards as we followed a truck through tunnels of dust on the road across the island, we agreed that we ought to have told them what the GI's said after they'd sat through the pictures. 'The pictures are like chow,' said the driver. 'You can't do without it but you sure do bitch about it.'

We stopped to see the new town the Military Government people were building up on the hill at Sinajaña to house the refugees from Agaña. It was mass production applied to the traditional Pacific island thatched hut. The doors and shutters were all made in one place. The frames for the sides were knocked together on jigs. Japanese trucks that Chamorro mechanics had gotten to running again went down daily to fetch coconut palm fronds from the end of the island. Groups of women chattering in soft birdlike voices sat under the tall dense trees up on the rising land behind the village weaving the palm fronds together into panels for thatching the roof and sides. When enough thatch was woven, roofing parties of men swarmed with it along the rows of skeleton huts and the houses were ready. The houses were laid out in rows over the freshly cleared hills. Already laundry hung on the line behind them. There were grocery stores and a big school in the hollow. A few houses had ruffled curtains in the windows.

We stopped at one house to ask a certain Mrs. Mateo if she would do some laundry for us. Mrs. Mateo was a sweetfaced little woman with something of the soft plump look of a baked apple. She beckoned us in without speaking and showed us the corner of the room stacked high with bundles of soiled suntans interspersed with a few navy grays. She made the gesture of one swamped with work. Her daughter got up from the table. She looked like her mother, except that she wore her hair loose around her shoulders instead of pulled back off her forehead. She spoke excellent English. 'My mother will do the clothes for the war correspondent,' she said. 'But instead of paying us in money, could you not get us some dresses by parcel post from Honolulu? We have more money than we need, but we have no dresses. I have been invited to teach school, but I cannot go because I have no dress.'

We drove on across the island through the dustcaked jungle, along the edges of highways under construction where cats and bulldozers and scrapers and graders worked in a blinding swirl of dust, until we came out on an untroubled asphalt road that carried us around high headlands and over a bridge across a narrow inlet where a smashed Jap freighter lay beached in the surf, past rivers where women were scrubbing clothes and sunburned soldiers were washing trucks, to a huge camp of marines that spread for miles among coconut groves along a beach. In the middle of it was a baseball diamond.

A regular big league game was going on between a marine team from Saipan and the local team of this division stationed on Guam. The grandstand was a row of 'ducks' set end to end. Marines, soldiers, and seabees were sitting and standing all over these olivegreen scows on wheels. The bleachers were trucks parked side by side with a row of jeeps in front of them. The fans were wild for the game. · We stopped for a look and found ourselves staying through two innings. Listening to the umpire bawling strikes and balls, watching the pitcher winding up, the way the runner's legs thrust out as he hopped back on base, shortstop running forward with short careful steps with his mitt out in front of him to catch a fly, you could forget the six thousand miles of ocean and the heat and dust and the sturdy little swarming Japs crouching in all these green jungles roundabout. Just for the batting of an eyelash you were home on a hot summer afternoon at the ball park.

As we drove on down the road, we passed a marine patrol home from the daily Jap hunt coming out from the jungle side of the road. Their shirts stuck to their backs. They were mudcaked, sticky with sweat, and grayfaced from fatigue. As they stepped out of the thorny underbrush and formed up on the hard road, the grim hunter's look, compressed lips and narrowed eyes, slipped off their faces.

We drove on through banana groves and overgrown coconut plantations into the little corner of the island that's still
untouched by war. There was a seedy village of long huts
with galvanized-iron roofs. On the porches shaded by masses
of coral vine and hibiscus people sat behind rows of flowering
plants in pots quietly nursing the heavy Sunday afternoon.
There were garden patches back of the houses. Bantams and
chickens pecked at the sparse grasses on the side of the road.
On the square was a big dilapidated Spanish-style church.
The next village beyond was neater. Here the houses were
whitewashed and scattered along the edge of the rising land
above a curving treeshaded beach. There were a few old
stone buildings with a Spanish look of elegance and good
masonry about them. Right off the shore in the still green
water inside the reef lay anchored the hulk of an old iron ship.

There was something familiar about the outline of the ram-
shaped prow. We asked about her and were told that hulk
was all that was left of the old *Oregon* of the Great White
Fleet. She was hush-hush. Her very existence was classified
by censorship as she was slated to play a part in a forthcoming
operation. We sat in our jeep in the shade of a feathery iron-
wood looking out over the clear oilsmooth water at the hulk
of the old *Oregon*. I guess I was the only man there old enough
to remember the *Oregon* as part of the legendary glories of
childhood, the pictures cut out of Sunday supplements, the
tales of the *Oregon* steaming on her long course from Puget
Sound through the Straits of Magellan to Santiago de Cuba,
and triumphal arches on Fifth Avenue.

The last town, in a deep bay protected by steep grassy hills,
is Umánac. There's the ruin of an ancient Spanish church and
an overgrown graveyard with stone monuments. A small
crumbling obelisk on the shore tells you that Magellan landed
here on March 6, 1521.

There's another monument in Umánac, a plaster niche in a masonry arch, marked in large letters UMANAC PRIDE, that contains a set of bookshelves and a little plaque announcing that this outdoor library was established by Mr. Q. F. Sanchez in October, 1933. It contains a selection of moldering American novels. There's *Penrod* and *Mr. Tutt* and *The Little Shepherd of Kingdom Come*, and books by Louis Bromfield, Ogden Nash, and Kenneth Roberts. A sallow frogfaced man in a scrim shirt has seen us looking at them and walks over. 'It is the result of the co-operation of the people,' he says proudly. We ask him if the Japanese bothered the books. 'The people hid them in their houses. They were locked up,' he said in a loud stage whisper, making gestures of secrecy with fat fingers around his lips. 'Now that they have gone, we can read again,' he ended with an oratorical flourish.

The fat sawedoff sergeant, who was the expert on local life and customs up at the Island Command, brought the news one day that there was a wedding going on up back of the town and that he knew we would be welcome if we could only find it. The rain had stopped, so we set out in a jeep, slithering over the black mud of the back roads. We plowed round the edges of cornfields until at last we heard the sound of a band and headed for a little shack made of propped-together sheets of galvanized iron. Under a sort of porch behind a thorny hedge a long table was set out with a white cloth ornamented with asparagus fern and hibiscus flowers. At the head of it sat Father Calvo, smiling his little smile. At a rickety stand in the corner of the yard the bride and groom, both very young and very brown, both dressed in white, were carefully cutting slices out of a highly iced and decorated American-style weddingcake and wrapping them in paper napkins.

We were all made to sit down at the head of the table where the embroidered napkins were while handsome elderly women, with hospitable grins creasing their lined faces, brought us each out, first a bottle of Coca-Cola, then a cup of chocolate, then liberal helpings of Spanish-style rice, barbecued suckling pig, spiced up C rations, and a magnificent American potato salad. To cap it off, everybody had to eat a piece of weddingcake. Meanwhile a bottle of tuba was moving round the table. Tuba is a white liquor distilled from the fermented sap of the coconut palm. It's strong and slippery. It tends to get people talking.

I was asking what it had been like in Guam under the Japanese. The small brown man with the Clark Gable mustache who sat next to me said that at first it hadn't been so bad. They had brought in Brahma cattle to improve the stock. They had made the people plant rice and gone to great pains to improve the methods of growing it. They had introduced a kind of wild tapioca that produced a great deal of starch. 'But then . . .' he paused and looked dramatically up and down the table. 'Leafhopper come and eat up all the rice. Afterwards Japanese army come and eat up everything anyway. Japanese no good.'

'They do not like us to have radio,' said a young man further down the table. 'More than forty receiving sets we kept all over the island. Japanese never find. They are very angry about Tweed. Maybe they think Tweed had a two-way set to send messages to America. Many Guameños think so, too. That is why they died rather than give up Tweed. Japanese beheaded Father Dueñas.'

'In February last year, we buried all radios,' took up the young man with the Clark Gable mustache. 'Japanese come to hate us because we like America better, persecute and kill many people.'

'Now we are happy,' said an older man with closecropped grizzled hair. 'We are Americans again . . . Tell the people in America, we do not want to be treated like Filipinos. We are different from Filipinos. We feel like Americans. . . . Now there is only one thing. Some of us like to farm. Before the war we were never hungry because every family had a little piece of land to plant taro, bananas, papayas . . . what they wanted. Our farmers worked in the country all week and came back to the town weekends. Even if we had business in town or worked for the Navy, we had a little farm to fall back on. Now we would like the Army and Navy to tell us where we can farm. Everywhere we start to work they come with the great machines and pile six feet of coral on our farm to make airfield.'

I tried to tell about the great plans for air and navy bases, for making a model town out of rebuilt Agaña, to explain how prosperous the island would be on account of the employment the bases would give. Up and down the table they listened smiling and nodding their heads.

The elderly man shook his. 'It would be very good,' he said, 'if they would tell us where we can plant so that we can raise fruits and chickens and pigs and feed ourselves.'

With the help of the tuba and a couple of GI's, the small band kept whooping it up. The players were grouped around an upright piano, carefully shined and polished, that had somehow been brought through the Japanese occupation and the fighting and the shelling without a scratch. Gradually the dusty little yard was filling up with khaki and battle-green. With unwearied hospitality the Chamorro ladies kept putting out the food and drink. The bride and groom were sleepily gracious. They had reason enough to look sleepy, as this was the second day of the party and they hadn't been to bed all night. Still the groom's white linen suit and the bride's voluminous veil didn't have a wrinkle or a spot. By the time we left, the party was fast being swamped by an infiltration of grinning bronzed marines. They had taken over the musical instruments. They were eating up the food and drinking up the tuba. They were dancing with all the best-looking girls. The Chamorros were outnumbered, but they weren't dispirited. 'Now really the wedding is turning out to be a success,' their smiles seemed to say. When we left, the band was playing 'Roll Out the Barrel' and the couples were dancing in the dusty grass and the old women were sitting in a row beaming on them and Father Calvo was leaning back in his chair at the end of the table looking thoughtfully at a piece of weddingcake as he smiled his small quiet smile.

The Japanese in Saipan

It's a breezy blue afternoon. We are sitting under a large thatched shelter in the middle of a green plain full of growing crops. Behind us is a mountain of gray rock split by a steep wooded valley. In front of us, beyond the fringe of tall trees along the beach, we can see occasional streaks of the Pacific. Overhead tall white clouds drift in the tradewind.

The people are coming in from the field to have their produce weighed. They are moving toward us in twos and threes along the edges of the fields, in single file along footpaths. A small stubby people with slow ungraceful movements. On the roads carts with solid wheels drawn by small slow carabao come creaking along. They come in through the sunny afternoon like people walking in their sleep.

First trudging on stubby bare feet comes a small boy with a basket of beans tied up in a piece of blue cloth, then stodgy little women with bundles of calabashes on their heads and men jiggling along with loads of onions on carrying-poles. The vegetables are tied up meticulously in squares of cloth. Lined up in a row outside the shelter the people unwrap them with unsmiling care. They are an outlandish dusty little people with wooden faces. There's an air of laborious routine about everything they do. The foreman weighs the produce in small parcels on a hand scale, noting down the weights in a book scrupulously as if his life depended on having every bean accounted for. 'They are a race of statisticians,' says the American lieutenant with an explanatory grin.

He's a blond man with a cosmopolitan manner who has been in the diplomatic service. He can't seem to get over his surprise at finding himself out here in the Marianas running a Japanese farm. Sitting in a sort of chaise longue the Japanese have built for him out of bamboo, he tells the story with a good deal of gusto.

A start was made in getting the farms into operation about a month after we hit the beaches. Saipan had a population of thirteen thousand Japs, a couple of thousand Chamorros, more than a thousand Koreans working on road gangs and a few Kanakas. The first idea was to make the Japanese population selfsupporting so that we shouldn't have to feed them. The Japanese here were Okinawans, people from the southern islands, who were considered more or less the Okies of Japan. They had been brought in by the NKK, the Japanese sugar trust, as indentured laborers to work in the sugar and cotton fields. One of the old section foremen had been very useful in organizing the farming association through which the produce was sold to the people in the civilian camp. The first thing they'd done had been to cut the land available for farming up into one-hectare plots. Each hectare was handed over to a head of a family. The families averaged about eight, counting men, women, and children. They walked out every morning to their fields and returned to the compound every evening. Now, after about six months, the farms were producing ten thousand pounds of vegetables a day. The surplus, after civilian needs had been met, was sold to army and navy messes. They grew beans, cantaloupes, watermelons, squash, tomatoes, bunching onions, greens, sweet potatoes, Chinese cabbage, and a number of local vegetables. Now we were beginning to get in fertilizer to take the place of the night soil they'd been accustomed to using. That night soil, so dear to Oriental farmers, had been one of the causes of the high incidence of dysentery on the island. It had been the worst place in the Pacific for flies until our planes had plowed the island over with DDT. 'Now it's a health resort,' the lieutenant said; 'the healthiest damned island in the Pacific.'

We walked around the edges of some neatly tilled fields. At a corner of a hedgerow a smashed tank halfsunk in the earth was rusting quietly in the sun. Two fat doves flew up from it. This was Hell's Corner, the scene of a great tank battle a few days after our first landings.

There were still plenty of Japs hiding out in caves in the hills. The lieutenant pointed up toward the cleft in the mountain. A few gave themselves up every day. Only a few days ago the farm manager had induced his father and a group of old people to come out. At night the soldiers crept down this great wooded valley we were looking up at to creep into the farms to steal vegetables. Our boys laid traps for them along the paths. Every night they shot one or two.

Had the Japanese civilians given us any trouble? Did they try to help their soldiers in the hills? The lieutenant shook his head. What could they do? They were the most docile people in the world. 'They are as scared of the Jap soldiers as anybody.'

'What's that?' I asked, as we were walking back to the jeep. A tiny shrill piping came from a thatched shelter beyond some trees.

'That's the small children singing. We run a school for the children too small to work in the fields. We haven't managed to get many Jap schoolbooks yet, so they have to spend a lot of time singing.'

We drove down through abandoned canefields to the compound where the Japanese live in shelters built largely out of materials salvaged from the wreckage of Garapan. It's a big dusty shantytown laid out with wide regularly spaced thoroughfares. The shelters are raised on stilts off the ground. The floors, on which people squat and spend their lives, are scrubbed clean and some of them are covered with matting. In the middle of every group of houses there is a kitchen. We stuck our heads into one to watch them getting ready the evening meal. In one room women were emptying cans of what looked and smelt like first-quality Japanese crabmeat into a big kettle. In another they were chopping vegetables. A severe old wrinkledfaced Jap, who must have been the boss cook, was beetling his bushy white eyebrows over the measures of rice he was scooping out of a sack. He'd see to it that not a grain was misplaced.

'We are feeding them on the stocks of food we captured here,' said Lieutenant Commander Schatele, a redheaded man who in civilian life was a police captain in Cincinnati, Ohio. 'They grow their own vegetables as you've seen. They are eating their own rice and canned goods, so they are no drain on our supply. We are even giving the Japs a taste of their own medicine.' He winked. 'We captured considerable medical stores. There's a Japanese judge in the Yakuba — that's the city hall. He tells us we are spoiling the natives.'

The shopping center of the compound is in a long low building with a corrugated-iron roof. It has been partitioned off into a row of stalls on either side. In each one a craftsman is at work. The minute you set eyes on them, you get the feeling that they live in a really different world from ours. I find myself remembering the feeling of utter strangeness I felt in the bazaars of Kasvin in Iran years ago. There's a repair shop to service the bicycles. There are a great many Japanese bicycles. Their bicycles were about the only piece of property these people were able to save. A tiny grayfaced mechanic in blue dungarees is tinkering away with deadly earnestness on a broken chain. He has the posture of one of the little pottery figures you used to buy for a dime in the Chinese stores at Christmas. There's a man laboriously whittling out wooden rakes. In the next stall a man sits beside a pile of clay kept wet by rags spinning the potter's wheel with his bare feet. Next door there's a cabinetmaker's. The saw the carpenter is working with works backwards. You pull it toward you instead of away from you. The same thing with his plane. He squats at his work. The motions he makes at his work are different from the motions Americans or Europeans would be making. The expression on his face is different.

There's a set of boilers where they make soap out of coconut oil and wood ashes. There's a candy factory. Women and children in a long irregular queue jostle for position outside. Inside behind the counter Japanese women are mixing sugar into a paste of mashed navy beans and laying it out to harden on trays like fudge.

There's a general store where the yellow storekeeper adds up the prices with quick fingers on the abacus. There's a cobbler and sandalmaker, and a store where they sell dressgoods by the yard, and a signpainter's, and a big shed where women weave mats and baskets out of the pandanus leaf. There's a dressmaking shop with battered sewing machines. A sign on the door says, 'Please take off your shoes before entering.' Over the counter, where the men's tailor squats at his work, is written in fancy lettering: 'No custom tailoring without a chit from the office.'

At a small forge heated by charcoal he keeps redhot with the quick flutter of a paper fan stands the village blacksmith. He's an old man with long white mustaches at the corner of his mouth, a stiff straight chinbeard and sprouting eyebrows. His face wears the fierce hieratic expression of the Japanese actors' masks people in America used to hang on the walls of their dens in the last years of the last century. Hammer in one hand, fan in the other, he stands with his feet apart and his knees bent and his flexed arms well out from his sides. It is the attitude of a man who is carrying out the ritual of his craft as he learned it from his father and as his father learned it from his father and so on back to the swordmakers of the samurai and the earliest workers of metals. He doesn't look up as we walk past. He is as far out of our western world as a plaster figure of a cavedweller in a glass case in a museum of natural history.

'They don't do so badly,' the Military Government officer was saying. 'They were in pretty bad shape at first from malnutrition diseases.' They were infested with worms. Yaws and dysentery were bad. Our doctors had just about stopped the yaws and dysentery and cleared up the worms. There was a good deal of tuberculosis we hadn't been able to do much about, but the people were already eating slightly better than they did during the last days of the Japanese occupation. Undernourished children got a card that entitled them to milk. At first the parents used to drink it themselves. Their attitude toward children was entirely different from ours. They seemed to think it was up to the child to live through and wait on the parents rather than up to the parents to do anything for the child. It had been hard getting them interested in sanitation. At first they used to let the flies out of the flytraps: 'Couldn't imagine life without flies, I guess. They have none of our notions about making life easy for women and children. They won't do anything for other people's children. A small child fell in a latrine a few days ago and nobody thought to pull it out. Just let it drown there.'

We were walking across a large dusty open space when we met a redfaced young American officer sweating so as he walked along that his suntans stuck to his back and knees. He was followed by about forty toddling Japanese children walking solemn-eyed two by two. 'I'm taking them down to the beach for a swim,' he said in an embarrassed kind of way when he was introduced. 'We have to do something to keep them busy.'

Last thing, we went to see the lepers. Two elderly lepers had turned up among the other problems our Military Government people had to solve when we took the island over. Temporarily they were housed in two little shacks in a barbed-wire enclosure. One of them had a wife to take care of him. He was a pleasant-faced man with a white mustache. At the doctor's request he unrolled the bandage off his red and ravaged arm while his wife hovered over it protectingly. His wife helped him roll the bandage back up. Then he stood up straight looking right at us with untroubled eyes and knelt and touched his forehead to the ground in a deep prostration.

Down among the ruins of Garapan we found the man who was running the fishing fleet. He was Lieutenant Stauffenbiel, a large cheerful young man who had been salesmanager in a Milwaukee brewery before the war. 'Beer to fish . . . seems a long ways,' he said, laughing, 'but I'm sold on this one hundred per cent . . . In my eyes this is the best thing being done for the island.'

The Japanese had run eleven boats before the war and had produced an immense amount of dried tuna as well as enough fresh fish to fill the island's needs. With modern refrigeration we could do much better. Already we were catching enough fish to supply the civilian population, and this was the off season, when the Japanese never used to fish at all. Some days we brought in four thousand pounds of fish. Gradually we were raising the sampans that had been sunk in the invasion and putting them back in service. I mustn't forget, if I wrote about this, said Lieutenant Stauffenbiel seriously, to say that the man who really got the fishing fleet afloat and put the industry back on its feet was Lieutenant George Taggart. He was home on leave now. He'd had his own schooner in the old days and knew the Pacific thoroughly. 'All I've done is follow through . . . But it's been great fun,' said Lieutenant Stauffenbiel, grinning.

We climbed up on the deck of a fishing boat that was drawn up on the beach in a cradle. Japanese ship carpenters were at work on the wooden hull. They had that air of knowing their business. From the deck we could look over the desolation of the town which, except for a few walls of reinforced concrete, had been stamped as flat by our naval gunfire as if a steamroller had run over it. Where the bulldozers had leveled off the ruins rows of huge galvanized-iron warehouses were rising on the smooth white coral.

We went back to the office, in a building of fresh-smelling new wood piled high with nets and buoys and fishing gear. There we talked through an interpreter to the Japanese foreman of the enterprise. He was a serious-looking little man in new dungarees. He had been an independent boatowner before the war. He had evidently done rather well, because he had just built himself a new house that had cost eleven thousand yen. He had worked and saved all his life to build that house. The lieutenant said he was a very useful fellow. We asked him what he thought about the future of the fishing industry.

'After the war,' he said, after a pause, 'I do not think there is much future in fishing for the independent man.'

To make conversation I asked the interpreter to ask the Japanese where his eleven-thousand-yen house was. Without a change in the grave obsequiousness of his manner the man pointed along the beach at the worndown corner of a cement foundation perhaps eighteen inches high. Beyond there was not even a pile of stones in the gray marl. That was where his house had stood. We didn't ask him any more questions.

A Night on the Bomber Strip

We were late getting out to the airstrip. We had given a lift to three naval officers who wanted to visit a friend in the marine bivouac area. We joggled along side roads around the windy flank of the mountain under a sky full of immense stars for a long time before we found the marine's tent. Then we had to have a drink with him. One drink led to another. Then there was a nurse who had to be taken back to her hospital.

Trying to find a short cut to the hospital, we found our jeep speeding in the wrong direction along a one-way road cut so deep into the mountain's rocky shoulder that the feathery growth of the scrub met overhead. The nurse seemed delighted. 'I bet this is where the last Japs are hiding out,' she said with a giggle.

We came out on a maze of roads that led down over the brow of the hill toward camps speckled with lights. Beyond, a great glare of working lights showed us where the bomber strip was.

We chose the wrong road and found ourselves in an immense quarry of white coral, where in a storm of dust white as steam mechanical shovels were loading trucks with crushed stone. From the quarry a brightly lighted fourlane highway roaring with two lines of trucks going in each direction led across the smoothly sloping valley to the airstrip. 'They used to load a truck every forty seconds, now it's every twenty seconds,' said the man who was driving. 'I don't believe it,' said the nurse. 'Neither do I,' said the man who was driving, 'but it's a fact.'

We backed up and circled around again through the darkness until at last we climbed up over the rim of a new airdrome where bulldozers were spreading out the freshly dumped coral. Scrapers, graders, sheepsfoot rollers, machines we didn't know the names of, moved evenly behind them. The glistening bodies of the men, dark from the tanning sun, were highlighted with streaks of white dust in the glare of the floodlights.

In the arch of the dispensary Quonset beyond the immense empty airstrips the doctor was waiting for us. Outside, the ambulance and the crash truck stood ready. While we were waiting for the bombers to start coming back from their mission over Japan, the doctor showed us his emergency operating room. Methods were improving, he said. Now two men on every plane were given the course of training of a hospital corpsman. Immediate action was saving a great many lives. At first there had been some trouble in administering blood plasma in the plane. So little room to move around. The veins tended to collapse in shock. They had worked out a method of administering plasma through the sternum.

'No, not there. The sternum's your breastbone.' The doctor burst out laughing. They had a special needle just long enough to reach the hollow in the breastbone. All you needed to do was lay the patient on his back and punch in the needle. The plasma was absorbed readily into the blood stream. Foolproof, could be done anywhere.

While we were talking, the superfortresses began to come in. Everybody grew tense. The doctor slapped on his helmet and drove fast along the edge of the strip to the hangar where more ambulances were parked. There he sat with earphones on in a car that had a two-way radio. Voices began quacking and squawking over it. A moon had risen to light up the clouds and to glimmer smoothly on the immense expanse of the airfield. Far overhead the sky was filling up with circling navigation lights. The bombers came in in pairs. Red and green lights hovered awhile above the dark shape of Tinian beyond the straits. Then the landing lights flashed on and the great planes roared up the runways, churning clouds of dust into the steady breeze. Our ears were numb from the roar of motors, cut by the sharp twang of radio voices. Driving white dust shot through with the glare of floodlights obscured the moon.

We drove out to a ship that had been hit. They were all laughing as they climbed out. The waist gunner had been hit in the chest, but the piece of jagged metal had stuck in his flak vest. Never touched him. Cabin perforated but nobody hurt.

Back in the hangar they are saying a truck has gone over the cliff. Men hurt. The doctor jumps in a jeep and goes careening off round the edge of the strip. On a road that cuts below the high rim of the narrow end of the airdrome, we find a group of silent men. Ambulances. A quiet voice says a truckdriver must have been dazzled by the lights of the incoming planes. Drove off the edge. They are bringing the men up now. Below us we can see the mashed shape of the truck hanging out over the white fringe of surf far below. Six men are slowly inching a stretcher with a shape on it covered by a blanket up toward the level road.

Another man is already in the ambulance. By the light of three flashlights we can see the waxy skin tight over his cheekbones and his broad bloodspattered chest. His open eyes are very dark. Beside him in the ambulance the doctor crouches with a bottle of plasma held high in one hand.

Meanwhile above our head in pairs the great planes slither smoothly in. Their long bodies, slender as the bodies of dragonflies, glitter with light. Every two minutes they roar in and vanish in the swirl of dust raised by the planes already on the ground that are taxiing to their dispersal strips.

Seventy-nine planes had already landed when we went down to the messhall. After the clamor of radio voices and the dinning of motors and the hurry of jeeps and ambulances the messhall seemed very quiet. The crews who had just come from their interrogation were sitting along the tables eating fried chicken. A few were drinking the spiritus frumenti the flight surgeon had brought out, but most of them were drinking Coca-Cola. Nobody had much to say. A routine operation. Weather might have been worse. Visibility fair. They were still tense. They were sleepy and a little grumpy. They sat gnawing glumly on their chicken bones until word began to go around that eighty ships were in. Only one unaccounted for.

'Eighty-one,' said the major and slapped down the telephone. His cautious smile kindled smiles along the table. Men's faces relaxed while you looked at them. Men leaned back in their chairs and stretched drowsily.

'Hell, this has been a lucky day,' somebody dared say at last. 'One man hit in the hand, well enough to walk to the dispensary, one man picked a souvenir out of his flak vest . . . a wonderful souvenir.'

'Of course,' said the major, 'we can't tell what we did till we see the photographs in the morning. Never talk till you see the photographs.'

Dunker's Row

A sleepy sailor with a command car picks me before day on the hillside outside of the Quonset. We plunge down the steep road toward the harbor and the lines of dark ships and the long pale stripe of the reef. A fringe of dawn is just beginning to glow along the horizon to the east. The ranks of warships and freighters begin to stand out sharp against it. The car leaves me in front of the control tower at the naval airbase. It's a Japanese installation set over a cubical shelter of reinforced concrete earthed up at the sides till it looks like a Mexican pyramid. Upstairs in a brightly lit whitewashed room several officers are looking over maps. They bring out silhouettes and overhead shots of the Northern Marianas from a pile of photographs. 'This is just a routine search,' they say. 'The other ship goes up toward Iwo . . . The one you're going on takes what we call the Cook's Tour.'

The pilot is a very skinny tall young man with untidy red hair. His manner is mild and vague. He wears shorts and a cartridge belt. On one hip is a jungle knife. On the other a forty-five. By the time we get alongside his flying boat and climb aboard, licking the salt spray off our lips, it's day. The boys of the crew have the shockheaded puffeyed look of just having been routed out of their bunks. After a few offhand questions about oil and some repairs on the radio, the pilot and the squareshouldered lieutenant who is his co-pilot settle into their seats before the instrument panels. The navigator leans over his little table scratching his long head with a pencil. The radio operator puts on his earphones. A whine comes from the starter as the props begin to spin. The prolonged roar of motors warming up shakes the ship, and we are off bumping over the choppy waves of the harbor.

We soar in a slow circle between the two islands crosshatched with runways of airfields, plunge through a rattling curtain of rain and head off over the empty ocean to the north. I put my mouth close to the navigator's ear to ask him if they are searching for any particular plane. He shakes his head. 'Always some floating around. If they can give us their position when they ditch, we can usually find 'em, if they haven't drifted too far,' he squeaks into my ear. Then he goes back to frowning down at the chart.

After a while he nudges me and draws me over by the arm to show me a shadow on the edge of the nervous bright-green radar screen in front of him. He points with his pencil to an island named Farallon de Medinilla on the chart. Smiling, he points forward past the pilot's head. Sure enough, you can see it already heaving into sight over the edge of the horizon.

We swoop and circle round the high narrow bench of rusty

coral rock eaten by the sea into crazy caves and tunnels and natural arches. Gulls and terns fly up in clouds as we pass. The pilot is searching the edges of the rock with his glasses. The tumbling surf and the sucking green eddies are empty.

What we are looking for is the fleck of yellow of a liferaft or a Mae West, a scrap of gray wood or a body. With a sense of relief we rumble on. Nobody there.

The next island was a beauty, an irregular green cone wearing a rainsquall like a plumed hat, beautiful sunny yellow beaches. We buzzed low over a clearing on a hillside. There were a few thatched houses and a trail down to the beach between regularly planted coconut palms. Friendly Chamorros were said to live there. You could imagine yourself landing in one of the quiet leeward coves and lying in the shade at the edge of the warm clean sand while the strength came back to waterlogged limbs. It would be fun to find survivors on a Crusoe's isle like this. We searched around the shores of every curving beach, skirted the dark lava cliffs. No living thing. The name of this island was Anatahan.

Sarigan and Guagan were tall immensely green cones. Almagan had great wooded craters. When the Spaniards explored these islands and called them Islands of the Lateen Sails, the aboriginal Chamorros had lived there sailing from island to island in huge sailing canoes. After the Spaniards had fought the Chamorros to a standstill, they had moved them all into the mission settlements in Guam. For centuries these islands had been empty. On a few of them there were said to be a Jap foreman or a Chinese family or two or Chamorros from Saipan sent up before the war to collect copra. Nothing stirred on the beaches. The deep shade under the huge trees was empty. Through the roar of the motors we could imagine the silence. Never a level spot for an airfield. It was tantalizing skimming and searching these faraway shores without a chance of a landing. You found yourself imagining climbing these green empty slopes, smelling the air, listening for the birds. You strained your eyes to catch sight of a raft, a man waving a rag, or a group of Americans sitting round a fire.

We gave the next island, Pagán, a wide berth. Through the glasses behind a trailing curtain of rain we could see the rectangular shapes of a village and a streak the boys said was an airfield. Neutralized, but the Japs still occasionally showed antiaircraft fire there. Perhaps it was only fancy gave it a grim gray look.

We had buzzed low to look at a log bobbing in the surf on a horseshoe beach between rocky pinnacles on Agrihán, forty miles beyond, when a column of spray rose up into the sunlight out of the blue sea ahead of us. Another. 'My! My!' said the pilot. The island soared out of sight as he banked steeply to get out of the way.

'B29's dumping extra bombs on the way home,' grumbled the navigator.

'Target practice,' shouted the radio operator.

'They are supposed to notify us,' yelled the navigator, with a shake of the head.

We soared and zoomed on northward.

I was looking drowsily out over the endless ocean, clear blue now except for an occasional cumulus sailing like a full-rigged ship over a shadowy squall, when he tapped me on the shoulder.

'Want to see a bogey?' he shouted.

He motioned for me to put my head between the eyeshades of the radar screen.

'The shadow's Asunción,' he said. Above it was a little tremulous fleck.

'What is it?' I looked up at him inquiringly. He made air-plane motions with his hands.

'Ours?'

He shrugged his shoulders and turned his hands over in a gesture of ignorance.

The bogey turned out to be a B29. Skirting the shoulder of the next volcano, we saw it far below us, long, shining, and slender like a dragonfly. 'Searching,' shouted the navigator into my ear.

North of Pagán the islands became steeper and wilder. Rainsqualls veiled them. On a smoking volcano we caught sight of a steep patch of yellow grass burning around the shoulder of the mountain. The trees were seared as if from a recent eruption.

Maug was a sunken crater that made a great round harbor hemmed in by ragged purple lava cliffs. We were looking at a house with an iron roof and steps or paths of some kind on the harbor side of the hill when the pilot noticed a burst of machinegun fire. He swerved and veered like a gull and high-tailed it out to sea.

The last island north the Spaniards named Farellon de Pajaros. High rock of birds. It is a tall smoking cone of bare volcanic ash that juts sheer out of the sea as if it had been thrown up yesterday. Not a speck of vegetation. We carefully scanned the surf stained gray and brown with ash. When his business was done, the pilot banked steeply and climbed up over the crater to give us a look. We dove so low we could see yellow streaks of sulphur under the swirling smoke and could smell the sulphurous smell of it. As we roared across the rim shoals of white seabirds rose up out of the pit. We explained to one another with words and gestures that they nested there and hatched their eggs in the warm

ash. Already the cone was trailing its steamy plume far behind us. After a couple of circles over the empty ocean to the
northward, which had already taken on a bleak and sunless
look, we set our course south. 'Next come the real Volcano
Islands,' the pilot shouted back over his shoulder as I leaned
over him. 'One more volcano bigger than this and then Iwo
Jima.'

Mission to Bombard

'Oh ho,' they said, kidding us when we came up the gangplank. 'Correspondents. That means trouble.' The executive officer found us cabins to sleep in. The gunner outfitted
us with battle equipment: earplugs, helmets, gloves, and
masks against flash burns. The doctor gave us tetanus shots.
The assistant exec found us places in the wardroom. The
Admiral invited us to dinner.

It takes you a long time to find your way around a battleship. The thing is stuffed with machinery like a watch.
Antiaircraft batteries occupy every inch of deck. Every
crevice between the working parts is full of men asleep in
tiers of bunks or swabbing the decks down or overhauling
gear. The bewildered stranger, trying to climb the right ladders, to follow the right passages, to go through the right
doors on his way from his bunk to his battle station, gets lost
in machineshops, in bunkrooms, in galleys full of the roar of
fans where lines of men are waiting for chow.

The scuttlebutt in the companionways is that the ship's
been lucky too long. This time she's going to get it. Correspondents. That means trouble.

The first night we lay at anchor between Saipan and Tinian.
The correspondents ate steak with the Admiral in his big bare

airy cabin high up under the bridge. We had just settled down to conversation over our coffee when word came that they were holding the movie for the Admiral. The Admiral excused himself abruptly and rose, his staff officers followed in a hurry. We correspondents straggled after. Outside, the sea and the night were inky blue. Stumbling along the narrow decks, encumbered with every kind of unfamiliar metal object, ducking under the long pointing fingers of the guns, plunging down ladders, stepping over unseen obstructions, you could feel as you made your way along it the bulging immensity of the steel bulk of the ship. It was like crawling along a ledge on the flank of a mountain. The deck was full of a wan glimmer of faces packed close like apples in a bin. Hands grabbed our arms and steered us into a row of chairs. Looking forward, we saw the towering central superstructure rising to the gridirons of the radar apparatus black against the sky. To the right and left the shapes of cruisers lay long on the water. Only the occasional stutter of a blinker signal or the red and green identification lights of homebound bombers circling far overhead pricked the blue night. Everything blacked out when the screen lit up with the vulgar candy colors of an Arabian Nights movie. Suddenly we were in the close childish dream of a picture theater back home.

Next morning a little before dawn, under a sky covered by a pearly overcast, the great mountain of steel swung out to sea in formation with three cruisers and eight destroyers. As soon as the last contact with the shore was broken, an announcement came over the public address system: 'We are leaving on a mission to bombard Iwo Jima, six hundred miles to the northeast of us. Cruising at a speed of twenty knots we will reach the island Wednesday noon and bombard from thirteen hundred till sixteen-thirty. From there we will retire at twenty-five knots to Ulithi. That is all.'

The next day it was already cooler. Up in the long slim bow of the great battlewagon you could feel the smooth power of her engines pushing her through the ruffled seas. Her motion was easy and steady. The sweep of the wind she made stung your eyes to tears. Looking aft you could occasionally see a flying fish take off from the surge of broken water pushed aside by the sharp clipperlike bow. I found myself standing next to a sailor with a square mature jaw who looked much older than the sunburned boys in their teens who made up most of the crew. We fell to talking. He came from Philadelphia. To say something, I said my father had come from Philadelphia.

'What about Philadelphia?' he asked, giving me a suspicious look.

'I don't know much about Philadelphia,' I answered haltingly.

'Well, we've all of us come a long ways,' he said, in a tolerant kind of tone. 'And I guess we've got a long ways to go.'

I was just getting around to asking him what he meant when the merry breathless stinging buglecall of an alert came over the loudspeaker. Immediately the decks were filled with scuttling figures in blue dungarees and helmets. I popped into the wrong door in my haste and found myself climbing the steep steel ladders inside the great central conning tower with all the trapdoors closing behind me, and ended up wearing somebody else's helmet in the lofty perch of 'sky control' above the bridge. 'Five bogies on the screen,' the young fellow with the earphones muttered between clenched teeth.

Looking down, you could see under your feet the broad fish-shaped platform of the battleship shearing through the rising seas under the gray sky, and to the right and left and abaft of us, the cruisers plowing great white furrows, and beyond, halfway to the horizon, the low angular destroyers spewing smoke from their stacks. A string of flags broke out from the signal halyards overhead and were immediately echoed in tiny bright specks from ship to ship. 'Planes identified as friendly,' said the young fellow at the earphones, giving me a wink. The all clear sounded. Immediately every part of the deck was full of men chatting and kidding as they strolled to their ordinary posts.

That afternoon we oiled the destroyers. The wind had freshened again and high bottlegreen seas were running. Even on the bridge you had to duck now and then to keep the fine spray out of your eyes. The whine of the wind dropped as the great ship slowed ponderously to ten knots. You could see the destroyer nosing cautiously up from astern.

'I bet that's the first time he's done it. Most of those boys on the cans are new,' said the skipper, and the fine lines around his eyes and the corners of his mouth deepened into an understanding grin. 'After a few times they get so it's easy as rolling off a log.' He had long sharp weathered features under the visor of a crumpled little green cap. There was a kind of tolerant skeptical look on his face as he measured with a gray eye the distance between the ships. Slowly the kitchen knife of the destroyer's bow jabbed further and further into the seas abreast of us. At every third wave her decks were awash. The men in their oilskins glistened with wet. A line was shot out of a gun from the deck below us. The first time it fell into the water and had to be hauled aboard again. The second time they caught it on the destroyer and began hauling the hawser aboard. 'Whoa!' shouted somebody on the destroyer when they'd hauled it in far enough. 'Whoa!'

The skipper, who had been watching the operation with the absorbed detachment of a father letting his small child fit a toy bridge together, burst out laughing. 'Hear that,' he said. 'Rich, isn't it? That's the New Navy.'

Then the black pipe weaving like a boa constrictor was swung out from the battleship on a derrick and the operation was complete. While the oil was pumped through, the two ships cruised on side by side keeping just enough distance apart to keep a little slack on the hawsers. Meanwhile twenty gallons of icecream were sent aboard the destroyer on another line and the crews looked at each other and tried to make an occasional friendly incivility heard above the seethe of churned water between the ships. 'Momma whale feeds baby whale,' said a redfaced ensign in an aside to the correspondent as if to put him at his ease when he brushed past him on the bridge.

Just as they were ready to cast off when the destroyer's tanks were full, the men looking down from the decks and turrets of the battleship saw that the drenched and dripping youngster on the destroyer, who was having trouble getting the hawser loose, had hauled out his sheathknife. He made a pass at the rope. 'No, no!' the cry burst hoarsely from a dozen throats. 'Can't you see it's a new line?' Flustered, he dropped the knife and puffing and spitting from another drenching sea got the hawser loose and fell back gasping. The skipper hadn't said a word. 'What can you expect?' he said, as he swung back into his cabin. 'Farmboys fresh from the plow.'

The battleship increased her speed and was soon chewing up the sea at twenty knots again. Columns of spray moved across the glistening gray decks.

'Well, what do you think of this life?' an officer asked me when I ran into him taking shelter from the wind and spray behind the great batteries in the forward turrets.

'Not bad,' I said.

'It's ease and comfort compared to the kids on those cans,' he said, pointing to the destroyers plunging along in a whirlwind of spray. 'Those kids really take a beating. Here we are comfortable and dry and we eat well. If we get it, we get it. On a big ship it's all or nothing.'

Back in the executive officer's cabin I settled down in the cool blast of the electric fan at a round table with a green baize cloth to get my notes together. The exec was sitting in his armchair with a big oldfashioned tambour frame on his knees busily embroidering a pattern of flowers on a piece of heavy material. His lips were pursed. He was so engrossed in his work that he didn't look up. It was some time before he spoke.

'Times like this there's always a little feeling of strain and tension,' he said in a brisk matter-of-fact tone. 'Work like this takes your mind off things. I'm doing my wife a set of backs for chairs.' He wrinkled his face up. 'If the war lasts long enough, I'll have enough for a whole drawingroom.'

Next morning breakfast was on the table before day in the wardroom. We'd hardly put away our bacon and eggs before the voice over the public address system came out with an order to man the antiaircraft batteries. Then immediately came a call to general quarters and then the bloodheating bugle call of battle stations.

Still chewing on last mouthfuls of bacon and toast, we scuttled up the ladders. The eastern half of the clear dome of the sky was beginning to glow a little at the edge with steely light. The wind was so cool the life preservers felt comfortable. Al Croker and I found ourselves stamping our feet to keep warm in the middle of the small platform called 'Sky Aft,' which had been assigned to us as our battle station.

Officers and enlisted men, all with earphones on their heads, who stood and sat looking out of immense fieldglasses in every direction, encouraged us with hospitable grins whenever they took their eyes away from their work. One of them dragged a cot out in the middle for us to sit on.

'It's nothing,' said the lieutenant. 'They've just got the mountain on the screen.'

'Just that damn volcano,' one of the men called down to the boys with the machineguns on the little turrets directly below us.

The young man with the hula girl under the word *aloha* tattooed on his forearm was reporting scraps of what he heard over the intercom from the radar report center. 'Iwo Jima fifty-nine miles away . . . Four submarines sighted . . . One plane down . . .'

'Ours or theirs?' asked the lieutenant.

He hunched up his shoulders to indicate ignorance. 'Our bombers already workin' on the airfield.'

We correspondents smoked and pulled our earplugs in and out of our ears and took our helmets off our heads and put them on again. Al Croker launched on a tremendous series of wisecracks. We even started telling over the United Press man's puns. People were beginning to get fidgety.

By the middle of the morning the sunlight had faded into a curdled overcast. Suddenly we made out the faint outlines of the volcano on the horizon. From a huge cone the color of cigar ash stretched a long straight plume of pallid smoke.

'That's the first of the Volcano Islands,' said the lieutenant. 'The next one's Iwo Jima.'

An announcement came over the public address system: 'Send one man down from all stations to secure coffee and sandwiches for each station.' The volcano had faded into the murk of the horizon again. The hot coffee and sandwiches made everybody feel wonderful. The lieutenant handed around cigars. We all began to feel cozy on our little platform.

It's thoroughly cloudy now. The wind is rising. The battleship's long bow occasionally digs into a gray sea. The cruisers and destroyers all have a bone in their teeth. Another faint outline has appeared on the northern horizon. A rock with two humps. 'Sure, man, that's Iwo.' Signal flags flutter at the halyards, are answered on the cruisers and destroyers. The flotilla makes a rightangle change of course. 'Bombardment postponed one hour,' says the voice over the intercom. Iwo Jima has vanished into the mist again.

'It's like waitin' to have a tooth pulled,' the boy with the tattooed hula girl, whose name turns out to be Ham, says, laughing. The lieutenant has opened a can of caramels. He tosses one to each of us. 'Here we sit and wait it out,' says the boy with the extrasized helmet over his headphone, flicking the wad of paper off the caramel at his mate with the big spyglasses.

'B29's.'

'I must be goin' blind. I don't see 'em,' says Ham.

There's a little flurry of bogies. Each time a new bogey is announced, all the antiaircraft batteries on deck swing around.

'I got an unidentified plane.'

'It's a Lib, it's a Lib.'

'The only thing we have on the screen now is land,' comes a voice cheerfully over the public address system.

Everything is suddenly very quiet. You can hear the thin hiss of the wind under your helmet.

'Sing me a lullaby,' Ham croons into his mouthpiece.

'How would you like a date with a beautiful blonde? Or a date with a blonde, period.'

'Life is good. Life is good,' comes a kidding voice from one of the antiaircraft batteries directly below us. 'Stand watch all night and sit out here all day.'

The sky has cleared. The wind is blowing half a gale. It's aft of us now. We are heading back toward the island. 'Sky Control says he wishes they'd mix cologne with their stack gas,' giggles Ham into his mouthpiece. 'Chokin' to death up there.'

'Raids one and two have dropped their bombs on Iwo Jima and are now re-forming at a low altitude,' comes the warm explanatory voice over the public address system.

'There it is. In fifty-five minutes we'll be tappin' on that door . . . One zero five six, oil slick on water.'

'Discolored water,' somebody is muttering. 'I don't like that.'

'What's our range goin' to be?'

'Six thousand yards.'

'Six thousand yards is too damn close.'

The boy at the interphone bursts out laughing. 'What's that one?' asks his mate, without taking his eyes away from the long spyglasses on a stand like a gunmount. 'Tell you later . . . There it is, low-lyin' plane at fourteen miles. It's a Liberator comin' in.'

'Nine miles.'

Another bogey.

'Damn right. Single-engine plane.'

'It's got a long nose. Detectors report have never seen a plane similar.'

All together the guns start barking. Fiveinch. Pompoms. Machineguns. The big white stoneware cups we drank coffee out of are dancing around in the corners of the deck. One of them drops off the cot and shatters. The correspondents are dodging burning wadding from the five-inch guns. Each detonation is like a blow with a baseball bat.

A tiny cross-shaped thing in the path of the sun that had seemed to be coming in has vanished. 'Perfect solution,' comes a voice over the intercom.

The destroyers are steaming back and forth across our bows like hunting dogs searching for the scent. The sharpnosed cruisers are buried in spray as they plow through the high cross-seas.

'A bogey. A bogey. We have the bogey. Two-engined plane flying low over water. It's a Jill . . . Torpedo plane. He's got a fish.'

The Jap plane swoops across the front of the formation. All the antiaircraft batteries are going at it hammer and tongs. Long streamers of flame spurt from the cruisers. The flash from the five-inch guns on the deck below flaps blinding across our faces. The Jap wiggles his wings as if saluting. He's heading for the last destroyer. There's a tiny glow in him. A broad sheet of flame trails out like a flag. He pitches into the water out beyond the stern of the destroyer and explodes as he hits. Nothing left but a curling brown pillar of smoke. 'The can got him!' shouts a happy voice like a voice from the bleachers at a baseball game.

'All we have on the screen is a group of friendlies that seem to be spotting planes,' comes the voice over the intercom.

'All hands man battle stations for bombardment,' warns the public address system. 'Set condition zebra . . . Fiveinch batteries loading in preparation for counter-battery fire as we go in . . . Prepare for three threegun salvos from the main battery.'

'Now you big bastards, go ahead and pop off,' Ham shouts in the direction of the sixteeninch guns in the turret astern of us.

We are right in on the island now, two meanlooking brownish gray piles of volcanic ash joined up by a tableland on which we can make out the light streak of an airfield, and, through the glasses, a tangle of wrecked Jap planes along the edge. We are headed into the wind and get choking gusts of gas from the great stack. Every time the sixteeninch guns bellow, it takes the breath out of us. The coffeecups in the corners of the deck are crumbling under the concussion.

Puffs of smoke and then great dirty smudges appear over the island. There doesn't seem to be a speck of cover or a green tree on it. Nothing but streaky piles of volcanic ash. Something blows up behind the nearer volcano. An immense mushroom of white smoke appears suddenly in the sky and then begins to swirl and churn. As we round the point of the island opening up the side where the beach is, we can see specks of flame against the billowing smoke.

The destroyers have gone in after three Japanese transports that lie anchored off the beach. They report one blown up and two beached and burning. The intercom reports the signal from the can's skipper. 'Sorry we can't blow the other two . . . they won't seem to blow.'

Meanwhile the battleship continues her zigzag course down the eastern flank of the island. When the sixteeninch batteries fire a ninegun salvo, the whole ship seems to move sideways in the water. Each time a salvo is announced, there's a tense crouched moment of waiting for the punishing blast. The teeth rattle in your jaw.

Astern the cruisers are cutting through the seas showing

long jets of flame from their eightinch guns. Smoke rolls behind them in great swirls.

'We expended ninety-one rounds of ammunition on that area. We are shifting to new targets on northeast corner of island.'

Now behind the burning ships we can make out the dirty curved beach where our landings will take place, the crumbling meanlooking hillside behind, the enfilading volcanic mountains that smoke as if they were in eruption from our shelling. Gradually the pillars of smoke and dust churning up out of the mountains join into a huge pall that hangs over the island and blots it out.

A cold front is coming down with the rain from the north. No visibility left for spotting planes. After a few last salvos at the northeast end of the island, the battleship and her cruisers pirouette majestically. The voice over the public address system announces cheerily: 'Destroyers report everything along beach wrecked . . . Rain and poor visibility make it advisable to discontinue bombardment. Retiring at twenty-five knots,' and suddenly there is silence. Silence except for the swishing crash of the seas over the bow and the whining of the wind under our helmets and the hard patter of the rain. We pull the plugs out of our jangled ears.

Ulithi, January 25, 1945

4

Floating Base

A Busy Corner

THIS MORNING our position is around ten degrees north
latitude. The sun glistens hot on the gray steel plates. The
tradewind has lost its freshness. Below decks, in spite of
ventilators and fans, the battleship is stifling. Any little
effort starts the sweat running down your face.

'Well, there's Ulithi,' somebody says. In the murk along
the light-blue horizon ahead you can make out a faint cross-
hatching of crowded masts and superstructures of ships. As
we draw nearer to the atoll, a few shadowy green streaks of
islands rise to the surface. Signal flags flutter on our halyards
and answering signals flicker and vanish on the foremasts of
the cruisers and destroyers. Blinker lights keep up a continual conversation. Three fighter-planes, rolling and tumbling
in the sky overhead, fill our ears with the roar of their motors.
As we slow down to approach the entrance to the anchorage,
radar grids and gray masts and stacks and turrets bristling
with guns rise out of the sea. We begin to make out a line of
battleships and beyond them the great barns of aircraft carriers, planes with folded wings crowded close on their decks

as bees swarming on a hive. There is a tangle of destroyers hull down far to the south behind ranks of long low tankers. In the broad lanes between whaleboats, bluntnosed landing craft of every size and description, tugs, destroyer escorts, patrol boats, stagger in a chain of white water through choppy seas. It's like steaming into a great port, New York or Liverpool, except that there's no land, only a few tiny drowned islets fringed with coconut palms along the reef.

At the entrance through the submarine net we cut down our speed. Our destroyers and cruisers go their way. The battleship with ponderous smooth dignity swings slowly into her anchorage in the line of battleships. As the chains rattle with the dropping of the anchor, a look of relaxation comes over the faces of officers and men busy with the shipping of accommodation ladders, the swinging-out of derricks and booms, the opening-up of hatches. The ship has made port.

The correspondents are strapping up their gear. Most of them are inquiring about the plane back to Guam. A couple of us want to go over to Azor Island. We hang around the accommodation ladder watching whaleboats and lighters bobbing and lurching in the steep blue chop while the officer in charge explains the shortage of small boats. Warships stripped clean for action can carry very few. 'This may very well be the largest collection of shipping ever collected in a single anchorage,' he says with awe in his voice. 'There aren't enough small boats in the world.'

The Admiral's barge has come alongside. It's a neat little speedboat with white duck seats and curtains with tasseled fringes that gleam white in a patch of sunlight. The Admiral and his flag officer appear on the upper deck, run briskly down the ladder to the quarterdeck, the 'scrambled eggs' shining on their caps. The Admiral salutes the Captain of the ship and his group of officers in suntans. The officers salute. The bosun blows a thin note on his pipe. The Admiral and his flag walk down the accommodation ladder, make the perilous leap into the stern of the speedboat when she rises on the wave, and disappear into the cabin as she shoots ahead and cuts a foamy V through the waves.

After a while the deck officer finds us a place in a whaleboat that's going for the mail. We tumble into it sprawling land-lubberly on top of our bags and crouch under the canvas awning as the boat noses into the steep seas. At every lurch warm greasy waves slosh in under the awnings. Immediately our seats are wet. The boat staggers ahead in a blur of spume. The young fellow in oilskins standing bareheaded at the tiller in the stern can hardly see for the lash of spray in his face.

We pass slowly in the teeth of the wind along the row of fifteen battlewagons at anchor. Across from them are ranks and ranks of cruisers. We duck under the beetling bows of the tall flattops that, seen close to, have a sawedoff look as if they were segments of some great industrial plant blown out to sea in a hurricane. Beyond the carriers, up in the northerly end of the atoll where the islands are closer together, we plow through a pack of Liberty ships, supply ships, repair ships, transports, converted tramps and liners, painted gray or green or striped and checked with various types of camouflage. Right up at the end, where the shallower water is green against the reef, lie destroyer escorts and landing craft and barges and scows, and off in an anchorage by themselves, a row of ammunition ships under their red flags.

The floating postoffice is a landing ship. With wet behinds and dripping trouserlegs we scramble up the ramp in the landing ship's open bow and find ourselves inside an electric-lighted tunnel piled high with mailbags on either side.

There's a smell of mold and damp planking. Lines of men, all as wet and dripping as we are, wait for their ship's mail along board tables worn shiny, while sweating mailclerks, stripped to their blue cotton pants, rummage in the great heaps for the grimy canvas bags. There's something merry about the place in spite of the crowding of sweaty men in damp clothes and the standing in line. The men waiting for their shipmates' mail, and their own, too, they hope, have a look of cheerful anticipation on their faces. Men from various ships smoke and kid and yarn happily. The clerks seem to enjoy their job. Anything to do with mail from home is cheering. The fact that there are such mountains of it gives the whole ship a homey holiday feeling like a department store on Christmas Eve.

I climbed up the narrow ladder to the deck and found myself talking to a brown young man with curly hair who's wearing a pair of khaki pants torn at the knees and a faded blue cotton jacket without any buttons. Beside him stood a small brown popeyed dog. The sky was overcast, but the scaling plates of the deck still reflected the sun's heat. We were both sweating as we talked. Asked if he'd ever been to sea before he joined the Navy, he laughed and said, well, he might have gone rowing a couple of times in the park.

He noticed that I kept looking out over the ships anchored rank behind rank as far as we could see in every direction. Out beyond, where the big ships were, the water was blue. Up at this end where it was shallower, it was emerald green. Small boats moved continually back and forth. They hung in a tossing cluster around the landing ship's bow.

'There's eighteen miles of it,' he said. 'I've been figuring out from the "ships present" list. I figure there must be at least three million tons of shipping in here . . . pretty good for a cannibal isle.'

'That must keep you busy with the mail.'

'Sure, they all come at once . . . There are still warehouses ashore packed with mail to the roof. If I said we were serving a population of three hundred and fifty thousand, I don't think I'd be lying.' As I started down the ladder again, he added, 'I like it. It's a busy corner.'

An Island No Bigger than a Peanut

We landed at a little pier of coconut logs filled with crushed coral. While we were waiting in front of a row of warehouses for a jeep to haul our bags up to the transient quarters, we watched a rusty landing craft coming in to the beach to unload. The beachmaster, a tall rangy man in sweatdrenched greens and a small visored cap like a baseball player's, was waving the landing craft in past the coral heads with the gestures of a traffic cop. At last it was in the right position and the ramp splashed heavily into the small waves on the beach. Several sunblackened men of the crew came wading ashore. They had that look of having been a long time away from home. They wore beards. Their hair was long and bleached out yellow. Several of them wore a single silver ring in one ear. They hauled on the cable to secure the landing craft in its position nose to the shore. Meanwhile a goodsized crane on a tractor was clanking down through the sand. The treads caught hold on the ramp. The crane tipped as it clambered clumsily aboard. It took some time to work the crane into the right position. The treads had to be blocked to steady it. Then a big sixwheel truck backed up the ramp and the unloading began.

The beachmaster turned to us. 'That's what we do twenty-four hours a day,' he said.

We asked what he was unloading. 'Dynamite,' he said, 'and beer.' He frowned. 'I sure don't like the beer. Too much responsibility to keep people from gettin' at it . . . We ought to have more hands, but it's Sunday. Handlin' cargo sure does give the average seaman a deep sense of religion.'

The beachmaster strode down to the waves' edge to signal in a second landing craft. 'And so it goes,' he shouted back at us over his shoulder.

Already the loaded truck was rumbling up to the road and another was backing its way down through the sand.

The sergeant who drove our jeep had a comical expression on his red face. 'Gentlemen,' he said, 'this fair emerald island is not without its historic landmarks. The pier at which you have just landed was built by the honorable krauts at the time of the first World War. The little control tower you can see behind the communications center was built by the Nips and evacuated by them at a dead run on or about September 20, 1944. We are now approaching Shady Acres, the best hotel in a radius of a thousand sea-miles . . .'

We had driven up in front of two Quonsets joined by a wooden porch that faced the surf pounding on the coral benches on the windy side of the island. Overhead the long spiny streamers of coconut palms thrashed in the tradewind. With the help of a drowsy colored boy we picked ourselves cots out of the row along either flank of the hut. We tore off our itchy wet clothes, managed to get a sprinkle of brackish island water out of the showers that had been rigged up on the shore, behind some bushes with reddish-green leaves like coarse oak leaves, swallowed a few salt tablets, and lay down in the breezy hut for a moment's rest. After the crowded days on the battleship and the pounding of the whaleboat over the short seas, the stillness was delicious. In the hut it was abso-

lutely quiet. Outside you could only hear the pound of the
surf and beyond it the distant buzzing unending monotone of
formations of planes on patrol. The colored boy had lain
down on the floor of the porch and gone back to sleep.

The quiet-mannered young Californian who was Public
Relations Officer came around in the afternoon to see how we
were faring. I asked him who ran the place.

'Commodore Kessing is atoll commander.'

'But who sees that all these ships don't run into each
other?'

'That's the port director. Suppose we drop in on him.'

The port director was Lieutenant Commander J. A. Ma-
loney. His office was in one of the headquarters huts, at the
end nearest the harbor. He sat at his desk opposite an immense chart of the anchorages. He was a humorous roundfaced man with a flicker of blue in his eyes. He talked slowly
and thoughtfully, as if it were somebody else's work he was
talking about. He hadn't been home in two years. He asked
me a little wistfully if New York still stood up on its hind
legs. He had worked for the Shipping Board there. He'd
had a little experience with the Port of New York, he said,
but his real training for this job had been at Espiritu Santo.
Eighteen months on Suicide Island. He'd moved up on October 8 and had operated off a destroyer tender. Two hours after
they dropped anchor they were routing a convoy in.

Of course we hadn't any charts of our own. We used the
Japanese charts. The little Nips had been kind enough to
leave a chart of the Ulithi minefields in Saipan when we took
the place. Thoughtful of them. This chart — he nodded,
smiling, toward the wall in front of him — had been made
by our survey ship, using the Jap charts as a basis. He turned
in his swivel chair and pointed out through the screen door

over the dense green water to a gray ship with a clipper bow lying at anchor off the pier.

It was pretty simple really, he went on, talking slowly with his eyes fixed on the chart. Of course the hours were long. No putting off till tomorrow in this work. He had thirty-two officers and a hundred men under him. They usually worked twelve to sixteen hours a day. A good many officers were sent to him for training. The main jobs were convey routing. At a certain point in the Pacific convoys came under the management of this port. Before that they were routed from Pearl. For one thing they had to be diverted out of the way of Jap subs.

Then there was berthing and control of harbor activities.

And communications between ship and ship and ship and shore. Communications were a tough nut. This office alone handled seven or eight hundred messages a day.

The biggest headache was turnaround. There was a saying in supply that if you held up a Liberty ship for eight days it was the same as if you sank one. Floating warehouses were a help — barges and obsolete freighters put aside for that purpose — but that meant double handling of cargo. Well, perfect turnaround demanded a daily miracle, and miracles just didn't happen every day. He smiled wryly and got to his feet and walked slowly over to the chart.

'You see these circles.' He pointed as he talked in his meditative tone. 'They show the space a ship takes up swinging on her anchor chain. It's kind of fun working this stuff out. Each ship has to be placed as near as possible to the ammo or the fuel or the supply as the case may be. There's a terrible lot of lightering. We have to cut down the distance the lighters have to go as much as possible. And then while a ship's in here loading, she's using up her stores. Suppose she's in here a week. Each ship has to be topped off before she leaves.'

Shaking his head, he walked slowly back to his chair. I could see him looking out of the corner of his eye at the yellow slips that had been piling up on his desk. He waved a bunch of the flimsy at me with a rueful smile. 'Just while we were talking . . . it piles up.'

After mess the Public Relations Officer took the correspondents to the officers' club to buy them a drink. It was a pleasantly arranged building open to the wind with a mural and a bar and a jukebox and some round tables set outside on a concrete terrace. At the bar there was most of the staff of the island and the atoll, a sprinkling of officers waiting for their ships, a few doctors, transients of various services, and a sprinkling of seabee officers from the stevedoring outfit.

'It's hard to believe,' one correspondent said, looking around at the lights and the rows of bottles and the chairs and the glasses and the young men in laundered uniforms, 'that we've only been on this island four months.'

'Took us two months to clean house . . .' One of the doctors spoke up in a reproachful tone, 'You men land here and say it's dandy and then you're gone again next day . . . You don't see the process. You couldn't imagine how much trash and litter there was on this island that's no bigger than a peanut, and the flies and the mosquitoes. A coconut palm makes as much litter as an Italian family on a picnic.'

'There aren't any mosquitoes now. Was that DDT?' the correspondent asked.

'No, we didn't use any here. Plain routine sanitary measures and plenty of sodium arsenate to kill the flies. We had trouble with mosquitoes breeding in the bases of palm fronds. But there wasn't any dengue. It's a simple process.

The first thing you do is isolate the natives. We moved 'em down to another island. You eliminate underbrush and marshy spots and you spray and bury your feces and spray and bury your garbage . . . Spray and bury . . . Then you screen your latrines and screen your messhalls, spray and bury and screen and screen . . . Fortunately, we've got a base commander who is thoroughly sanitation conscious.'

'Were you here when we had the typhoon?' somebody asked.

'We expected Japs, but what we got was a typhoon . . . most of our landing craft and small boats piled up on the reef.'

'Does that mean,' asked the correspondent, fishing in the damp breastpocket of his shirt for a notebook, 'that we will have to move out of here before the typhoons start again next fall?'

'Might be.'

'A typhoon sure would pick this place up and dump it into Greasy Creek,' said the doctor bitterly.

'That's just what happens,' said a skinny young man with a Dixie drawl who belonged to the seabees. 'We just get a place fixed up nice when they tell us, "Gentlemen, we've got a nice little pile of manure for you to clean up a thousand miles across the water. So shake the lead out of your tail and git goin'." '

'Wasn't Ulithi part of the same change of strategy that landed us in Leyte instead of in Yap and Mindanao?' asked the correspondent.

'Uh huh,' someone answered in matter-of-fact tones. 'The biggest base in the world five hundred miles inside enemy territory.'

'I don't see why it isn't the biggest story in the war,' said the correspondent.

'Try and tell it,' somebody said.

'Who said territory?' came a sour voice. 'The damn place is all afloat.'

'I didn't come here to talk shop,' the doctor was grumbling. 'I want to hear what it's like stateside among the white natives.'

Later we found ourselves up at the bar with the skinny seabee. 'You come on down with me,' he said, putting his arms around our shoulders, 'to have a snack at our messhall and meet the Bougainville Bastards. Damned best outfit in the Pacific. This whole atoll was lifted right out of Bougainville, commandin' officer and all. We're lucky in havin' an atoll commander who understands seabees. Tough as hell, but great to work for. We've got the best setup on the island. Come on down and see our setup. The boys'll give you a snack.'

He piled us into his jeep and plunged into the cloudy night. Passing the pier, he stopped a moment so that we could look out at the dark bulk of the ships stretching out across the lagoon. Their masts and stacks and superstructures stood out against the moving fingers of searchlights. 'Eighteen miles by eight,' he said. 'They have to signal by searchlight instead of by blinker, so many of the ships are hull down from one another.' He threw the car into gear. 'You folks are probably sick of sightseein' and want that snack.'

The seabee camp was about a block further along the beach. 'Well, here we are at the other end of the island . . . no kind of an island,' said our friend. After he'd been recognized by the sentry, he led the way up some steps into a messhall where, under a bright light over an immense gleaming refrigerator, a group of men sat at a table. At one end of the table was the half-demolished carcass of a turkey, at the other a section of an immense pink ham, and between a great white pile of army bread.

These men were older and varied more in feature and expression than the navy youngsters we'd just been talking to. Their faces were lined and creased by the experience of years, jobs, trades, skills learned, businesses started, techniques undertaken. They'd left families and broken off careers. There were short men and tall men, big bullchested longshoremen and slender longfaced machine operators. There were tough beefy men who had been around, smart quiet sinewy men who had knowhow. They were scarred with the scars of old accidents. Their necks were weathered and leathery. The sun and wind had tanned their hides. Some of them wore undershirts. Some of them were stripped to their shorts. They sat sweating round the table chewing on thick ham and turkey sandwiches and arguing with their mouths full as they chewed.

'Who wouldn't have a bitch,' a brickcolored man was saying in a deep growling voice, 'a goddam serious bitch? Here I thought all my life I was an engineer and they've got me smashin' crates like a nigger.'

'You're drunk. We knowed when we practiced stevedorin' way out on the prairie on the good ship Neversink, we'd have to smash a hell of a lot of crates. Stevedorin's the bottleneck, ain't it? We joined the Navy to go where we'd do the most good, didn't we? Well, where's your bitch?'

A seriouslooking darkhaired man caught sight of us and got to his feet and said hoarsely in a loud stage whisper to the young man who had brought us, 'Take 'em to see the lieutenant . . . He'll straighten 'em out. We don't want 'em to listen to this crap.'

'At least we can let 'em have a snack . . . I brought these gentlemen down to have a nice sociable snack.'

'Make the boys a sandwich, can't you? I'll get some butter,' whispered the darkhaired man, reaching for the refrigerator door.

'Make 'em a sandwich for crissake,' shouted several voices.

Big mitts grabbed carving knives and started hacking off hunks of turkey. Butter was slathered on bread.

'Give 'em some stuffin' for crissake. Can't eat turkey without stuffin'.'

'Here,' the man who'd been bitching roared out of his barrel chest, 'that ain't enough.' He slashed off a pair of drumsticks and handed them to us. 'I don't 'pologize,' he growled, 'but I won't let you boys go away hungry.' He winked an enormous wink. 'If you want chow, come to the seabees . . . If you want to know about the seabees, ask the marines. You know what they say.' He got heavily to his feet and spouted with gestures:

> When we march into Tokio with our cap at a jaunty tilt,
> We'll walk in the roads that the seabees built.

'He's quotin' poetry, he must be awful drunk,' hissed the darkhaired man.

With our mouths full and a sandwich in one hand and a drumstick in the other, we followed our friend down a path between the palm trunks to a lighted tent. A tall narrow-faced man was sitting at a table writing under the unshaded bulb.

'Lieutenant Newcomer,' shouted our friend, 'meet the press.'

He got unhurriedly to his feet and opened the screen door for us. 'Well,' he said. 'Well, well.' His eyes narrowed as he looked us each in the face for a moment. Then he smiled a slow smile. 'Come right on in,' he said cordially. His drawl, the burr in his *r*'s, his way of putting his words together, were pure Kansas.

While we chewed on our sandwiches, he listened to our friend telling him he was the man to straighten us out about the seabees.

'Well, the first thing to remember about the seabees,' he began, 'is that Uncle Sam didn't have to pull any of us in by the scruff of the neck. We enlisted, and most of us not only didn't have to go, but could be makin' real big money now if we'd stayed home . . . This bitchin' don't mean a thing. If the boys didn't get it up their nose sometimes an' kick the gong around a little, they'd get the Asiatic stare . . . You watch what they do when there's work to be done.'

And it was good tough work, he went on. Not a fourth of his oufit had done any stevedoring before they came out to the Pacific. Only two of them had had dock experience. They learned to run tractors. They learned to operate cranes and winches and they learned to supplement the heavy bull work with knowhow . . . Getting a twenty-ton tank off a ship wasn't just a matter of heaving and hauling. It was a skilled operation and it took brains and experience. That was what reconciled most of them to the work . . . Damn little rank in the seabees. Sure, they all of them wished sometimes that they had a job with more headlines in it. He did himself. He was county road commissioner back home. The folks were keeping his job open for him . . . Well, he couldn't help thinking sometimes that folks back home might wonder why he just stayed a lieutenant when other fellers got to be commanders and majors. Maybe the folks might think he wasn't doing such a good job . . . But, hell, a man's only real satisfaction was in knowing himself he was doing a good job. Was that so or wasn't it? He came from plain people back in

Kansas. His folks had been in every war since the Revolution. When they saw the old flag in danger, they just naturally had to go. 'Well, if you are goin' to serve, you serve, and way down that's what all the fellers work for me think' . . . He put his long hand on my arm. 'Don't imagine for a minute we do only stevedorin', we build roads, we build camps and wharves and piers. We built every damn thing on this island. And if the Japs poke their noses into our business, we got some pretty good sharpshooters itchin' to get a shot at 'em. You ask Scrappy Kessing how long it took us to put up four hundred and fifty buildings for him. He'll take you to see the recreation building we put up for the men. He likes to show that . . .' He paused, and his voice slowed to a slow rural drawl. 'But I'm gettin' off the track. What I started to say was: If you're goin' to serve, you might as well serve where it does the most good.'

Atoll Commander

Everybody tells you about Commodore Kessing. Ashore and afloat he's affectionately known as Scrappy Kessing. He commands the anchorage and the miles of submerged reef and the few scraps of land scarcely above high-tide level that make up the atoll. He's not a man you find very often sitting at his desk. He's always plunging out to see how the work is going. His jeep with its single star is everywhere on tiny Azor Island. Or else he's storming around the bigger island where the airport is or buzzing in his Piper Cub from one thin strip of land to another along the fringes of the rough over-populated waters of his domain. In the late afternoon you can see him playing a desperate game of softball on the sandy diamond between the recreation hall and the movie theater.

Evenings after mess he's usually sitting in a big chair in his square hut on the windy corner of the island at the table in front of the refrigerator entertaining old friends from among the horde of admirals and captains riding at anchor on the lagoon. The talk is all navy, bluewater yarns, reminiscences that stretch back to Annapolis and to drowsy old days before World War One when warships were painted white with yellow stacks like yachts, through the period of spit and polish and diplomatic cruises and uniformed routine, through stifling leafy summer months in Washington, oldtime Army and Navy Club gossip, and stories of Guam and Manila and the China stations, to the day when the Jap bombers rumbling in a shuttle through the mountain gap on Oahu touched off the immense energies of the new Navy and put every manjack on his mettle for life.

'Yes, he's in there,' they say in the outer office when you go to call on him, indicating the open door to the inner office with a somewhat cautious gesture of the head, as if they were referring to a charge of dynamite or to a valuable but cantankerous bull. The commodore jumps up from his desk like a jumpingjack. He has a round head of closecropped grizzled hair set close to a pair of broad shoulders. There's a look of almost childlike energy in the quick glance of his eye and the pugnacious set of his mouth. His attitude is that of a man ready to jump down your throat, but when he speaks the tone of his voice is unexpectedly considerate. While he is listening to what you have to say he is sizing you up.

Today the first thing he asks is, 'Have you seen our new recreation building?'

'Yes indeed I have.'

'Have you seen my seabees?'

'Yes indeed.'

'A great bunch to work with . . . You have to keep men active. That's my job. If you don't they start to run down. The hardest time in a base like this is when the tough work is over. Every officer has to play softball or something every afternoon. Hard work and plenty recreation . . . that's what keeps off the Asiatic stare.'

Service Squadron

We made the leap for the ladder out of the bucking whale-boat and clambered breathless up the side of the ugly green freighter. We stood dripping on the deck wiping the spray out of our eyes with damp handkerchiefs. 'Boating in Ulithi . . . How do you like the watersports?' the officer on watch asked, laughing.

'Watersports is right.'

'Let's go up in the wind and dry off a little,' said the young man who was guiding me around. 'I'll try to give you a notion of what a service fleet means.'

We stood in the tepid breeze up in the bow looking out at the floating city about us. Anchored not far away was a big green vessel that looked like a Noah's Ark with a large sign alongside of the house that read Ritz Carleton.

'That's the barracks ship,' he said, laughing. 'Replacements. The old notion was that the fleet went back to a base for supply. Now the base comes out to the fleet. We operate thirty-eight different types of ships. The ship we are on is a floating office building, only one of them; it would take the *Normandie* to house all the feather merchants in the Service Squadron . . . feather merchants in the Navy are the people who do the paperwork. . . . We handle everything the fleet needs from beans to bullets: food . . . a thousand men will eat

more than three long tons a day . . . medical stores, clothes, repairs, servicing of radar and radio equipment, ammunition, sundries like toothbrushes and toiletpaper, moving-picture film . . . there will be more film shown in this anchorage to-night than in the whole of New York City . . . We supply everything but the fight. The figures are so big they leave off the last three digits when they type off their reports.'

A battered green landing craft passed slowly under our bows, its square front end sending up sheets of spray as it slapped into the seas. A bunch of men in blue pants huddled, trying to keep dry, under a tarpaulin aft.

'That's a working party going to load supplies. We couldn't get to first base without those little landing craft . . .' He spread out his arms to let the wind get at his arm-pits. 'Well, I guess we're as cool and dry as we're going to get . . . Suppose we go below and visit some of the leading feather merchants . . . The first man I've got lined up is the Supply King of the Pacific.'

Belowdecks the ship is a tangle of cramped dimly lit passages opening out into rooms crammed with tables and desks where men pale with perspiration stoop over stacks of papers under a whir of fans. On every bulkhead and partition hang charts and graphs that tell the story of the work being done.

The supply officer, Captain Novinski, is a man of about fifty with faintly crinkly light hair and an office pallor on his face. He has a serious unassuming way of speaking. He worked his way up in the Navy from apprentice seaman. He first enlisted when he was fifteen, then he was a civilian again for a while, a bookkeeper for a meatpacking firm. 'Always in the office game,' he says deprecatingly. He was in the oil business when World War One brought him back into the Navy, this time as a payclerk. He stayed on after the war and passed his examination for the Supply Corps. After that he was disbursing officer at San Diego, supply officer on a tanker, was sent out to Bermuda to help commission the naval operating base. He'd been out here with Service Squadron 10 since October. He'd never worked so hard in his life. 'We don't have hours on board here. If a message comes at 3 A.M. we take immediate action. We don't even know what day of the week it is.'

A fleet, he explained, required the same variety of services as a great city, and the further you had to bring the stuff, the more the problem grew, not in arithmetical but in geometrical proportion. Many thousands of items had to be on hand all the time. The storage problem was immense. 'You can't substitute a fourpenny nail for a twentypenny nail . . . We've got to have the type of nail the fighting ship needs on hand when she needs it. We aim to take the worry about supply off the shoulders of the men on the fighting ship. Our motto is: If we've got it you can have it. But in this business there can't be any "if." We've got to have it when it's needed.'

A tall lieutenant commander with beads of sweat standing out on the white peak of his forehead above the brickcolored line of sunburn was hovering around the corner of the captain's desk. He was evidently in a hopping hurry about something. Time for us to move on.

The fuel officer, a young blond man from California named C. T. Munson, asked us up to his cabin. He handed us each a bottle of Coca-Cola and talked while he washed his face and changed into a dry shirt. He'd been in the oil business all his life. Had gone with Shell when he left college. The twenty officers he had under him were straight out of the oil business — about every American company was represented — but none of them had ever done anything like this. He spotted

with his finger on an imaginary map the continuous train of
evenly spaced tankers bringing out oil across the Pacific. It
was a lot of oil, but to increase the flow on a given day meant
planning three months ahead. What kept the oilmen up
nights were the unpredictable factors. Suppose Admiral Hal-
sey suddenly had to chase the Japanese fleet at full speed for
five hundred miles; that meant he'd use two and a half times
the oil that had been earmarked for that particular operation.
And the wingwalkers, the aviators, they hardly knew from
one day to the next how much high octane gas they were
going to need. The solution was to keep floating tank farms
— Dirty Gerties they called them, old cargo boats condemned
for one reason or other and turned into tankers — as far forward as possible as a margin of safety. Sure, he'd been in the
oil business, but the oil business had never been up against
anything like this.

We had trouble running down the ammunition king, Captain Palmer, because he was busy with the British. A British
cruiser had anchored inside the atoll that morning and the
Admiral and his staff were aboard the floating office building
moving about from department to department asking the
Americans to explain how their fleet managed to get along
without fixed bases. Wherever we went in the offices crowded
into the holds and packed between the narrow decks of the
old freighter, we'd find a Britisher in gleaming whites, red
knees sticking out from his shorts above his white stockings,
sitting at a desk with his long lanternjawed sportsman's face
uptilted while around him pressed a group of American officers
in sweaty suntans, explaining, describing, pointing to the
pictures of little men or little ships on charts, indicating with
stubby fingers the curve of a graph. At last Captain Palmer
managed to slip away and to join us in a corner between two

maps for a moment. With the leisurely politeness of a very busy man who has his work well in hand, he recited again part of the story he'd been reciting to his British opposite number.

In a nutshell, he said, the thing about ammunition was that just enough wasn't half enough and you always had to have all types. Suppose the fleet ordnance officers had figured out the needs for a shore bombardment and a couple of Jap battleships unexpectedly stuck their noses into the party, you'd have to have armorpiercing shells right away. Your figures on the ammo would be knocked screwy. That meant that you had to have floating storage for velvet, for a margin just in case. 'We try to make this a science, but a lot of the time we are gazing into a great big crystal ball.'

Already a chubby little curlyhaired yeoman was at the captain's elbow with a paper in his hand. Captain Palmer took the paper, and immediately he had forgotten us and was edging his way back to his desk, reading it as he went.

We climbed sweating up the iron ladders again on our way to freshen up a little out in the breeze on the bow. It happened that we stepped out on deck out of one hatch just as the British admiral and his party came out of the other. 'By Jove,' he was saying in awed tones as he cast his eye along the banks of ships, row on row as far as you could see in every direction. 'I've never seen anything like it since the Imperial German Fleet lay at anchor at Scapa Flow.'

That evening, in the conversational period over coffee after dinner in the narrow salon under the pilothouse where the senior officers ate, I found myself sitting across the white cloth from Commodore Carter, who commands Service Squadron 10. He's a quiet grayhaired man with a round seagoing countenance and an unruffled rather scholarly manner. He's a man who has seen a great deal and thought privately about it and read a great deal and formed his own notions about what he's read. His people came from Yarmouth, Maine. There's still a little of the salty flatness of the State of Maine in his way of talking. His father was a sailingship captain and his mother was a schoolteacher. He was born out in the Pacific, on the clipper ship *Storm King* outwardbound from Seattle to Honolulu. He rounded the Horn as a child. He had his schooling in the old shipbuilding town of Bath on the Kennebec. He still owns a white frame family homestead down in Maine, though most of his recent life ashore has been in Washington. Since the war he hasn't been ashore at all. In the last fifty-six months he's been home exactly twenty-four hours.

He's skeptical, he says with a smile, of the value of articles in magazines and particularly of articles by laymen on the problems of supply in the Navy, but he can't help touching on the daily business of his life as we talk about other things. He's eaten and drunk and slept and breathed supply all day and every day in these fifty-six months. He admits in that grudging downeast way that Nimitz has been heard to say that supply is his secret weapon. The fact that we've been able to establish floating bases halfway around the world has thrown the Japanese off balance and upset all their calculations. Obviously, without having invented a system of supply undreamed of in naval history we couldn't be threatening them in their home islands today. But it was equally obvious that the further we went west, the tougher the problem would become. The answer probably lay in increased speed in the service fleet and in continual tightening-up of efficiency all around. Nobody had believed we could do what we'd done up to now, and now perhaps it was hard to believe that we would be able to do what remained to be done.

'You think we can do it?'

He allowed himself a cautious scrap of a smile. 'You've been around here all day, you answer that.'

'I suppose the time will come when this whole floating base will move on west.'

'It's conceivable,' he said.

'How long would it take,' I asked as I got up to say goodnight, 'to move out of Ulithi?'

'Maybe twenty-five hours.'

Island of Baseball and Beer

The native Micronesians had a fine village on Mog Mog, with thatched huts and great canoe sheds along the pleasant inside beach and highpeaked ceremonial huts supported on forests of pillars of dark carved wood. Our forces have moved the natives away to an island across the lagoon and cleared the underbrush and scraped up the litter and built a pier for a smallboat landing and set the island aside for a recreation area for the fleet.

Charley Speidel from Pennsylvania, a chunky little barrel of muscle with a flattened nose and cauliflower ears, who used to be a famous college wrestling coach, is the big chief of Mog Mog now. He drives you around to see the ceremonial hut that's been turned into a bar for the admirals, and the canoe sheds that have been turned into clubs for the commanders and lieutenant commanders, and the various shelters that furnish tables and drinks for junior officers, and the beergardens laid out for warrant officers and chief petty officers, and the picnic grounds with fireplaces for broiling steaks and roasting wienies for the enlisted men, and the tennis courts and volleyball courts and rings for boxing and wrestling and baseball diamonds and bathing beaches. Swing music swirls out from jukeboxes and loudspeakers. A band is playing on a platform under the palms along the beach.

The pier is jammed with men bringing up boxes of chow from the boats for their outfits. There are long lines of men at the beer counters. The green water off the beaches is a brown tangle of swimmers. Baseball games are in progress on the diamonds; men with golf clubs practice putting in corners; under the shade of the palms groups cluster round crap games and poker games. In the scrap of untouched jungle on the far side of the island, a few more retiring spirits are drinking their beer quietly in the tangled underbrush. Out on the reef solitary wading figures with watergoggles are searching for shells.

'We've got everything for recreation we've been able to think of,' says Charley. 'We had some kids the other day wanted to shoot bows and arrows; by gum, we're going to get some . . . we even got cardsharpers . . . I got a detail to keep an eye on the crap games. We take six thousand men a day, a batch in the morning and one in the afternoon. And on the whole they don't give us much trouble . . . Somebody'll break an arm or try to get himself drowned in a tide rip, but mostly they police themselves. They know what they want to do before they come. Kids come ashore who haven't stepped on dry land in three or four months . . . some longer . . . Some of 'em just want to roam around and stretch. On the whole the enlisted men give me less trouble than the officers.'

After he'd finished the circuit of the island, he drew up in front of a screened thatched shelter at the edge of a gleaming shallow channel through the reef. Inside was a neat little clubroom with tables and chairs and a bar. 'This is where we come to get away from recreation,' he said. While he brought out the drinks, we sat looking out over the water. Here it was quiet. The music and the rooting at the ballgames were far away. It was hard to remember we weren't at a fishing camp somewhere down on the Florida keys.

'Well, what's Miami got that we haven't got?' he asked, creasing his brown face up into a grin.

'I could tell you what Miami's got that we haven't got,' said a longfaced man in a chief petty officer's uniform who had just come in.

Charley raised a thick flipper and pursed up his lips. 'Don't say it,' he said.

Cannibal Island

It's just the way we used to read about it when we were children. The local inhabitants come out to the tug in their gaudily painted outrigger canoes to ferry us in across the clear water that's sapphire, then emerald, then topaz along the beach. On the beach two grizzled brown men in red geestrings, with a tiny herringbone pattern tattooed in blue on their arms and chests, shake hands with us and smile. The huts thatched with plaited brown palm fronds are tall with steep pointed roofs and are raised on foundations of carefully laid coral slabs. A path bordered with scarlet hibiscus leads inland through the village. In the huts a few old people sit on grass mats and pound food in wooden bowls. Their only utensils are a few finely woven baskets and wooden trays and coconut shells. Spreading breadfruit trees with handshaped light-green leaves shade a few patches of taro here and there among the dense growth of coconut palms. Beyond the village there's nobody stirring. No sound but the rustle of the wind through the palms. A big fruit bat swinging its obese mousecolored body through the air on slow wingbeats flies over our heads, then another.

The path comes to an end at a canoe shed on a bright beach. The big outriggers, painted yellow and pink and ornamented with delicate geometric patterns, are carefully covered with matting. The long spearshaped paddles are hung from the ceiling overhead. We sit on the coping of the stone foundation and look out over the lagoon.

'One reason why this village seems so quiet and odd,' the man with me is saying, 'is that the Japs carried away all the young men and women to work at Yap.'

When he spoke I saw two brown eyes looking up at us out of a weazened darkbrown face out of the brown shadow under the canoes. An old man was sitting on his heels laboriously polishing a stick of wood with a smooth stone. Beside him was an adze made of a metal blade lashed to the end of a stick exactly the way the stone blades are lashed in the stone implements that you see in museums of Neolithic work.

'This place,' my friend was saying, 'is in the polished stone age. How many thousand years ago was that?'

The old man isn't looking at us any more. He's stopped rubbing the stick with the stone. He's looking out over to the horizon of the lagoon cut in every direction by the gray and green metallic masses of ships. A carrier steams by fast in front of us, immense, black, abrupt, its beetling flightdeck tightpacked with planes, the high bow cutting sharp as a knife through the sunny blue water. The old man sits on his heels staring straight ahead without moving. We can't read the expression on his face, or maybe there is no expression on his face. When he notices we are watching him, he drops his eyes and sets to polishing his stick again.

Peleleu, January 30, 1945

PART TWO

Theatre of War

1

The Road to Manila

Tacloban Evening

'ALL RIGHT, MEN . . . Fasten belts. We're in the Philippines.'

The flight orderly stuck a tousled head out of the door to the forward compartment. His eyes ran down the line of faces on either side of the cabin and he closed the door again. The men closepacked into the rows of bucket seats stirred drowsily. They stretched and yawned. They twisted their necks to look out over their shoulders through the smudgy windows. The plane was flying under a lowering overcast. Under us a heavy cloudbank rolled soggy and flat as bread dough on a board. Ahead this floor was beginning to ravel out. In the patches of inky shadow you could already see, faintly far below, the green bristle of densely packed trees. As we lost altitude the warm air that seeped into the cabin began to smell of woodrot and drenched leafmold. The mouth of the man next to me was moving. 'Samar,' he said, making repeated downward motions with his thumb.

The cloudfloor under us had thinned to a streaky haze flecked with gray curds of mist. Under it knobbed hills, bright green and bunchy as freshcooked broccoli, hurried past. Flying low, we crossed a drowned reedy shoreline orna- mented with the odd scrolls and spearshapes of fishtraps, and then a scattering of sailboats and tiny islands, and sped out over smooth inland waters streaked with waving lines like galvanized iron. Gray and tiny and looking exactly like models in a toyshop anchored ships lay in rows beneath us. Busy as waterbugs landing boats left V-shaped streaks as they moved in and out. Overhead the sky opened up higher and brighter. Great sagging inkstained clouds sailed free under a silvery mackerel ceiling. Beyond the far-scattered shipping the steep hills of Leyte rose bluegreen into a steam of rain. Against them writhed a tall pillar of smoke from something burning.

Clouds and ships and hills and a long strip of beach stippled with landing craft and the roofs of a town swung past the window as we circled for the landing. Everything was gray and glistening with wet. At the end of the long dark metal runway of the airstrip, the busy brown swirl of smoke rose straight up from a curling red cluster of flames.

As each man, balancing himself under the heavy load of his gear, stepped down the ladder from the plane, his face turned inquiringly toward the column of smoke.

'Raid?' somebody asked a mechanic in greasy greens who was watching us land. He shrugged his shoulders.

'Oil tank,' he said. Nobody asked any more questions.

Over the operations hut was a lettered sign: *Tacloban, the World's Busiest Airport*. Under the overhang of the dripping roof a row of men with rifles sat perched on their gear waiting to be sent off somewhere. Their faces were yellow from ata- brine under the tan. They were spattered all over with half- dried mud. Their pants were muddy to their knees. Their boots were lumps of mud. One man had a little gray monkey hunched on his shoulder. On the back of a wet jeep, driven by a bareheaded man in a dappled poncho, sat two bright-green parrots.

When the rain stopped, we all piled with our unwieldy duffle into the back of a truck that was going into Tacloban. Taking the left side of the road, the truck plowed through deep puttycolored mud, past dispersal areas and checkerboards of tents and piles of matériel draped with green canvas and antiaircraft guns ringed with sandbags, and turned into a slow-moving line of trucks and jeeps flowing in a river of mud past rattletrap houses on stilts with flimsy balconies under sagging tin or tile roofs. All the motley traffic drove to the left. Between verandas you could see canoes with long sharp-pointed bows like the boats in Chinese paintings that little men in pointed straw hats were poling across the slick gray harbor. The air was heavy with warm moisture. As we advanced slowly, stopping and starting in the packed train of traffic, mudspattered buildings of peeling stucco and bamboo houses, toppling at crazy angles on their stilts, edged in closer on the two unbroken lines of traffic. Behind shattered shacks a few large buildings, with stone arcades that had a battered reminiscence of forgotten old Spanish or American administrations, stood up among the palms. The truck stopped in front of a gateway. There was the unfamiliar word, USAF-FE, and yellowfaced sentries in wet helmets. We were in Tacloban.

'I suppose you want to get to Manila,' they said, when I stamped sweating and dripping gray mud from every pore up the stairs of the Public Relations Office. 'According to the communiqué the First Cavalry entered the city Saturday night.'

'What's today?'

'Monday.'

'Any way of getting off this afternoon?'

'Transportation's tight . . . Everybody's dreaming of that drink at the bar of the Manila Hotel . . . We'll see what we can do in the morning.'

The young officers kindly found a cot for me in the house they were occupying on a back street in Tacloban. It had been the house of a local businessman of some importance. It was a cramped tall house with stained glass set into shaky woodwork that had a darkbrown waterlogged look. There were tiled floors and narrow windows closed with gawky wroughtiron grilles. Everything had a look of damp and verdigris about it. A shower had been rigged up out of an oildrum set on stilts back of the kitchen door. Standing out in the hot steamy air, so saturated with wet you felt almost a chill in it at times, under the tepid sprinkle of the shower you could look out over the top of the curtain of gunnysacks into a confusion of little yards and back porches and open-trellised rooms full of a hidden bustle of housekeeping. Through cross-slats of broken blinds you could see small women carrying pottery jars, yellowfaced children with shoebutton eyes, old men in rumpled linen suits who sat, with solemn faces wrinkled in circles like the faces of monkeys, looking out at nothing. Slender barefoot porters with oilcans slung on carrying poles passed quickly and quietly through the yards. There was a cackling of hens and an occasional crow of a rooster and a low hum of chirping voices. An old old woman in a yellow gauze blouse with puff sleeves tiptoed out, carefully picking her way between mudholes, and dumped a bowl of banana skins into the pen of a black razorback hog. A sour reek of wet slums rose into the heavy air.

My friends were setting themselves up to a treat that night. Their Filipino houseboy, an elderly man who had about four words of English, was frying up some chickens. While the gray bead curtains of the rain pressed dense against the windows, we sat in the dark diningroom gnawing on skinny sections of tropical chicken and talking about Westchester County, New York, the Bronx River Parkway, and the Boston Post Road. When the rain cleared, it left blue twilight. Immediately there was a red alert. A few antiaircraft guns fired far away. We couldn't tell whether some distant thumps we heard were bombs or more of our guns.

After the all clear, a Chinese correspondent came to call. His manners were pleasantly American, with a difference I didn't know China well enough to define. He'd studied journalism at the University of Missouri. Somebody remembered that he had a bottle of Scotch and we moved upstairs to drink it. We sat on cots in a glassed-in upper porch talking about China. The atabrine had given an outlandish yellow cast to the faces of the Americans. We all felt very far from home. Those little lizardlike creatures with cupped toes and popeyes they call geckos ran up the windowframes and made upsidedown dashes across the ceiling after insects. In the pauses in the conversation you could hear their throaty clucking call. From outside, the sour closeness of crowded people and stagnant water and mildewed wood seeped into the house. As we talked I kept thinking to myself, 'This is Asia.' The word was full of millions, of a sense of helplessness, of crowded bound lives as choking as the still airless heat of the night that held us by the throat.

We had sat there talking and drinking up the Scotch whiskey for a couple of hours when we began to notice that the house was shaking under us. The loose panes rattled in the windows. Glasses jiggled on the floor. The sills and timbers creaked like the timbers of a wooden ship in a gale. 'We have them every night almost . . . much pleasanter than Jap planes,' somebody said. Everybody began to laugh. 'A nice cheerful little earthquake.' The shaking increased, died off, and then started up again.

Observation Flight

We got up long before day. Two tall darkhaired men met us in the half-light of the airport.

'So you want to get a look at Manila,' they said. 'We're going to give the town a buzz. The story came in last night that it's burning . . . Fires can be seen twenty miles away.'

'The communiqué announces that we have occupied the city,' said Norman Soong, and smiled his Chinese smile.

We were walking down a row of Mitchell bombers decorated with Indian heads. 'Well, we'll go check up,' said Captain Brigham, and waved a long hospitable hand toward a plane with open bomb-bays. 'We'll take up one correspondent with us and two of you can ride with the waist gunners.'

Before we knew it, we were off the runway in the cloudy dawn and skimming low over the densely grown sopping green hills of Leyte. I sat on my musette bag beside a tangle of radio equipment looking backwards out of the window past the machinegun and across the sleek bulge of the motor out along the wing. When Leyte dropped away, we came out into sunshine and an airless inland sea over which steep islands hung at intervals under silky cumulus clouds. Spidery square-sailed canoes with outriggers hovered motionless between the islands.

I sat with a lot of little points and angles sticking into my neck sweating quietly in the clammy embrace of my Mae West. Across from me were the faces of the gunners, chubby with sleep, and Krolich hunched in a nap with his head on his knees. Beside me the radioman in his earphones wore a withdrawn subjective look on his atabrine-stained countenance as he fingered the knobs of his instrument. Through the opposite window the nose of another plane swayed gently into sight. The Indian head painted on it gave us a cozy feeling of being in company.

The other plane has peeled off and gone. For a long time we have been skimming close to the glassy smooth water. Suddenly we bank and slide sideways up over a little beach jostling the palms with the wind of our propellers. After that, small steep hills terraced in intricate green patterns of fields speed under us. Populous country. No look of war about it yet. Roads, bridges, thatched toy huts at the corners of fields or grouped into villages.

'Manila in twenty minutes,' comes the pilot's quiet voice over the intercom.

When the photographer opens one of the round escape hatches to set up his camera in it, immediately we smell smoke. Over converging roads and towns that grow together into suburbs, we are cruising through a thin murk of smoke from the burning city.

The pilot noses the plane down toward the houses. He gives something we can't see a burst out of his forward machineguns. Immediately we are buzzing low over streets under the pall of smoke. The city is whizzing past below us, seen palely in the amber light. There are regular blocks of stucco buildings enclosing yards and gardens. In broad streets there are men, women, and children in lightcolored clothes, pink, yellow, pale blue. Big hats. We are buzzing so low we can see faces tilt upward. A man waves his hat. The people are standing about aimlessly in the streets with a look of waiting for something.

Behind a roadblock in an open space stand green trucks, uniformed figures, guns. Ours or theirs? Before I can formulate the question, we are over a cemetery, great trees, pink pagodas, oddlooking pinnacles of stone. We are so low I wonder for a fragment of a second whether the pilot isn't picking us a final resting place.

The plane swings in a breathless halfcircle. By a river — must be the Pasig — what looks like a factory or a warehouse burns briskly beside an intact iron bridge. Beyond are crowded blocks of an American-style business section. Across the river rise the big stone cubes of government buildings, among grassy spaces backed by an ancient wall. We are skimming the crowded tiled roofs of the old city. An elaborately carved Spanish window set in the corner of a building whizzes under us in the blur of smoke.

The dirty green water of the harbor, scarred and tangled with wreckage, swings up into the sky. Rows of steamers lie on the mud, sunk at their anchors. As we bank for another dizzy turn, two grimy blobs of smoke smudge the bay shore.

There's a light popping noise somewhere in the plane.

'Anybody hurt back there?' comes the pilot's inquiring voice over the intercom.

'Nobody hurt?'

'Cylinder blew off righthand motor,' he explains quietly. 'Prepare for crash landing.'

He straightens the plane out and heads away over flooded paddyfields. In the waist compartment nobody moves. Each man sits looking straight ahead of him.

After a while the pilot's voice comes again, very quiet, full of fatherly concern: 'Under control . . . better move as far forward as you can.' The tail gunner is crawling toward us up the tunnel with a light deprecatory smile on his face. We wait. A little ooze of oil appears on the smooth aluminum casing of the motor outside of my window. Beyond it I get a last glimpse of the serrated skyline of downtown Manila, ringed with crinkling columns of smoke. 'All right, we can make Lingayen airstrip in twenty-five minutes,' comes the voice of the pilot over the phones again, briskly this time. 'Unload ammunition' . . . then thoughtfully fatherly again: 'Better throw out everything you can to lighten the tail.'

The photographer has pulled his camera in and is putting the round door back in the escape hatch. Somebody works the lever to open the bomb-bays. Working slowly and deliberately the gunners lift and drop the heavy ammunition boxes. Looking down through the open bomb-bay under your feet, you can see that we are crossing dry fields now, yellow with rice stubble. The fields are flat, but they are scrawled over with low dykes used in flooding the rice crop. Not so good for crash landings. In the back of your mind a picture trembles, like something projected on a screen, of a crashed plane, twisted metal, smashed bodies, fire. From the bulge of the wing outside the window the oil wells thick and black out of the righthand motor, trickling down over the smooth aluminum like blood out of a wound.

It's slow work pulling the belts of big cartridges back out of the machineguns. The snaky belts of ammunition snap the whip brightly in the sun as they drop earthward. On the roads now we can make out friendly unmistakable American jeeps. We begin to breathe. The gunner closes the bomb-bay doors.

Twenty-five minutes passed.

Swaying a little the plane came in on one motor for a perfect landing over the rattling steel matting of the airstrip. As we ducked blinking out into the hot sunlight from under the belly of the plane, I heard one man grumbling, 'Who said there weren't any Japs left in Manila?'

The crash truck with its fire extinguishers and an ambulance were there to meet us. We walked toward them, each with two arms, two legs, a head, eyes, ears, unscratched. They looked at us and we looked at them. 'You caused a red alert,' said somebody reproachfully.

Transportation to Headquarters

We were on Lingayen beach in Luzon. The sun beat down. The air was dry and sweet. When we got over into the shade of the operations hut, our navigator started slapping his thighs and saying, 'By God, I saw them in front of that big building with kind of columns in front, jeeps and trucks and tanks and GI uniforms, and all the people crowding around waving, and that flag, the old Stars and Stripes aflying.'

'I'll probably catch it for tearing up that motor,' said the pilot, with a frown of concern. 'It's a good thing I was able to feather the prop.'

We shook hands. He was going back to Leyte on the first plane out. Our problem was to get to Manila. After a while Krolich promoted a truck to take us to Dagupan, where the communications ship was.

It was pleasant riding away from the airstrip in the front seat of a truck through the quiet late morning sunlight. The driver said yes he knew where Dagupan was, but first he had to deliver a message. Couldn't he phone the message, asked Norman Soong, who was in a hurry to file his story. The driver pulled up the truck and scratched his head. Naw, he drawled, he couldn't phone because he didn't know where the officer was. He was unloading a landing craft somewhere along the beach.

So we set off along the broad sandy road fringed with palms and hibiscus hedges and a scattering of pink and yellow stucco seaside villas smashed like eggs dropped from a basket. We passed large ruined public buildings with columns that had a faintly U.S.A. look, and an unmistakable American high school. 'That was the state capitol,' said the driver.

We crossed a little bridge over a green treeshaded creek full of dugout canoes and came out on the bank of a broad river. A few peeling green landing craft were drawn up on the beach. Some loaded trucks stood beside them. The driver slipped down from the seat, and we sat there waiting, watching him roam in a daze from one group of men to another. He was slow in leading up to his question. Each time he asked it, the men shook their heads. Finally he had a long conversation shouting up at a man perched in a sentrybox on a high bamboo platform. He was in no kind of hurry at all.

We sat there twitching. We were itching to be off toward Manila. We hadn't managed to get any breakfast. We were hungry, we were thirsty, we wanted a cup of coffee. Norman Soong wanted to file a story. 'Who was the wise guy,' groaned Krolich mournfully, 'who said that in war you were either scared to death or bored to death?'

The driver came shambling back through the sand, shaking his head. 'Things move so fast around here,' he was drawling in slow apologetic tones, 'you can't keep track of nobody.'

'We are far from moving fast toward the communications ship at Dagupan,' said Norman Soong.

The driver clambered into his seat and started up the truck.

We rambled back along the waterfront past the ruined public building again. After a couple more fruitless stops, Krolich gently pointed out to the driver that the correspondents really had to get to that communications ship to file the cables five hundred million people were waiting for, and to get to Manila to see what the hell was happening there. He added that that officer was probably at mess and wouldn't want the message now anyway.

'Couldn't you take us to Dagupan right now,' asked Norman Soong tactfully, 'and then search for your officer?'

After one more stop at a tent area, the driver reckoned yes maybe he had better take us to Dagupan, and we went rattling off along a dusty road through the sunny green beaten-up countryside. Dagupan had a gray Spanish look. There was a big dusty square and a smashed church of solid stone construction with a stumpy baroque tower. The communications ship was a landing craft tied up to the bank of a river between Chinese-looking houses. When you walked up the gangplank, you could feel the heat of the metal deck of the ship even through the heavy soles of army shoes. In the deckhouse two fans made a breeze. There was a shower. There was chow and good navy coffee.

We sat eating and sweating and drawing little maps on scraps of paper and trying to tell each other what we'd seen over Manila. The group of big buildings where the flag was and the tanks must have been the University of Santo Tomas . . . that's where the American civilians were interned. There was one undestroyed bridge still standing over the Pasig. We had counted seven separate fires. The downtown business district was intact. Nothing seemed to be burning but wharves and warehouses and oildumps. No new damage had been done to the old city within the walls. The residential section along the bay and the Manila Hotel seemed unhurt. The Japs must be evacuating the city. 'By God,' somebody said, 'we'll be having that drink at the bar of the Manila Hotel before night.'

After lunch I sat on a bit under the awning in the bow waiting for a jeep to take me up the valley of Luzon and fidgeted and looked at my watch and tried to imagine what was going on in Manila. Here in Dagupan the afternoon dragged heavily on in immense quiet under the crushing weight of the sun. Across the greasy brown river longnosed lighters of dark wood with a peaked thatched shelter over the stern were tied up against the bank. There were dogs aboard and children and women in brightcolored shirtwaists and immense pointed straw hats fussing over pottery jugs and bowls and baskets of rice. In the bow of one lighter two ragged barelegged boatmen stretched out side by side were drowsily trying to get two bantam chicks just growing pinfeathers to fight each other.

A thinfaced officer with a black mustache walked toward me down the deck. 'Ready,' he said. 'Say, I was wondering if you would like to stop off at the Sixth Army to see the prisoners of war we sprung at Cabanatuan the other day. Those fellows have got a million stories.'

'What about getting to Manila?'

'The Sixth Army P.R.O.'ll get you into Manila in the morning.'

The road was strangely empty. Little military traffic. An occasional carabao drawing a wagon shaded with matting or a painted-up twowheeled cart drawn by a tiny buffcolored Filipino horse. A few country people with big conical hats plowing in their sandals through the thick dust of the roadside. Battered American road signs were still standing.

'Sure, the Japs had to leave our signs up,' said the officer.

'They even had to use English for their proclamations. They tried Tagálog for a while till they found that only a few people around Manila could read it . . . Look, they were here a month ago and they've hardly left a trace.'

We were crossing a series of temporary bridges across a broad dry riverbed with intermittent channels of slimy green water. Beside us was a railroad bridge. Every other span was blown up.

'See that bridge,' the officer said. 'I met the man who blew it the other day. One of our engineers blew it back in December, 1941, when we were retreating from Lingayen. He found that bridge just the way he'd left it. Japs never repaired it. They didn't do a damn thing on this island. Here they didn't even put back the road bridge. They used a ferry.'

We turned off the main road into a lane through a sparkling green jungle made up of a thousand different varieties of palm. We reached the headquarters camp in time to duck into a tent out of a blinding downpour of rain.

The Men from Cabanatuan

After supper a sergeant drove me down a railroad track between banks of steaming green jungle becoming dense as boiled spinach in the dusk. 'I been over here three times today,' he said. 'It's the most interesting place I've ever been. I look at those fellers and I ask myself, How the hell did they live through it? You can live through anything, I guess.'

We turned off the railroad track, plunged sharply down the embankment through a tunnel of tangled creeping plants with big leaves, nosed up a muddy road between some bamboo houses and came out in a drowned-out encampment. The drab green tents were sagging with wet. Slipping and sliding in the mud we picked our way among the stakes and tent ropes. Inside the tents men sat on cots, their hands hanging between their knees, looking out into the rosy gloaming. They were not talking, they were not moving. They sat there with their eyes fixed on something straight ahead of them.

They all looked strangely alike. Their heads looked very large for their bodies. Gray skin hung in folds from skinny necks. Their eyes were large and sunken, the whites clear, the pupils sharp and small, the iris bright. It was as if all the life left in their bodies were concentrated there.

We talked to a chaplain. He spoke of digging out excrement from the Japanese latrines to put on the land, of the helpless humiliation of the first months after the surrender and the march out of Bataan, and the shootings and the beatings and the abject sick misery of men too weak to move, and the glum preoccupation of the starving. He told of the way some men pulled themselves together and kept their nerve. A young officer had written some remarkably fine poems before they shot him. He'd buried them under the pumphouse. He hoped somebody would go back and find those poems. They shouldn't be lost.

He was a tall quiet man with a scholarly rather meticulous way of talking. I could see it was tiring him to talk. As we left, we asked him how it was that any of them had lived through those three years. 'Faith in God,' he said, in an off-hand tone as if the matter were too obvious to need explaining, 'and the daily observance of religion.'

We talked to a major. He was sitting on his cot looking down at legs like a pair of golf clubs that stuck out pitifully from his ragged shorts. The prisoners wouldn't be alive today, he said, if it hadn't been that the Japs had gotten panicky and pulled out of the camp three weeks ago. 'They told us we would be shot if we left the area, but they left us in charge of the camp. There was quite a store of food. We started eating and that's why we were strong enough to be able to walk out when the rescue party came for us. We are still dazed. There are things we can't remember, particularly about the time before we started to eat.'

'How do you suppose so many lived through?'

The question seemed to please him. He smiled a thinlipped smile. 'I think most of us who lived lived out of pure meanness. We didn't want to give the Japs the satisfaction . . . The old army discipline helped.'

We left the officer's country and went slogging through a gulch of bottomless mud and, taking advantage of the roots of an enormous spreading tree, climbed up the rise to the enlisted men's quarters. It was already dark. In a glare of searchlights a stalled truck was being hauled up the hill by a cable. The rows of tents were lit up by bright lights strung here and there from the wet boles of palms.

The men in the enlisted men's section looked less exhausted than the men in the officers' section. Most of them were younger. The three years hadn't borne down quite so hard on them. We roamed around among the tents looking shyly in men's faces when we passed them, but we couldn't bear to ask any more questions. There seemed no way of phrasing a sentence that would bridge the gap between the life we knew and the life these men had known. Here and there the sergeant stopped a man whom he had seen before, but at the word correspondent their faces froze. They immediately remembered something they had to do.

There was a truckdriver from Miami, a husky redfaced man. He'd gained twenty pounds in the last three weeks, he said. But he hadn't been so bad off as some of the others to begin with. He'd driven a truck for the Japs building airfields. Truckdrivers and mechanics who worked away from the camp hadn't been treated so badly as some of the others. 'They wanted to git work out of us, so they couldn't let us git too weak, could they? . . . Excuse me, won't you,' he added politely. 'I'd like to stay here talkin', but they are goin' to put on a movie for us. I haven't seen a movie in three years.'

'I guess it's time we went back to camp,' I said to the sergeant.

'I don't want to stay here long either,' he said, 'but as soon as I get away I want to come back.'

The Taste of Victory

Next morning the sky was cloudless. There was a racket of noisy birds in the palms above my tent. The Sixth Army camp was in a grove of tall palms screened off here and there by twenty-foot clumps of bamboo. When the sun rose, the golden light streaming through the shining swaying bamboo shoots trembled in bright splinters on the dark green canvas of the tents. Soldiers with carbines swung across their backs strolled briskly to and fro on morning policing jobs. Bright amid the shining greenery the flag fluttered on a tall pole in a clearing. The air had a cool smell of freshwashed foliage. It was war in the Philippines as you had imagined it as a boy.

When the driver and I walked out to the jeep that was to take me up to General Headquarters, we found a young lieutenant in a new uniform sitting hunched up in the back seat.

'Mind if I ride up to headquarters with you?' he asked.

When he looked up at me he blinked as if the bright sunlight hurt his eyes. While we were backing out of the parking lot, he added in an apologetic tone: 'My head's in a kind of whirl. There are things I can't remember. Just now I couldn't remember my mother's maiden name.'

'What's the trouble?'

'Malnutrition, I guess. It seems to have hit my eyes. Most of the time I feel kinda weak and dizzy.'

'Cabanatuan?' asked the driver.

The young man shook his head. 'Came in from the hills a week ago,' he answered in the same explanatory apologetic tone. 'Been out three years.'

'Jeezus!' said the driver.

Then as we drove through the dust and clatter of the crowded road up toward headquarters, across hastily repaired bridges, over green rivers, through towns stamped flat by the fighting, past the neatly ranked piles of white ash that is the only trace a village of bamboo huts leaves when it burns, he began to talk.

He came from a Connecticut mill town. He had enlisted at nineteen and been sent right out to Manila. Air Force ground troops. He had gone through the bombings and the retreat to Bataan. When Bataan began to look hopeless, they had offered a commission to any enlisted man who would take a chance and try to get out into the hills to keep up resistance. He had gone through at night with some other guys, but they had gotten scattered, and then there were only two of them, and then he and his friend got separated, and later he heard his friend had been killed. In some villages people took you in and gave you food and a place to sleep; and in others they drove you out like a dog. Some of them would turn you over to the Japs if you didn't keep moving, and your shoes wore out, and your clothes wore out, and you got sores on your legs from the cuts of the sword grass, and the leeches got on you when you hid in the underbrush, and you were all the time scared that at the turn of a trail you'd meet a snake or a Jap patrol. And then you were barefoot, sweating and stinking, and worn down with ulcers, sloshing up through the rain, in the mud of the steep trails that follow the terraced paddyfields up into the high green hills. Up in the mountain province the people treated you all right, if they didn't cut your head off the first time they saw you. The Igorots were all right. They were sore at the Japs because they closed up their schools. They were crazy about American schools.

He had broken his arm in a fight with a Jap patrol and had come down with fever, and for seven months they nursed him in one of the villages up there. They respected white men up there. They liked to have white blood in the family. They wanted you to take their girls. It was kind of embarrassing because you had to fix it up with the father first.

'I've got two children up there,' he said, in a puzzled sort of way.

As we proceeded up the road, the traffic got heavier. Through driving clouds of dust we wound in and out of long convoys of army trucks. There were more pony carts, each one jammed to the roof with small roundfaced people with shoebutton eyes. There were carabao wagons with solid wooden wheels that creaked dolefully. There were men with baskets slung on carrying poles trotting along with the jerky hip motion men use in walking races back home. There were little girls with bunches of flowers and venders with peanuts and fruit running along the lines of stalled trucks and jeeps each time there was a traffic jam. Country people looked up at us laughing and made the V for victory sign as we passed through beaten-up villages. Overhead in the sky full of high white clouds the only planes we saw were American. There was a holiday look in people's faces and an air of applause and enthusiasm that made you sit back in your seat and puff your chest out and say to yourself, 'By gum, I'm on the winning side.'

In a town full of beautiful mango trees, our friend the lieutenant said, 'There are some nice Spaniards living here, a family that did everything in the world for me, lent me food and money and put me up in their house when it was hellishly dangerous . . . Suppose we stop by and see them.'

I said I was sorry, but I was under contract to go through to Manila.

'Well, some other time, amigo.' He let the notion drop without an effort. These Spaniards were good people, he drawled. The rich Spaniards were most of them collaborating with the Japs and definitely shall we say antidemocratic, but the medium Spaniards were people you could trust not to turn you in. He leaned forward out of the back seat and put his hand on my shoulder. 'You can't explain what it's like to be a hunted man day after day, week after week,' he said insistently. 'Some things I'm clear about, but mostly my mind's fuzzy. I did a lot of drawing and painting. They are keeping them for me up in the hills. Maybe I'll get up a book . . . If my head would only clear up. They ought to send me home for a rest, and instead they are returning me to duty.'

In a place called Paniguí we heard a sound of what sounded like a hillbilly band. 'That's the all-day nightclub,' said the driver, drawing up beside a row of army trucks in front of a roadside tavern with lattice windows and balconies.

'There's a whorehouse around the corner,' said the lieutenant dreamily. 'Want to take a look at it?'

'I been overseas twenty-three months,' said the private firstclass who drove the jeep. 'I've held out this long and I guess I might as well hold out a little longer till I get home among the white natives.'

'Wouldn't take a minute.'

'They got good rum here,' said the driver.

I suggested we have one drink in the tavern and then push along. I had to get to Manila, I explained again.

We went in. The place had a dark look of damp tropical wood. Through the thin board ceiling you could hear the band stamping and jingling upstairs. A stout soiled half-Spanishlooking man poured out drinks of very good rum for us at a peso a drink at a curving bar made of a solid chunk of mahogany. At a heavy square table four truckdrivers were sopping up the rum while a sallow girl with bags under her eyes buzzed around them like a fly round a sugarbowl. There was so much of the oldest profession in the way she jiggled her hips as she moved that as you looked at her the tavern became any tavern, behind any battlefront in any war since time began. We had some trouble getting away from the truckdrivers who were at the 'you take a drink on me or I'll smash you in the jaw' stage of drunkenness.

They started to pick on the lieutenant after pouring a number of drinks down him. A 'son of a bitch' snarled without a smile shook him out of his daze. He had his dukes up and was ready to fight them when the driver and I cut in between and got him out to the jeep.

'Let the M.P.'s take care of them. That's their business,' the driver was saying philosophically as he stepped on the gas and whizzed up the dusty road again in the flaming noontime sunlight.

Tarlac was a wilderness of broken cement and twisted iron

roofing. A smell of burning and death from the recent fighting still hung over the place. Wherever the rubbish had been cleared away, little Filipinos with baskets of withered fruits and vegetables were starting up a ghostly revival of chaffer and trade. A little way out of town at a Tex Cal sign over a white American filling station, empty but intact, we turned off the road, followed an avenue of red identical bungalows and drew up before a long building with balconies shaded by low eaves of galvanized iron painted a dull red.

'Glad to have met you. You don't know what it feels like to meet somebody from home. I got so I didn't believe in home any more,' the lieutenant said drowsily as we shook hands. 'Gosh, I'd like to go home and see my folks just for two hours. I guess I'd lock the door on the inside and throw away the key.'

Strategic Highway

At the Public Relations Office they said a jeep was leaving right after lunch for Manila. A radio commentator, a big quiet determined man from San Antonio, Texas, named Pat Flaherty, was waiting to go. They issued us helmets and canteens and a very special pass to get us past the convoys on the road, and off we went. The driver was from northern Alabama, a deeply tanned young fellow with narrow eyes who seemed to be having the time of his life.

At first we breeze along a stretch of empty cement road. 'We'd call this all right back home,' says Alabama exuberantly. The road cuts through ricefields pale yellow with stubble where the Japs got in the crop before they retreated. To the left a high conical hill stands out against distant cloudy mountains. To the right is the Zambales range dark under sagging cumulus. Already we can hear artillery and make out the white puffs of phosphorus shells exploding in the ridges above Clark Field.

We pass a guerrilla outfit, a long string of little men padding along the side of the road softly in their sandals. First come two flags, an American flag and a Filipino flag, proudly carried on poles by two barefoot brown boys. Then a few older leaders in suntans. Then a string of mildlooking smooth-skinned boyish little men with almond eyes. Some have swords, some have pikes, some brandish Jap rifles as they pass. Next come a group of girls, in slacks or in bright print dresses, walking in pairs with their arms round each other's necks.

'Ain't that somep'n,' says Alabama, almost stalling the jeep. He nudges me softly with his elbow and makes a kissing sound with his lips. 'Oh boy, Manila tonight,' he sighs.

Next come some men in fragments of GI uniforms, shouldering the parts of an ancient U.S. machinegun. There follows a procession of decorated pony carts piled with baskets and bags of provisions, and stuffed in among them occasionally an old party in a sun helmet with dark glasses and a face full of wrinkles like a withered russet apple. Some of the carts, instead of being pulled by the usual small buffcolored horses, are pulled by men and boys. At the end comes trailing a string of wiry dark barefoot fellows with carrying poles on their shoulders balancing big jars or packages wrapped in matting. Last in the procession a small boy hurries along with a tiny squealing black pig under each arm.

We cross a river in a rocky defile encumbered with the red broken fragments of a blown-up railroad bridge. The shallow pools are full of women doing their washing and naked yellow and brown children bathing. From up the valley comes the stutter of a machinegun. Alabama points out the caves along the cliff face where the Japs were still dug in a week ago. At the next crossroads an M.P., his face red as a beet from the sun, tells us to put on our helmets and get out our guns. There's a ground alert ahead.

From now on the roadsides are encumbered by convoys of trucks waiting to get through. The dust rolls in white clouds from under the wheels of the vehicles in the urgent lane. Grinning from ear to ear, holding our orders between his teeth ready to show to the M.P.'s, Alabama cuts figure eights through the traffic jams.

Stalled behind a recon car between the stone walls of a road leading through dusty gardens into a village, we fall to talking with three sweaty youngsters who have just crawled out of the open hatch. 'You ought to ride with us,' they say. 'Drives like a Packard. Yesterday we took seven direct hits and not even a headache. You men are goin' to get sunstroke out there in that jeep.'

Rumbling forward into open country beyond Bam Bam, we begin to see the smoke of artillery fire again in the ranked hills behind the airfields. Along the grassgrown strips near the road we can see rows of Jap zeros smashed like bugs in their dispersal area. We begin to understand why we see no enemy planes overhead.

Off to the right, over a patch of rolling country tufted with big bunched trees that might be mangoes, three of our fighters are weaving in and out like midges over a stream strafing something that hides under the trees. A little further along there's a group of soldiers fresh from combat asleep in a close-cropped dry ricefield. Each man lies with his gun in his hand where he fell in the middle of the sunbaked field. Outside of one man, who sits smoking with his gun on his knees under a tree, every man in the group is asleep. Their faces have a sweet defenseless childish look asleep. Propped against the road embankment a thickset curlyhaired man with a broken nose sleeps with his mouth open, his face flushed and smiling like a baby's in its crib. Meanwhile up in the hills behind Clark Field the unheard battle goes on. The dense white blobs of phosphorous smoke and the dark smokesmudges from the guns bloom out and hover and merge together into a streaky haze over steep barren hills sharpcut under lowering clouds in the bright afternoon.

Out of the dry dusty country we have come into a flooded region of paddyfields dotted with white herons that feed peaceably among the grazing carabao. Here and there one sits perched on a carabao's back. There are ducks and little fuzzy ducklings in the ditches. The bamboo matting and thatched houses standing up on stilts and the long canoes shaped like half a stringbean on the quiet rivers are off the Willow Pattern. The landscape is out of a Chinese painting. The old towns full of hibiscus and bougainvillea with gray stone churches fronting small plazas are right out of Spain. Scattered along the deep ditches sprawl wrecked cars and trucks, Japanese and American, and around each wreck swarms a group of eager villagers busy with the salvage. Old women cart away a wheel or a tire or a section of crankcase on their heads.

The wreckage increases in patches as we get nearer Manila. There's a long string of burned freightcars on an embankment and in the middle two locomotives buckled head to head where they collided. It is like a still from an oldfashioned movie.

When they burn, the flimsy houses leave hardly a trace.

Only the tin roofs remain. One rather elaborate villa has vanished except for the curved stairs and the balustrade of its concrete porch and the garden full of shrubs with variegated leaves. A young man in immaculate white ducks wearing dark glasses is combing through the gray ash with a rake.

The road becomes crowded with Filipinos. There are families with their goods and chattels leaving Manila to take refuge in the country and there are lines of men and women going back into town with bags of rice on their heads. There are people on bicycles, people pushing wicker baby carriages and varnished twowheel carts and every conceivable type of rolling contraption contrived out of automobile wheels or bicycle wheels or wooden wheels or rollers. Every one is piled high with bags of rice or baskets or old women and children. A tiny yellow bus, marked Palace Auto Cab in red letters, has broken down. It's stacked with people and goods. A great crowd of men and boys is happily pushing it along the road.

For a long time now we have been watching a pillar of smoke on the southern horizon ahead of us. It's dark and towering and spreads out like a pedestal under a pile of milky white cumulus cloud. Every time the road heads direct toward Manila the smoke beckons ahead of us.

'There's more smoke than there was yesterday,' says Pat Flaherty. 'I guess they are burning up the Manila Hotel all right.'

'How about that drink we were going to have at the bar?'

'The first thing I'm goin' to do in Manila is git me a gurl,' croons Alabama. 'I'm goin' to git me the purtiest gurl.'

Outside of a crumpled tannery on a riverbank we came to a dead halt. The road ahead was blocked by a file of great tanks working their way past the trucks and halftracks and the short howitzers uptilted under their canvas covers of a train of artillery.

Just before we stopped, we heard a light ping overhead.

'Could that be a sniper?' whispered Pat Flaherty thoughtfully.

'They wouldn't shoot us,' drawled Alabama. As soon as he took his hand from the wheel, he reached back for his rifle.

This time we seemed stalled for keeps. The men in the command car ahead had been there since six o'clock that morning. We walk along the line of jeeps and trucks and halftracks to reconnoiter and to get away from the clatter of the long column of thirty-ton tanks that is nosing slowly past us. There's another bridge out. From the shade of the big buildings of the tannery we look out across a brown river at a bridge of pontons the engineers have just completed. The bridge ripples like a watersnake under the weight as the great tanks move cautiously across.

A redeyed major of M.P.'s haggard from lack of sleep is directing traffic from the end of the broken stone bridge. We stand near him waiting for the right moment to show him our orders while a constant stream of officers, from various outfits stalled along the road, their faces and their damp greens gray with dust, flows past him. There's a row of cars from the FBI. There's a convoy of Civil Affairs trucks loaded with food for the civilian population. 'People are dropping dead in the streets from starvation,' the man in charge says desperately. There are headquarters detachments and radio units and signal corps units.

The major is sleepily polite, but very firm: 'Tanks and artillery have got to go first.'

'If the Japs had any planes, they sure would have a field day,' somebody says under his breath.

Nobody argues. Nobody complains. Each man goes back patiently to his outfit. All the while a little way upstream from the ponton bridge an old woman stands quietly fishing from the grassy dyke. In one hand she holds a long bamboo pole. In the other a Japanese parasol. She never once looks our way.

When there's a lull, Pat Flaherty gets into slow drawling conversation with the major about nothing in particular. It turns out that the major has a gasoline can full of beer in the back of his jeep. He offers us a drink. 'It's from the brewery up the road,' he explains with a smile. 'Tastes good when you haven't been to bed for thirty-six hours . . . Once you get past this bridge you won't have any trouble,' he adds soothingly, 'except a slight traffic jam at the brewery.'

While we are talking to the major, Alabama has somehow managed to get his jeep up out of line and appears pokerfaced right at our elbow. I slip him a tin cup of beer and his grin breaks through the white mask of dust on his face. The tanks have all crossed. It's the howitzers' turn. All at once there's a gap between two halftracks.

'Just follow along,' says the major casually. 'Drive on the bulge on the bridge. Stick to the artillery and you'll get through.'

Before we know it we are across the river and jolting along a worn macadam road in a swiftmoving line of traffic.

For some time we've been meeting empty trucks passing to the rear with beer signs tacked on them. At the next traffic jam there's a big intact brewery. The courtyard is packed with every type of vehicle. Men come running out with buckets and gasoline cans and helmets full of beer. Among truckloads of infantry, bottles spurt as they are passed from hand to hand. The boys on the truck ahead reach us down an armful of open bottles. The beer is warm and flat, but it is incredibly refreshing in the heat and dust of the afternoon.

The sun is low. A breeze has come up. 'Put on your helmets. Do you want to get shot?' an M.P. shouts at us as we round a corner. Ahead of us against the sky rosy with evening stands up the pink obelisk of the Bonifacio Monument. 'Boys, we made it,' says Pat Flaherty. 'This is Manila.'

As we spin around the grass circle, everything is suddenly very empty and quiet. Down a wide avenue of scattered suburban houses in lightcolored stucco we can see that the pillar of smoke we've been following all afternoon has become many smokes. They fill half the horizon. As we look, a burst of white spurts up into the middle of the brown and spreads into a towering mushroom over the end of the street. 'Burnin',' mutters Alabama. 'They didn't lie when they said Manila was burnin'.'

Nightfall in Manila

As we drove in through the fading light under the thin brown smoke pall, we came to the cemeteries. The pink pagodas that had looked so strange seen from the air the morning before were the buildings of the Chinese cemetery. We crossed a railroad track by a big market building. Outside of it the people with big hats and pastelcolored clothes we'd seen from the air stood in little knots chaffering over bags of rice and piles of withered fruits. They had a haggard hungry look, but they went about their business without flinching at the sharp thumping of nearby gunfire. The Japanese were shelling this side of town with antiaircraft. There'd be an explosion and a blur of smoke in the sky above the buildings and pigeons would fly up and flutter awhile against the highpiled clouds white as curds that rose into the bright sky above the low murk that gave an amber gloom to the streets.

The city wore a wan look of danger. We drove slowly into town along Rizal Avenue. Here and there were American or Filipino flags. Under the shabby arcades men, women, and children stood looking out with round eyes at the trucks and the Americans cruising about in battlegreen with rifles and tommyguns. There were a few civilian cars parked at corners, each one packed with young Filipinos with guns. The cars flew Filipino flags or were draped with banners lettered with the names of various guerrilla organizations: Huk Bala Hop, Markings, Hot Spot Kids. Down side streets you could hear the occasional crisp snap of rifle fire.

As we drove along the trolley tracks over the pitted illpaved street toward the burning downtown district, the smell of smoke rasped in our nostrils. The streets were empty now, lonesomelooking. We caught a glimpse of a group of tall Spanish-style buildings off to the left. The University of Santo Tomas. Picking our way through the littered side street, we heard machinegun fire behind a block of low square buildings with tiled roofs. Inside the gates, past the sentries and the sentinel tanks, the ranked tents and the parked trucks and jeeps, and the easy loafing attitudes of the men in battlegreen gave us a sudden feeling of security. The central tower of the main building rose up purple into the last rosy dusk. The doors were open in the tall entranceway. A sound of dance music came from a radio truck standing outside.

Inside, the cavernous lobby is barely lit by two acetylene flares. A big broad stairway goes up into the darkness. Immediately I am in the middle of a gently milling crowd of white people. I can't stop looking at their faces, so chalky white in the pallid sideways light. For weeks all the faces I have seen have been yellow or brown or brickcolored from the sun or stained with atabrine. These people's faces have the waxy white of plants grown in a cellar. Long noses, lantern jaws, cheeks that sag away sharply under sharp cheekbones. Light clothes scrubbed threadbare hang limp on bony frames. So many of them are women. Children run this way and that. Young girls move through the throng with an abstracted overserious look in their eyes. There are tall gangling youths that have made weedy growth on insufficient food. Old people move by inches.

On the stairs they sit in ranks, looking straight ahead of them. Shadowy figures move slowly up and down. They pull themselves up by the banisters. At each step they pause to get their breath. There's a hum of low voices. You can hear scraps of desultory conversation. There is something polite and restrained in their tones like in a crowd in a church or at a funeral back home.

They can't seem to stand still. Nobody hurries or jostles, nobody pushes, but they move wearily back and forth with a humble sort of exhausted politeness. It's as if they have lived so long enclosed, overcrowded, waiting in line, for food, for water, to go to the bathroom, that they have developed a special way of behaving unobtrusively in a crowd. There are odd individuals who walk with their eyes fixed on something straight ahead of them. Some have strange twitches and tics. People make way for them without looking.

Every now and then a brisk voice says, 'Make way for the stretchers, please,' and dim figures pass through under blankets carried by ruddyfaced wellfed boys in uniform. The crowd gives way gently and closes again behind.

They look you right in the face with clear eyes when they

talk to you. There are people of all European nationalities, but most of them are so American it's as if you had known them before. They start talking quite naturally as if taking up an interrupted conversation. I find myself conversing, as I would at a party back home where there were too many people to allow for introductions, to a lady from a small college in Ohio. She shrinks a little when she notices I'm a correspondent. She talks very precisely. She's anxious for her statement to be accurate. 'Don't mention me, please,' she says. I can't help looking at her arms. They are shrunken to the bone. She points down at her pathetically swollen legs and feet. 'Beriberi,' she says.

There's a tall gaunt Englishman who is very anxious to be helpful. He's been terribly busy all day, he explains, getting out report cards for the children. 'Oh, yes, we have quite a good school system right up to college,' he says.

'How did you keep them fed?' I ask him.

'The Japanese only gave us half a ration. In the last months, that's been half of seven hundred calories,' he says. 'We divided the available food to give them each a full ration, but mostly it was the milk and parents starving themselves to feed them. They don't look bad, do they?'

A small boy comes running up to me with a roll of Jap issue hundred-peso Filipino bills in his fist. 'It's Mickey Mouse,' he shouts. 'Have a souvenir.' He presses a bill into my hand. I can't find anything in my pocket to give him except an American dime. He goes skipping off hugely delighted.

'They are quite out of hand tonight, I fear,' the Englishman says apologetically. 'By Mickey Mouse he means Japanese issue. There's a story that somebody put a Mickey Mouse in the watermark.'

There is such a restless stir in the high dark hall of people moving back and forth, with humble, lightly shuffling steps, that it is hard to talk consecutively. Before you are half through they forget what you started to talk about. There's a timid sort of happiness about them. Nobody seems to notice the snorting bursts of the occasional mortar shells the Japs are throwing in round the university buildings.

'Wouldn't you like to go up on the roof? It's quite a sight,' the Englishman asks me in a hospitable tone as if he felt he ought to be doing the honors of the building.

'Won't it tire you?' I ask.

'Oh, no. I've remained quite strong for some reason.'

He led the way up three steep flights of stairs. In the upper halls flickering candles light up rows of cots with sleeping figures in them veiled in white mosquito netting. When we stepped out on the roof beside the central tower, a halfcircle of flaming buildings lit up our faces.

'Let's see, where are we? Oh yes, that must be the Great Eastern Hotel,' he said pointing to a perpendicular grid of fire to the southward. 'I say, they are doing a job.'

'Every building in the Escolta — that's the downtown business district — is afire,' came the voice of a sentry out of the shadow of a doorway. 'There don't seem to be much burning on the south side of the Pasig River.'

As we looked, new fires budded soundlessly and glowed and gradually brightened like hot embers when you blow on them. Ragged smokeclouds hung overhead fringed with orange and rosy light.

'How's the Manila Hotel?' somebody asks the sentry.

'They say it's intact, sir,' he answers smartly.

I find myself roaming around the huge building. The arcaded courts are divided up into little thatched shelters with tables and chairs. People have managed to make them-

selves fragmentary imitations of home. In the light of candles
and of an occasional kerosene lamp you see them sitting reading or chatting or putting the children to bed or cooking up
little messes on gasoline stoves. There's even an occasional
potted plant.

Two soldiers brush past me. 'Well, I got the showers going,' one of them is saying briskly to the other.

A man with cavernous eyes in a bigboned face comes up and
asks me what the navy anchor on my collar means. I explain
it's the naval insignia for correspondents. 'Shake,' he says,
'I work at Cavite Navy Yard. Anybody who's got navy
insignia is all right by me.' He asks me if I have any place to
sleep. No, I haven't. He says he can give me a cot in his
dormitory that belongs to an airman that has just been evacuated to a hospital.

I remembered that I hadn't had any supper either, so I
asked him to wait for me while I went out to the jeep to get a
box of K rations I'd left there. As I stepped out of the door, a
new burst of flame blooming dully beyond the low buildings
in front of the university shot a tongue of light among the
parked cars. Groping my way round our jeep, I make out a
whiteclad figure sitting beside Alabama's sinewy dark form
on the front seat. It is a girl. It is a white girl. I can even
imagine in the faint glow of the fire that it is a pretty girl.
His arm is around her waist. Our big guns back of the university are making such a racket that they don't hear me. Alabama's voice is whispering something mellow. There's the
crack of an incoming mortar shell somewhere in the compound. I grab my box of K rations and run back into the
building. The couple on the front seat of the jeep don't stir.
When I get back into the hallway in the light of the acetylene
flare that shines on a row of pale patient faces moving past the

information desk, I look at my watch. Exactly seventeen minutes have gone by since we arrived at Santo Tomas.

Night under Fire

The dormitory was full of breathing. Stretched out under the privacy of the mosquito netting I could feel the furtive stirring in the cots all around me of men who had adjusted themselves even in their sleep to life in closely packed rooms. The place was clean but stuffy from the crowding of dull inactive underfed bodies. It smelt of confinement.

A sharp explosion had waked me up. A mortarburst. Another followed pretty close. Fragments went rattling across the roof below. At the same time the ruddy light of a new fire filled the windows on the side toward the bay. Men stirred under their mosquito bars. There were some racked bronchial coughs. Somebody who was having a hard time digesting the army rations broke wind prodigiously. A man got up and clacked gently in wooden clogs out into the hall. The night dragged on. Mosquitoes had got in under my net. Our howitzers behind the building kept up a continual banging. Every few minutes a mortar shell burst near. Slapping at the mosquitoes, I lay on my back looking up through the netting at the waxing and waning glow of the fire on the whitewashed ceiling, thinking of the women and the very old people lying in their beds listening to the shells combing their way toward them. They must be afraid of the fires. They must be anxious about the children they had nursed with such heartbreaking care through three years. The people I'd talked to last night had been full of pathetic confidence. The Army had come. They were safe. Mail had come. The Red Cross had brought in twenty-seven thousand letters linking them back to the America they had almost lost hope in. They had their letters under their pillows as they lay there, while the enemy sought them out with the groping pattern of mortar fire. They were free. Soon they were going to be sent home. It was hard on them to be caught in war's vise right on the edge of safety. In the dormitory the men lay quiet under their mosquito nets. Nobody said a complaining word. Every quarter-hour somewhere in the building a clock chimed sweetly with an oldfashioned faraway sound.

When I woke up, it was light. My friend from the Navy Yard was sitting in his drawers on the edge of his cot. His skin hung so empty over his bones his body looked blue. 'You wouldn't have any more of those ration biscuits, would you?' he said, with a dry little cough of apology. 'I can't seem to get enough to eat . . . I'm hungrier now than I was when I started to eat.'

The box was empty. He took it from me and put it carefully with the little pile of belongings on the chair beside his bed. I told him I'd bring him some more K rations next time when I came back to Santo Tomas. I pulled on my shirt and pants and went out.

The huge stony lugubrious building was full of early morning stir. The corridors were already filled with the long patient queues of men and women waiting for breakfast. At the washroom and toilets men and boys waited in line. There was no impatience on their faces. They chatted in relaxed and customary tones. They had forgotten the time when they hadn't had to wait in line.

In the lobby there was the same gently milling crowd. Stretcherbearers were carrying out a young man in battle-green. His face had a greenish-yellow cast from atabrine but there was no color under the skin. He was quite dead. A new shocked look of sympathy came over the faces of the interned civilians as they made way for the dead soldier.

Manila, February 7, 1945

2

Headquarters at San Miguel

Filipino Village

'LET'S TAKE A TURN about the barrio,' suggested the dark thinfaced Aussie. It was a morning of breathless heat. We ducked through the dust churning up from a line of fastmoving trucks to cross the main road and strolled slowly, so as not to sweat too much, down the village street.

'The barrio is the basic Philippines,' the Aussie was saying. 'It makes me wonder sometimes if you blokes have much to be proud of in your colonial administration.'

We were walking slowly so as not to scuff up the thick dust. The oblong thatched houses on stilts were evenly spaced on either side. Sicklylooking people squatted among their scanty utensils on mats in the shade under the houses. A few small pigs rooted in the grass along the edges of the street. Here and there a crosslooking Philippine toy horse grazed in a bamboo corral. Between the houses in the shade of broadleaved plants of banana and hemp, women were pounding rice with heavy longhandled pestles. In one place they had rigged a machine to husk the rice that had a succession of small pestles on a wheel which was worked by turning a handle. The people seemed vastly amused when we stopped to look at it. Some of the houses had porches shaded with bamboo blinds with plants in cracked pots round the edges. There was almost no furniture in the houses. The barrio had a look of longstanding scarcity and want.

'The want was there before the Japanese,' said the Aussie. 'You can't blame it on the Japs. These people worked on the sugar plantations. Sugar and poverty go together all over the world.'

At the end of the street a little girl with pigtails came running up to him. 'Mabuhai, Teresita,' he said. 'She's my little friend,' he explained bashfully as he disentangled his leg from her grasp. 'I bring her tucker. She's just the age of my little girl.'

A holloweyed woman was looking out at us from the house opposite. 'Mother has T.B.,' he whispered, 'but she keeps the little girl clean as a pin . . . There's a lot of illness here.' He waved his hand in the direction of the woman in the house. 'Mabuhai,' he called.

The street ended in a riverbank of trodden mud. Some women were bathing at the turn of the stream. Through the intense green canefield on the other bank came shambling a prehistoric-looking carabao with a small naked yellow child perched on its huge black neck. Beyond the canefields the hills rose very blue into the haze of heat.

'They drink that,' said the Aussie, wrinkling up his nose as he waved his hand in the direction of the slimy water.

We walked back through the other street where the better houses were. Those nearest the main road had all been burned by the Japs in their retreat. There was nothing left but fine white ash and a scattering of calcined pots and pans. Some houses had stood on concrete posts. In most of them the stool of a watercloset still stood up on a pillar above the cesspool as a forlorn sort of monument to the American standard of living.

I pointed them out. 'Progress!' said the Aussie scornfully. 'That's all you Yanks can think of.'

We stopped at a little booth kept by an old yellow squaw-like woman. There were some cigars, a few piles of dried shrimp, dusty tomatoes arranged on broad leaves, a jar of tiny shellfish, and a few salted mullets hanging by their tails that gave out a strong reek in the heavy air. 'It's a tiny little life they led in the barrio,' said the Aussie.

The railroad station of San Miguel was intact, though full of litter and rubbish. On the walls were fragments of posters. We could still make out part of a proclamation of martial law signed by President Laurel, and a piece of a Japanese propaganda poster that said:

> . . . In Nippon sports are not regarded as an individual amusement, they are looked upon as physical training of a national character . . .

'Have you seen anything the Japs actually built in the Philippines?' I asked.

'Not a bloody thing,' said the Aussie.

Across the empty tracks were the mashed galvanized-iron roofs of a warehouse marked *Hacienda Luisita*. As we looked, the rails began to sing in front of the station. From down the track that led out of Tarlac a jeep came rollicking toward us running on the rails at a fast clip towing a string of freight-cars. A group of sunbaked men in khaki waved as they passed. Some ragged barrio-dwellers who had been sitting hunched on the edges of the track got to their feet and looked after the little train with round eyes. Smiles broke out on their faces.

'Oh, you Yanks,' said the Aussie with a shake of the head. 'You're always at it.'

'I Shall Return'

Most of the offices of General Headquarters are up on the hill in the low buildings and the bungalows set on grassy knolls under big trees that used to house the Spanish managers and foremen of the great sugar hacienda. There are gardens with brick walks. There's a swimming pool where, whenever the water is not full of tanned Americans diving and splashing and whooping, beautiful red and blue kingfishers skim saucily over the surface. From the porch of the main building you look out across the flatlands of the valley of Luzon, hazy from an occasional white pillar of smoke where canefields are burning. There's always a little tang of burnt straw in the air.

The officer I have come to see sits at a plain deal table on the lower porch of the main building. His red face with little wrinkles at the corners of the mouth is a face you would expect to see in the office of a contractor or factory owner rather than the face of a soldier. He's an old Manila hand of many years' standing who has transacted many kinds of business in the islands. I'm asking him how it was we got back to Manila so quickly.

He frowns as if the answer were too obvious to be worth making: 'We are in Manila ahead of schedule because we have the support of eighteen million Filipinos who believed Mac-Arthur when he said, "I shall return." '

He turned to the roundfaced colonel at the next desk as if for confirmation of what he had just said. The roundfaced colonel nodded vigorously. He cleared his throat and went on: 'From the time we started back from Australia our policy has been one of boldness and disdain of the enemy . . . Japanese propaganda was countered by aggressive leadership and by getting the truth to the Filipino people in our radio broadcasts . . . Sure, everybody listened in. Japs never could stop 'em.' He stopped to clear his throat. The roundfaced colonel was smiling approvingly.

'The Japs were confused by our unconventional methods. They expected conventional undercover stuff. We threw the idea of secrecy overboard. We only preserved enough secrecy to protect our vessels. Everything else has been done as openly as possible.

'Our relations with the Filipino people have been directly under the Commanding General's chief of staff. MacArthur would handle even the most trivial questions for himself. When we were getting up the sewing kits and little mirrors and packages of chewing gum and candy and matches with his picture and "I shall return" on them to broadcast over the islands, MacArthur decided every detail himself . . . everything except the flavors of the chewing gum.'

He paused and tapped thoughtfully with his pencil on his desk. 'MacArthur knows the Filipinos and they know him. They knew his father before him. That means a great deal in the Philippines. Personal and family loyalty mean a great deal here. From the moment of his arrival in Australia, his messages to the Filipino people were personal messages . . . The wrappers off chewing gum with the General's picture and his message were selling in Manila for ten dollars apiece. That's how much people thought of him.'

He gave me a challenging look as if to say, 'You answer that one,' and went on: 'The basis of our work was the guerrilla movement and the groups of Americans at large in the islands. About a thousand Americans came through . . . Of course lots of them aren't in yet . . . but nothing would have been possible without the passive resistance to the invader of the masses of the Filipino people and the profound spiritual leadership of General MacArthur. It was due to the people's co-operation that we were able to establish weather stations and coastwatchers and a network of intelligence . . . By the time we landed in Leyte, we had literally millions of agents. They sent us reports of troop movements and shipping. We could have the guest list at the Manila Hotel any time we wanted it. We knew where every can of gasoline was stored. Yamashita held a meeting of his high-ranking officers in Manila on December 16. On the twenty-sixth we had the complete minutes in our hands . . . Without the intelligence agents we could never have carried out our hop-skip-and-jump campaign.'

He pushed his chair back and got to his feet. 'Does that give you a start?' he asked. He looked from me to the round-faced colonel next him. The Colonel nodded. He cleared his throat. 'By the way, if you should see the Commanding General,' he said, 'tell him I've covered the matter of personal leadership.'

The Character of the Enemy

'Be sure and see Steve Mellnik,' several people had told me. He was a hard man to get hold of because he was always on the move. I finally ran into him in front of the army postoffice in the main building of General Headquarters. He led me up the brick path into the screened messhall.

'Maybe they'll give us a cup of coffee,' he said.

'No, sir,' said the mess sergeant firmly. 'There's no coffee ready.'

Steve Mellnik seemed immensely amused. 'Oh, well, we'll drink a glass of ice water . . . You don't mind if we sit here, do you?' he asked, laughing.

Colonel Mellnik has straight black hair and a scar on his face and a sharp light in his eyes. His manner of talking is kidding and explosive, half irritable, half affectionate. His people were Slavs. He was born in Pennsylvania and raised in Rochester, New York. He went through West Point and served a postgraduate course as a Japanese prisoner in Cabanatuan. He got away. Fevers and captivity and the hairbreadth escapes of the last few years have beaten the Philippines into his hide. He has matched his wits against the Japanese and they interest him.

He kids me for taking out my notebook. 'What's the matter? Losing your memory already?'

When I ask him why the Filipinos seem to like us so well, he bursts out laughing. 'What's this? An interview? . . . Seven months of Japanese propaganda clinched the business . . . I suppose it was in the summer of 1942 that white prestige in these islands reached its alltime low. But by October and November of that year, the Filipinos had discovered what it was all about. Respect for Americans has been rising ever since . . . It was the schools and the schoolteachers that came out around nineteen-four who laid the foundation for it. A lot of able honest Americans came out to these islands and the rural population — the population is ninety per cent rural — learned to respect them, called them *apas*, fathers. They have an instinctive trust in the fair dealing of the old Americans. You are traveling in out-of-the-way districts and the word goes out over the bamboo telegraph and the people come out of the barrios to meet you. The most stupid American automatically becomes head man. Why, one elderly American officer, so sick he can hardly leave his bed, has been running the Zambales section for years.'

'Why didn't the Japanese make a better showing?'

The Japanese were too rigid, he explained. They had an immensely rigid caste system. Their language was rigid and full of formality. They couldn't understand how other people thought and felt. Their language was so unbending, so full of politenesses and decorums and facesaving circumlocutions that they hardly understood each other. There were different forms of address for different castes. If a man was your social equal you spoke to him one way, if he was your inferior another, if your superior still another. There was no way a Japanese could bawl out an inferior without losing caste. There just wasn't any form of address for it. That was probably why they did so much faceslapping. Take this business of bowing to the sentry. All Japs bowed to the sentry because he represented the Mikado. The Filipinos couldn't get that through their heads. The Japs chopped off heads of people for using improper forms of speech. Then they were trying to build an empire on a shoestring. They didn't have anything to give. All they could do was take. Their police system was wretched. They proved themselves incapable of preserving law and order. Many of the guerrilla organizations grew up among the Filipinos for mutual protection against looting. They were police units in small communities. The Filipinos thought the Japanese were maddeningly dumb. They weren't so dumb as all that, but they did have a rigid archaic kind of mentality and their language went with it. The Filipinos felt that they were smarter than the Japs. It wasn't long before they began to yearn for good old Uncle Sam.

He'd had some experience outsmarting the Japanese himself, hadn't he? I tried to ask him a leading question.

He laughed. 'I was driving around Manila with a car and a chauffeur a year and a half ago,' he said. But that was all he'd say. As soon as the conversation got around to himself, he began to stir restlessly in his chair. He began to talk about Australia and in a minute he was up and gone.

The Work of Preparation

General Willoughby, the Chief of Intelligence, had his office in a corner of the broad upper porch. He was a tall man with thin dark hair parted in the middle. He had the scholarly somewhat sarcastic manner of an oldfashioned German professor. He sat at a plain deal table like a teacher in a college seminar facing his class. He spoke with few words arranged in precise wellorganized sentences. His slight foreign accent intensified the scholarly tone. I felt as if I were consulting a specialist on a problem of research. This was a good time, he said, smiling his small thin smile, to talk about what had been done in the Philippines. Two months ago, nobody in Intelligence would have had time. They were all working eighteen hours a day. A few weeks from now they would be up to their ears in it again, preparing for further campaigns.

Already, he said in a thoughtful tone, they were forgetting the arduous nature of the work of preparation for the Philippine campaign in their pleasure in seeing its results. But it was all in the past. To tell the truth, they were more interested now in sending a Mohammedan holy man into Borneo than in the guerrilla movement in the Philippines. Their work was a work of preparation. He spoke in the objective tone of a man who has completed his writeup of a laboratory experiment and now has another under way. 'Meanwhile,' he said, waving a flat hand at the folders in blue covers piled on the corner of his desk, 'I have had a few documents on the guerrilla movement collected for you to study at your leisure.'

Resistance Leader

Headquarters, poised as it was on the edge of Manila, was full of walking documents. On the porch of President Osmeña's yellow house on the hill I was introduced that afternoon to Governor Confesor of Panay, known affectionately among the Americans as Tommy Confesor. He had come in from Panay to join MacArthur's forces in Tacloban a month before. Since then he'd flown to the States and back. Four days each way. 'This life is very different from my life as a guerrilla hiding from the Japanese,' he said, laughing.

He was a small stocky man with rumpled black hair, rather broader in the shoulders than most of his countrymen. When he got excited as he talked, he made the pumping motions with his arms of an habitual public speaker. Immediately he began to tell his story. He was caught in Manila by the Japanese occupation on January 2, 1942. The Japs wanted to use him in the puppet government, but he managed to escape by mailboat to Iloilo. He had once been Governor there before the war. A month later, the Japs landed in Panay and he had to take to the hills. His idea was to keep the thread of the legal government of the Commonwealth going at all costs. After Wainwright's disheartening surrender of all the USAFFE forces, resistance collapsed. From his hiding place in the hills he issued a proclamation assuming the powers of government. Colonel Peralta took over the military command. The courts, the police, the whole machinery of civil government they carried on from the hills.

'Here in the Philippines,' he explained, putting his hand on my wrist to hold my attention, 'we have an official. We call him *teniente del barrio*. You know the barrio is the small town. It is our unit of life. He is appointed . . . he is elected

. . . ' He shrugged his shoulders with a little frown. 'Any-way'. . . his eyes twinkled as he smiled broadly . . . 'he is head man of the township. I made it my business to keep always in touch with the tenientes del barrio to see that they remained faithful to the Commonwealth. It was they who led in the saving of American flyers. The behavior of these flyers kept people from forgetting what Americans were like. In Romblon it was a typical instance . . .' He smiled his twinkling smile. 'There was an American flyer who had been saved by the people when Japanese sailors came swimming ashore after the naval battle. The American flyer gave them cigarettes. "But why?" the people ask. "If Japs catch American flyer they cut off his head."'

The people wouldn't submit to the Japs. They seemed inferior. Their American-trained schoolteachers kept the people together. Wherever the Japs came, the people fled into the hills, and with them went the tenientes del barrio and the schoolteachers. The Japs found empty towns. They burned the towns and the nipa huts of the guerrillas, but after that there was nothing left for them to do but move out again. The people lived on crops they grew in the hills. The people's backbone was never broken. Even the very poor people would give one salmon can of rice a day to feed the guerrilla soldiers.

'I myself,' he exclaimed, spreading out his arms, 'was a year and a half in the hills with my wife and little children. Often we were shot at and had to climb to safety up steep trails in the rain at night. One night I fell asleep in a hut in a mountain valley and dreamed that somebody knocked on the door and said the Japanese were coming. I thought this foolishness, but an hour later my boys came to say the Japs were really coming and we had better run for it.'

He paused and looked at me with a reminiscent smile. 'When the first bombings by American planes came, our people were very happy. You will not believe it is true, but people cried, danced, knelt down in the street, mothers held their children up to see the planes so that when they grow up they could tell their children about it. "America has not failed us," they said.

'When an American flyer drops in Panay the people come to meet him with flowers and a brass band. American soldiers bring gold, the Japs bring bad paper. Americans bring food, Japanese take away food. When an American seaplane was landing in Negros, hundreds of people rowed out in bancas and canoes. Yes, yes, during the Japanese occupation. The people brought them food and fruit, what they had. The boys in the plane gave away all their cigarettes and then they were sorry because the people were so ragged and gave away clothes. We have no clothing in three years. They gave them their jackets and then they pulled off their trousers and undershirts. They gave away their blankets and mattresses. They went home in their drawers. The people as long as they live will have a soft spot in their hearts for Americans. No Jap can come to the island of Panay for fifty years.'

Disciple of Jackson and Lee

On another cool screened American-style porch up on the hill, the Five Star General sits in his rocker smoking his corncob pipe and looking out at the streaks of late sunlight gilding the grass between the great trees. When the Public Relations Officer bustles a visitor through the door, he gets to his feet. You see a tall man remarkably slender and erect for his age. He wears dark glasses. He has a long head of closecut chestnut hair. On his thin cheeks and his sharp chin the rosy skin is surprisingly taut and smooth. There's an air of breeding about him. He stretches out a small dry hand and greets you with somewhat oldfashioned courtesy. He waves you into a chair and when you are seated he unhurriedly sits down in his rocker again and starts to talk. He talks looking straight ahead of him. His sentences are long with carefully balanced clauses. He rarely pauses for an answer. It's as if our arrival had merely caused him to speak aloud the thoughts that had been working rhythmically in his head as he sat there after the work of the day smoking and looking out at the failing afternoon. Only gradually you discover from the turn of his language that he is acutely aware of his listeners and of their interests and affiliations. There is something disarming in the direct way his rather elaborate thoughts take shape in elaborate phrases.

Gently and without undue emphasis he uses again the words we had heard that morning: 'boldness and disdain of the enemy.' . . . He speaks of the destruction of Manila and of the amazement that sometimes comes over him that men should find it in their hearts to do such things. It is amazing to him sometimes, he says musingly, that his own life should have been spent among scenes of slaughter, he has never been able quite to accustom himself to them. . . . Robert E. Lee and Stonewall Jackson have been the great prototypes on which he has modeled his life. Neither did they ever get over their amazement that men should find no other way than war to settle their disputes. . . . He has been often criticized for speaking so much of the power of God in his communiqués, but without God's help and guidance we would never have prevailed as we have over the enemy. He has merely given credit where credit was due. . . . Manila would rise again from its ashes. . . . A new six-million-dollar power plant was already on its way from the States. . . . In a year we would see a great change. He personally invited us to come back in a year and see for ourselves.

The Public Relations Officer makes a rasping noise in his throat. His chair scrapes. He's on his feet, smiling discreetly. The General smiles his bittersweet smile. I am outdoors again among the dusty shrubberies and the dense trees full of the evening chatter and flutter of birds.

Lincoln's Birthday Dance

Back at San Miguel behind the lacy green trees the last of the sunset shines through streaks of cloud, yellow and purple and tinsel strips, bright as ornaments on a Christmas tree. Small bats swoop and twitter above the dusty road. Round the sentry at the gate an endless chaffer and dickering goes on. There's a little girl who wants to do somebody's laundry. There's an old woman with a bantam chicken. There's a small child with a basket of eggs for sale. There are two serious dusty young boys of about ten who are offering their older sister's charms to a soldier in no uncertain terms. 'Naw,' says the sentry sententiously. 'Five dollars is too much.'

A guerrilla detachment is passing in single file, ragged little smoothskinned beardless men with carbines slung over their shoulders.

'That's the hot bellhops comin' for the dance,' says the sentry. 'Those boys'll make trouble, and I don't mean maybe.'

Up in the Public Relations Office beside the railroad tracks the moths blunder about the weak electric-light bulbs. Sweating correspondents sit under them stripped to their

pants, straining their eyes to clack out their stories on their
typewriters. In the inner office the censors brood over a pile
of copy under a yellow shade. From the colonel's desk you
can hear a voice full of rank at the telephone ordering somebody to prepare three box lunches for three colonels who are
going into Manila tomorrow.

Down the road in the stripped hotel beside the empty filling
station, other correspondents sit on their cots in their underdrawers drinking a hideous pinkish rum that tastes like juicy-
fruit gum and cursing out the censorship.

'The shelling of Santo Tomas is the biggest story in the
whole war and they won't let you write about it.'

'Why the hell couldn't they have gotten those people out
of Santo Tomas instead of leaving them there to be blown to
pieces with shells?'

'Might as well pull out and go back to the States if you
can't write the news.'

'I've got an appointment to take it up with the Commanding General in the morning.'

At the door downstairs I meet the neatly dressed barefooted
woman with mournful circles under her eyes who took my
shirts to wash. She makes a little speech in remarkably clear
English as she receives my two dollars. 'You see, sir,' she
says, 'I have to do washing to feed my children. My husband
is in Manila. I have brought the children because of the danger, but I must do washing to buy them food. The Japanese
have been very cruel. They take all food. They burn the best
houses in the barrio. And now the price of rice is so high . . .'

The tenniscourt opposite has been decorated with flowers
and freshcut palms. The infantry outfit that is giving the
dance has rigged up a stand for the band and the Filipinos

have banked it with greenery. The court is lit by two flood-lights that get their juice from a portable generator on a truck. Sweating prodigiously, the divisional band is striking up boogie-woogie. Round the edges of the court are grouped all the girls in the barrio that have any best clothes to wear. They have flowers in their dark hair. The guerrillas have gotten themselves into suntans and army boots. The round Filipino faces look strangely pale and smooth beside the deeply sunburned windroughened faces of the Americans. They all have their guns. The Filipinos even dance with them slung over their shoulders. The glaring floodlights throw the sharp shadows of the guns among the weaving shadows of the dancing couples. The darkness all around is an inky blue.

There are only enough girls for a few men to dance with at a time. I'm standing in a group of Americans who are looking rather glumly at the proceedings over their comrades' shoul-ders. When the conga stops, there's a shuffling silence. We hear in the distance the roottootoot toottoot toottoot of an American locomotive. There it goes again. From the tracks up the road comes the ringing clank of an approaching freight.

'By godfrey,' says one boy, 'they've opened up the railroad line.'

The engineer hoots again as the train passes the railroad station. The freight rattles off up the line. The sound of a last whistle dies away in the night. The men around me stand very quiet.

'Jesus, boy,' says a voice that is almost a sob, 'don't that carry you home?'

San Miguel, February 12, 1945

3

The Fighting in the City

Noncombatants

OUT AT THE EDGE OF THE CITY the morning dawns sunny and cool. In an empty stucco villa on a hilltop near the Bonifacio Obelisk the advanced echelon of a noncombatant unit is setting up an office. Corporals and sergeants are carrying in tables and folding chairs. Soldiers are unloading desks out of mudcaked trucks. Inside the empty cobwebby rooms officers are stringing mosquito netting over their cots. The politician-in-uniform, in command, paces up and down smoking a cigar. He's a pudgy flaxenhaired man who greets you with a sweetish smile that fades instantly into tiny wrinkles of self-centered peeve round his mouth and eyes. He is attended by a Filipino liaison officer, who has just brought up the owner of the house, a broadfaced tobaccocolored civilian in a white linen suit and white pith helmet. The owner of the house is making an elaborate smiling speech, saying that to welcome an American officer into his house lifts up his heart within his breast upon this day of the liberation of Manila, which is the happiest day of his life. The politician-in-uniform has lost interest and resumed his abstracted pacing.

Meanwhile a battery of 155's somewhere back of the villa has gone to work again. Each time the Long Toms shoot, it's like being hit on the head with a baseball bat. The Japanese reply with a few dual purpose antiaircraft shells that burst grimly over the road into Manila. In the midst of the din a straightbacked young officer has appeared on the porch steps. He says something about this house having been picked out by the Fourteenth Corps. The face of the politician-in-uniform becomes sourly blank. 'Nope . . . Assigned to my unit,' he says, and turns on his heel. The straightbacked officer tries politely to insist.

While the exchange of military courtesies is going on, something has started to happen on the hill beyond the radio masts the Japanese didn't manage to blow up before they left. People drop what they are doing and turn in that direction. An alert professional look comes over the faces of the enlisted men. One man reaches for the rifle he's left leaning against the side of the house. There's a machinegun burst. A couple of rifles crack. People edge a little toward the shelter of the stone wall behind the house. Everybody is looking at a red barnlike building half-hidden by the bulge of the hill. A tiny gray figure is moving out from it, pointing in our direction with a tubular something held from the shoulder. On the hill groups of Americans in battlegreen kneel or fall flat behind the sights of their guns. The machinegun speaks again. The tiny figure drops out of sight. A group of men in battlegreen moves cautiously forward spreading out over the dry grass as they advance toward the red barn. Already men are coming back our way swinging rifles at the end of relaxed arms. They have a little the air of boys coming in from the outfield at the end of an inning in a baseball game.

'Got him,' somebody says cheerily.

'What was it?'

'Jap sniper. Somebody forgot to clean out that barn last night.'

On the porch the politician-in-uniform, puffing heavily on another cigar, has settled down to his pacing again. His face still wears the skindeep smile. 'I have ordered up extra guards,' he is saying emphatically to one of his junior officers. He squares his shoulders and thrusts out his chin. 'I confidently expect a banzai charge.'

Amid the long grass of the hibiscus-hedged yard in back of the house the cooks are setting up a portable kitchen. A ring of spindling small Filipinos stands around looking on with cordial interest. The gasoline stove flares up in a puff of white flame. Everybody edges away except the roundfaced sergeant, who advances on it with a frown of resolution. He kneels down beside it.

'Don't those things blow up?' asks one of the Filipinos.

'Sure, they blow up,' says the sergeant. He gets to his feet with the sweat streaming off his red face. He holds out his right hand. 'See that hand! Six weeks in the hospital. I can't open the fingers no more. I got that the last time one blew up.'

'Why don't you use kerosene stoves?' asks the Filipino. 'They are very much safer.'

The cook is busy adjusting the burner with the fingers of his good hand. 'That's why Uncle Sam took me,' he roars into the flame . . . 'to blow these goddam stoves.'

The View from the Steeple

A young man from the First Cavalry has come in a jeep to pick up two correspondents. He's a rawboned youth with glasses and a way of throwing his shoulders around when he talks. His name is Bill Shields. 'My! this is great luck for me,' he splutters as we shake hands with him. 'I've just been put on this detail. I'm going to have the time of my life driving you people around.'

We drive out a broad avenue with stone curbing and lots marked out with white posts through a region that looks like the next to the newest suburb in any California city.

'This is the Quezon City development,' Bill Shields explains with enthusiasm.

At a traffic circle he stops to point out the tanks scattered at intervals among the clumps of evergreens through a rough parkland grown up in long grass. Their guns are pointing away from the city.

'This is where we are expecting a counterattack . . . All hell may break loose any moment now.'

He shows us a fold in the valley where the foothills hunch up to meet the cloudy mountains.

'The Japs are up in there,' he says. 'If we're lucky maybe we can take in the excitement on the way back from Manila this afternoon.'

He turns off the road into an encampment among nipa huts and low buildings under the shade of dense evergreens. One thatched building is full of new and used American automobiles packed around with sandbags. Some dealer has evidently hidden his stock away there. At the command post in the trees just above we meet a marine major who offers to take us dive-bombing.

'It's the greatest sport in the world,' he says. 'We lay down a smokescreen on either side of the target and dive-bomb between them.'

We explain that we have to go into the city today. 'Thank you very much,' we say.

Driving in through a prosperouslooking section of pink and green and blue stucco houses with redtiled roofs set among hibiscus hedges and buried in masses of bougainvillea, we stop on a side street to look at the twisted skeleton of a Sherman tank.

'They ran on a mine,' explains Bill Shields. 'We never did find the crew. The Japs are planting regular marine mines in the streets. That's really more explosive than you need to do the job.' Torn sheets of metal are scattered all about the wrecked stucco houses. 'All these streets are full of mines.' He waves his hand across the quiet suburban hillside. 'You have to stick to the dotted line.'

Looking out across the city to the north, we see back lots and trees and streets, and in the distance the gray husks of the buildings of the Escolta district standing up against a brown smudge. There are no big fires, but the whole city is smudged in a sullen haze of smoke.

We plunge into an ancient irregular thoroughfare that leads into town between garden walls and gray stone Spanish churches and convents set behind big trees. As we drive in, we begin to meet the people coming out.

Looking straight ahead of them, they come straggling out along the edges of the street. They walk with their eyes on the ground as if they were afraid of stumbling. There are men and women, a great many children. Some have bandaged heads, arms in slings. They all look very much alike, eyes hollow, jaws sagging. They put one foot shakily before the other with slow dogged weariness. They push carts piled high with furniture. They carry heavy baskets full of odds and ends of household goods. There's a Chinaman slogging along with two stacks of Chinese restaurant dishes swung on a carrying pole. There are ambulances and painted twowheel carts and jouncing trucks full of wounded. We pass a truck-load of wounded American soldiers.

'Gosh,' says Bill Shields, 'they are using trucks to bring our boys out. That shows how busy the ambulances must be.'

Driving slowly we grind past a convoy of weapon-carriers. They are packed with men in torn smokegrimed battlegreen. The men's faces have a hollow look. Their faces and their arms and their bare chests are gray with ash and dust. Their eyelids are narrowed to slits. Their lips are compressed into a hard line. Their eyes have a black look. There's no release of tension on their faces yet. They look resentfully about them as they are driven out from the skirmish line into the fresh-smelling suburbs full of flowers and green leaves and shade. 'That's First Cavalry,' says Bill Shields between clenched teeth. 'They are coming back sore. It's rough in there.'

The Pasig here is a narrow muddy stream. Engineers are still working on the bridge. Two streams of traffic, military going in, civilian coming out, have to wait while the engineers explode a charge of dynamite under a piece of masonry they are clearing away. It's a little jumpy waiting because we are within range of mortar fire. 'They killed three of our sentries here this mornin', right on this here bridge,' says the M.P. who is directing traffic, greeting us cordially as he stalks past our jeep. In the silence before the charge goes off, we can hear the grumbling explosions of mortars and the rattle of machineguns from the fighting ahead of us.

When the traffic moves again, we enter a burned-out district where nothing is left but galvanized roofs scattered along the ground like a spilt pack of playing cards. People have gone back to their homes and are trying to live in the ruins.

You see women crouching under propped-up bits of scorched roofing or threading their way through piles of still smoking cinders, carrying cookpots or gasoline cans full of water. Here and there a few bits of ragged laundry flutter from up-ended scraps of metal. Occasionally amid the sour smell of ashes there's a new sweetish reek that clutches horribly at your throat. It's the smell of the dead rotting fast in the hot sun.

In front of a new cement building marked PACO GRO-CERY stands a Japanese staff car that a shell has stamped flat as a tin toy when you step on it, and in the gutter beyond on a heap of old iron a dead Jap swells in the heat.

The gutted city blocks have the look of lots cleared for new construction. We can see in front of us the row of modern American buildings along the bay. The sharp drilling of the machineguns echoes back from them.

Bill Shields has stopped the jeep and is scratching his head. 'Let's see,' he says, 'there ought to be a command post around here somewhere.'

'Where's the fighting?' we ask breathlessly.

'This morning it was along the edge of the burned-out area . . We've got a command post up in there somewhere I thought you might like to go to.'

We've caught sight of a church steeple off to the left. 'Isn't that the Singalong Church? Suppose we go there first.'

'Sure,' says Bill Shields cheerfully. 'I'll take you any-where you say.'

He slews the jeep around to the left toward the church. On the way we pass a little wooden booth set up on the edge of a row of flattened houses. There's a sign above it: *Information*. Beside it is strung on poles a poster, harshly painted in green and black on thin canvas like a circus poster, of a Filipino with bulging muscles slaying the inevitable cartoonist's spectacled bucktoothed Jap with a bayonet.

The church is a big barnlike Catholic Church in superannuated Gothic style. It stands alone more or less undamaged in a region of small houses razed by the fire. There's nobody outside, but inside it's like the waitingroom at a railroad station. People are scattered in groups among the benches and over the tiled floor as if they had never moved from the spot where they first fell when they came in. The floor is littered with filth and rags and broken objects that have lost all shape. In the corner stands a small wrecked hearse, elaborate and dusty, beside a wax figure of the dead Christ in a cracked glass case. There are piles of household possessions, things wrapped in napkins and tablecloths. Here and there is a heap of charcoal where someone has been cooking. There are live chickens in a basket tied up by their legs. Near the holy water font two white goats are tethered. A little black dog trots around on three legs.

A sluggish silence shrouds the place from the sounds of battle outside. There is no talking. When you start to look at people one by one, you see that nearly everyone has been hurt. Near the door there's a greenfaced woman stretched out in a sort of express wagon on bicycle wheels. She was wounded four days ago, someone tells you. She's wearing a frilly party dress. Her breathing is heavy and rasping. Her fingers move endlessly around a heavy brass crucifix that lies on her chest.

There's an old man in a wheelchair huddled over a mass of dirty bandages. There's a pretty half-American young woman with a pretty little boy and girl. 'We're all right,' she says, smiling. 'We ran all the way.' There's a Russian wounded in the belly who lies writhing in a pale sweat of fever on a long bench. Next to him we find an elderly American couple. He's a tall wasted man. His lips are blue. He lies back on a bench fighting for breath.

'You see, it's heart disease,' his wife explains hurriedly, while she fusses over him making him sip from a glass half full of liquid. 'At least I was able to save his medicines. The Japanese let us go back to our house from Santo Tomas because he was so ill. Couldn't you get an ambulance for him? He'll die this way. We were burned out. We lost everything. At least I was able to save his medicines.'

A haggardlooking little man shows us the ladder up onto the roof of the church. It is a long climb. It is a relief to step out on the warm stone coping round the steeple into the sunlight and the smell of burning and the racket of battle after the reek of misery that fills the church. We are looking out at the Bayview Hotel and the apartment houses of the Ermita and Malate quarters along the shore of Manila Bay.

'Look,' says Bill Shields, stretching out his arm. 'Our advanced posts are somewhere along Taft Avenue. That's just at the edge of the new buildings. It's all First Cavalry here,' he adds proudly.

The flashes from shells exploding among the buildings are followed by smudges of black smoke. Over to the left our artillery has been throwing in a screen of white smoke to mark a target for dive-bombing. As we look, a plane drops dark and sudden out of the sky and climbs with what seems like desperate slowness over the brown bay up out of sight again. Its bombs make a sullen rumbling snort. There's a hollow distant popping of grenades. Distinct from all other sounds, the machineguns keep up their intermittent staccato conversation.

Family Chronicle

I was the first one to climb down from the steeple. The small haggard man was waiting for me in the loft of the church.

'I live in Laveriza Street,' he said. 'I am a physician. Before the surrender I was medical officer in the forty-first Infantry of USAFFE. My name is Doctor Mariano Arroyo.'

'Glad to meet you,' I said blunderingly, and held out my hand.

He went on talking without paying attention, looking straight ahead of him out over the dusty rafters of the church. When I drew the damp notebook out of the pocket of my sweatsoaked shirt, he gave me a quick nod of approval. 'One evening,' he was saying, 'the Japanese military police came to our house because they claim somebody says I am a guerrilla. My mother-in-law — her husband was American citizen in Santo Tomas — tried to save me saying just physician, curing the people. They said she was American citizen and took her away to Rosales Station and decapitated her.'

He was talking so fast I could hardly follow him. 'Then the soldiers seize me and my wife and tie us up and throw us on floor and pour gasoline over our bodies and throw match on it, but they are in a hurry and match will not light. My wife she managed to untie her hands and feet and called for help, so we escape.'

'Look,' he said. He held out his wrists and showed me where the rope had rubbed the skin. 'And look.' He pulled up his trouserlegs and showed me the skinned places on his ankles. Without a pause he went on talking. 'Now the shelling was constant. We lived in open air in shelter on back side of street, very afraid because the Japs threw a hand grenade wherever they saw a group of people collected. Then everybody said we must evacuate. At the first cross-street my wife was hit in head by a shell and was dead. I came to hospital to help care for wounded. A direct hit in the operating room killed many doctors and nurses and helpless wounded. . . . Now I will stay here, but I have no drugs, no instruments, nothing. . . . Perhaps you will get word to my father-in-law in Santo Tomas. He is all I have left. But here is something that may be interesting . . .' He turned and looked me in the face and began to speak slowly and clearly. 'When the Japanese took me to see the second in command of the military police in Manila, Colonel Nishimura, he says to me, "I know you people are waiting for the Americans." Then he look at me very angry. "If the Americans come back to Philippines, we die. Don't forget that if we die you all die."

'I've often thought of that during the last few days,' the little doctor added in a normal conversational tone. 'Come.' I followed him downstairs into the church again.

Near the high altar there was standing a handsome Spanish-looking girl. Her eyes were red and puffy, but otherwise she looked quite well. 'Here is the American press,' the little doctor told her in a severe tone. 'You must tell him.'

She gave me a frightened half-smile. 'My name is Gloria,' she said. I couldn't catch the last name. 'We were all in an airraid shelter,' she began shakily in a low voice. 'And the Japs came and told the men to come out, and they took them to one place and we heard shots, and later on they were all dead. The shelter had two entrances. We were all women in the shelter. They told us to come out through one door and as we came out they bayoneted us. I fell down from fright and they just hit me in the leg.'

'Look,' said the little doctor. She showed me the inflamed red stab wound in her leg. 'A wound in the calf of the leg,' insisted the little doctor. It seemed to make them both feel better to see me making notes in my notebook.

She waited until I stopped writing. Then she went on: 'I rolled away as fast as I could across the ground and crawled to the other entrance of the shelter and pretended to be dead. Later on, I saw my mother very severely wounded. The Japanese struck her through one shoulder and then through the other and then through the right chest very deep. My mother was dying. She and our maid managed to crawl back together into the shelter. She was full of blood and dying. The Japanese poured gasoline down one entrance of shelter. There were mattresses there that caught fire. I told my maid, my other maid . . . my maid that was with my mother was severely wounded . . . I told her to pour water on burning mattresses. And then another Japanese came to look at us inside shelter and I had a cushion over my face and hid under my mother for five hours. The smoke was terrible. We nearly suffocated. My mother was calling for water, and then my mother died, but Japanese were still there. They would not leave us. They wanted to see if some of us were stirring. They pillage. They got my watch, and our things from the house and food and chickens. They broke the big jar of drinking water. Then, when the Japanese were gone, my maid and I we heard the Americans were in Singalong and we got all our things and ran here.'

It was hard to leave. We distributed the water from our canteens as best we could. All the time we were in the church there was an old woman with a black shawl over her head kneeling motionless in the middle of the floor with her back very straight and her face toward the altar. At the door two elderly men with round faces and straight gray hair, who had evidently given each other up for dead, were greeting each other and embracing with those benign smiles the elect wear in old pictures of resurrection morning.

Just outside we found a big rawboned whitehaired German. He had a Nazi passport in his hand and he waved it indignantly under our noses. It was outrageous, he kept saying, the Japs had burned his store, and on the street they'd jostled him off the sidewalk and a Jap soldier had spat in his face and called him 'You white monkey.'

'Now,' said Bill Shields, 'shall we try and find that command post?' He waved a hand vaguely in the direction of the smoke and clatter along the fringe of buildings in front of us.

'I better go back and file some copy,' said one correspondent thoughtfully.

'Let's get out of here for a while,' I heard myself saying.

'Any way you say,' said Bill Shields. 'Driving you men around is all wonderful to me.'

Resurrection

Just as we reach the Bonifacio Monument on the way back to our quarters, we meet the first of the trucks bringing the rescued American prisoners from Bilibid Prison out to safety. Bill Shields stops his jeep and stares after them without speaking. After the small roundfaced people of Manila we'd been seeing all day, these haggard American frames in their ragged clean-scrubbed clothes seem incredibly tall and gaunt. Their faces have a long lanternjawed look. The skin on their faces is transparent as waxed paper, but the thinlipped mouths under the hollow cheekbones are relaxed and happy. They wave as they go by. An old man flips a small American flag about as if he were in a Decoration Day parade. I think of the long faces of crusaders carved in stone on their tombs in European churches and of the faces of the ancients of the Grand Army of the Republic I used to see go by with awe and commiseration when I was a boy.

Eyewitness Account

Back in Dave Sternberg's nipa hut in Santo Tomas, we were sitting talking quietly and slowly in voices a little hoarse from the hammering of the guns in the compound when a young woman in a white dress walked in. I was struck by the wooden way she walked, as if she were walking in her sleep. She was rather handsome except that her face had a curious blue puffy look. 'This is Helen Botenko,' said Sternberg in his cheery offhand way, 'she's just come in.' All at once the people sitting around the table stopped talking. Something that they knew that I didn't know made their throats stiff and their lips tremble.

'You are journalist?' she said, looking into my face with glassy eyes. She spoke English well with a slightly pedantic-sounding Russian accent. 'You want to know what is happening?' She sat down beside me and borrowed a pencil and a sheet of paper out of my notebook. With pursed lips, holding the pencil very tight, she made a map of some streets. Her fingers didn't tremble, but they seemed strangely rigid.

'This is beginning,' she said when she had finished. She gave a spot on the map a didactic little tap like a school-teacher explaining something on the blackboard to the class. 'Eleven-seventy-nine Pennsylvania Street. That was our house . . . We had not been able to leave house for several days. Noises we heard made us feel there was battle. Jap guns in Harrison Park . . . American guns in Santa Ana area. My brother said barking of Jap guns was like barking of mad dog. It was like bowling alley over our heads . . . guns shooting first from one side then from other.'

She paused and sat there rigid and motionless. Suddenly she started to talk again. 'Friday, it was a week ago, started a new element . . . They had roped off Pennsylvania Street as supply area. They had left a few puny Japs making holes for mines in street. By Jones's Bridge there was big fire, other fires moving northeast . . . American army moving in through Santa Ana . . . Friday American plane flew over and bombed dancing academy which was empty at corner of our street. Saturday morning plane flew over and dropped bomb on our house. Nobody hurt . . . not fire-bomb. We were machine-gunned from plane. Mistaken information. Nobody hurt. I felt nothing could touch us.'

She carefully marked off a few more squares on the map and wrote in the names of streets. She spoke as if she were trying hard to repeat exactly a lesson she had learned by rote.

'There were guerrillas shooting machineguns. There was an odd sound in the machineguns. Morse code messages? Perhaps. Anyway, that is how we took it. Japs caught them in a house on Pennsylvania Street. There was a young Filipino hero. His name Miranda. He said he was guerrilla giving directions to Americans. They had beheaded his three brothers. They had tried to cut off his head. He bled terribly. He was brought into our garden where we were hiding. We tried to locate Syrian doctor who lived on other side of our block, but doctor wouldn't come out to give first aid. Relatives came over, but they didn't dare move him. We took young man with us when we had to leave because pieces of shrapnel were hitting house. That was Japs shelling house.

My brother, he is chessplayer, he could figure out. Jap gun pulled by men moved around all time. Every time they moved gun we went to the other side of wall.'

The effort of trying to remember exactly was too much for her. She began to talk fast in jerky random sentences. 'Then we were shelled by Americans trying to knock out Jap gun . . . We were sheltered in stranger's house in middle of block . . . My mother was hit in chest by shrapnel. She died instantaneously. We carried her back to our garden hoping to bury her, but my brother saw snipers crawling about both sides of street. . . . We went back and joined crowd that had gathered in center of street . . . Already corner of block was set on fire. A white cloud enveloped a group of buildings. It was an incendiary chemical. There were no detonations. Just suddenly a white cloud. They set fire to other corner. There was fire on next block in corner. It looked as if we would be caught in circle of flame. We couldn't cross street because snipers shot anybody on sight . . . My brother tried to address group, but they were too panicky to listen. We ran across Taft Avenue to grass lot on other side. There the labrador in nipa hut said the whole lot was loaded with gasoline in hands of the Japs . . . My brother said to drop the money and to let the dogs loose. We cut branches to camouflage and to beat out sparks. It was already dark. On return dash to first lot we had to jump through ring of fire . . . House was live coals . . . My brother slipped and fell down. I tried to lift him off and couldn't carry him. I ran to woman in a little lot the size of a garden surrounded by burning buildings . . . There were people hiding . . . I tried to get hold of men to carry brother out of burning building, but he found his way out and crawled to us. There was constant shelling . . . Syrian doctor didn't help . . . Filipino medical student tried to help. My brother died in awful agony at one P.M.'

The gunfire had stopped. We sat there in the crazy intensity of absolute quiet.

The young woman had her voice under control again. 'Perhaps here,' she said, 'I should express to the Americans profound thanks for our liberation.' She made a stiff little bow in my direction and went on.

'We hid in dugouts. Whenever somebody poked his head out of shelter, Japs would machinegun them. Several people injured. Tuesday morning a Filipino came crying with joy, saying he saw tall American soldiers crawling among débris. We took petticoats and baby things to hang on trees for Americans to see and not shoot. Order came to stay in dugouts. Americans said stay in dugout. An advance guard of thirty-one men under Lieutenant Rogge came. All that night Tuesday and Wednesday they were on lookout for snipers. They killed five. They warned us that they would blow up building where Japs were hiding. Japs burned it first. As they retreat they burn. We feared to go into buildings where Americans were. Wednesday morning there was real confusion. We received report that a hundred and fifty people had been massacred on road out. When we started, everything was still infested by snipers. Ten times on way to Singalong Church we had to lie flat on account of snipers. I came out from Paco by Calle Dart. I followed the streetcar line to Santa Ana Church. I came here. As soon as the Americans saw me, they recognized me because I had worked as nurse. I was admitted to camp. These friends here are all I have now. My mother's body was burned. My brother died saying God Bless America.'

She got to her feet and edged away stiffly between the cot and the table toward the end of the hut. Nobody could find anything to say to her.

Thoroughfare

Rizal Avenue, the street that leads in from the great supply road from the valley of Luzon into the city, has become the main stem of liberated Manila. Already groups of men are filling up the fresh shellholes between the trolley tracks. As our troops push the frontier further south in the quarters across the river, under the arcades along Rizal stores open, booths appear. There's a tailorshop with no goods for sale, a bowling alley, a few dark drugstores. Old women set out tables ranged with sticky-looking sweets and a few cigars and cigarettes. Anemic tomatoes and shriveled eggplants are displayed in pyramids. Old tobaccocolored countrymen in peaked hats preside over little bundles of sticks for cooking fires, laid out in neat piles on the edge of the sidewalk. Newspapers are already circulating, dimly legible on mimeographed sheets. In one tall stone doorway an enterprising fellow has drawn a crowd with a game of lotto.

The people don't look any too well fed. By contrast with the Americans in Santo Tomas, they look fat, but there is many a face puckered with hunger in the crowd and many a monkeyfaced child with the swollen belly of starvation. Long lines wait silent and heavyeyed outside the feeding stations Civil Affairs has set up.

In spite of the storm of dust raised by trucks and jeeps, there is a faint carnival air down the long, dingy avenue that hasn't been repaired in three years of Japanese occupation. Women have come out in bright dresses in patterns of orange and pink and green. Aged, dark duennas wobble along wearing the starched gauze sleeves and sober hues of the oldtime Philippine Sunday dress. Everywhere you see men and women who have walked barefoot miles in from the country with sacks of rice on their heads and are arriving drenched and dusty, but with the gleam of trade in their eyes.

Groups of idle men and boys stand at the corner curb watching the trucks pass. Already as if by magic American cars of fairly recent make, hidden away for three years by their owners in stacks of cornstalks or in clumps of trees in the jungle, have appeared on the streets. Every one is shined up and glittering and sports a flutter of American and Philippine flags. The skinny barefoot penniless laborers, waiting hungrily for somebody to find them a job, smile and give each other little looks of triumph as the American cars go past.

Public Relations has settled into the cement basement of a dwelling house on a street off the main stem out beyond the market. Sweating newspapermen ply their portables, crowded elbow to elbow at the long deal tables of the mess. The place is dark and airless and full of flies. Every day more correspondents arrive to cover the Manila story. Outside, a broad flight of steps with a landing under an awning leads up to the porch where most of them sleep in closepacked cots. On the landing there is a settee and some bamboo chairs that are always full of men of all ages and dispositions, redfaced and dripping from the heat. They talk, they drink, they make notes, crowded into each other's laps. They shave and bathe in the tiny yard beside the house. They sit in a shamefaced row on the scantily draped latrine in the adjoining back lot in full view of the civilian crowds moving up and down the avenue.

Meanwhile, half-submerged by the military routine domestic life goes on. Packed into the upper part of the house a welltodo Filipino family carries on its daily round. Meals are prepared and eaten. A young woman practices her scales at the piano. Morning and evening the doors onto the porch open and a brown man, wearing a striped pajama top and tan slacks, walks out leading on a threeway leash three incongruous little dogs of somewhat doubtful ancestry. There's one with English bulldog blood, there's a sort of a King Charles spaniel, and there's a fat and aged black-and-tan. For half an hour the man solemnly walks them up and down the street between the parked jeeps and the generator trucks and then he leads them back up the steps again.

Under the trellis beside the pump on the edge of the street a barber has set himself up and is cutting the correspondents' hair. Around the edges of a tiny trampled shrubbery there lingers a fringe of vendors of rum, of out-of-work local newspapermen looking for jobs and women looking for laundry and small boys looking for handouts of food. Among them is a withered party who might be half Chinese who seizes you by the muscle of the arm and asks you if you don't want the services of a masseur. He has a little black kit full of perfumes and oils and some dogeared testimonials on which the ink has long ago faded. He doesn't work for money, he explains with a snaggletoothed smile, but he will be very glad to work for canned goods. You disentangle yourself from him gently and try to find a cool place to sit.

The basement is full of a continual restless moving about that makes it impossible to collect your thoughts or to carry on a conversation. Every few minutes, when the battery of howitzers on the street in back goes to work, all talk becomes impossible. Through it all the seasoned newspapermen work away oblivious with abstracted faces and fingers busy at the keys of their typewriters.

Roof Garden

When you take advantage of a late afternoon lull in the noise of battle to walk downtown on Rizal, you find that below the street that turns off to Santo Tomas the crowds suddenly begin to thin out. You pass some smashed-up blocks of stores and restaurants and movie theaters and suddenly you begin to feel lonesome. Except for a Filipino family laboriously pushing along a stack of salvaged furniture on a two-wheeled cart, there's nobody in sight. Every way you look the walls of seared buildings stand up around you, warped and brittle as burned paper. Down the long street that used to be Chinatown, you see nothing but gray ruin blurring into a tired haze of smoke.

In the shelter of a wrecked bridge beside the sentinel tank, you can peer across the Pasig River at the postoffice and the smashed government buildings that are still full of Japs. In spite of the fires that have been burning all week, the destruction as yet doesn't seem so complete over there as in this north-side business district.

The sun is setting and the glowing west is reflected in streaks of green and orange on the greasy quiet surface of the river as we climb the nine flights of the calcined stairway that still clings to the blackened wall of the Great Eastern Hotel. At the top in front of the sooty shaft of the elevator a sign still respectfully invites us to visit the roof garden. We step panting into the burnt-out shell of a big hall shot as full of holes as a Swiss cheese. Against one wall the statue, coal-black from the fire, of a thick-hipped girl dancing, still stands on one toe over what once was a fountain.

On the balcony from which diners used to look down onto the dancefloor below a group of young men in greens from the

Thirty-Seventh Division crouch with their spyglasses and their telephones. Craning our necks timidly toward the jagged shellholes in the wall, we look out over their shoulders at the fighting area across the river. To the right we can see the gray masonry of the walled city and the plumcolored tiled roofs and the noble domes and cupolas of the ancient Spanish buildings. The Japs are still there in force. One of the artillery spotters points out an arched gate and tells a tale of a naked girl seen tied to a lamppost in the street beyond. Across a band of open grass we can see the lightcolored crumble of masonry at the foot of the wall where our Long Toms are starting to hammer out a breach. A shell bursts there with a heavy thump and the spreading smoke obscures the wall.

Across the smoking city blocks further to the left, the spotter shows us the two white Florida-style towers of the Manila Hotel standing up against the leaden streak of the bay. A column of smoke has started to curl up lazily from under the tiled roof at the corner. 'There goes our drink at the bar,' one correspondent whispers to the other.

On the south bank of the river right below us is a region of beaten-up factories and warehouses. 'Want to see a Jap?' the spotter asks in a low dry voice. 'Look . . . there's a kind of a gray wall and an open square beyond . . . They start running back and forth there about this time of day. There's one . . . Look. There they go.' I can make out creatures scuttling back and forth like tiny waterbugs along the base of the wall. 'Now . . . watch . . . our machineguns'll reach out after 'em.'

Sure enough, the sharp familiar rattle starts up on the riverbank below us.

It is almost dark. Our shells flash bright as they burst among the modern office buildings beyond the square. Out of one dim white structure corkscrew flames lick out suddenly like the flames in an oldfashioned oleo. Overhead the whirling canopy of smoke is stained with reflected glare. Along both sides of the river now the machineguns keep up their stuttering argument.

'Better keep away from the openings,' whispers the captain in a low considerate tone. 'They might send a burst up this way. It's about this time they swim across the river and try to raise hell back of our lines. We bagged three of them last night in a canoe drifting down to blow up the pontons. The sentry spotted them and knocked off the one that was paddling. We managed to blow the whole business before it hit. Damn lucky because the explosion was so powerful it blew the sentry clean off the bridge . . . No, you can't see the bridge from here. It's around the bend in the river.'

We whispered goodnight and wished him luck and crept breathless down the stairway again.

Garden in the Suburbs

Out in the suburbs the rumble of battle comes to us muffled by the heavy night. In the garden outside the house where we found a downstairs room where we could pitch our cots and spread our mosquito nettings, a candle set in a beercan on a small table lights up a circle of intent smooth coppery faces and the edges of the stiff banana leaves overhead. Beyond the hedges on either side are other little groups of townspeople lounging in wicker chairs round flickering lights. A cheerful chatter of Tagálog comes from them. There's a sweet smell of lush foliage and nightblooming vines in the air, soured now and then by streaks of the stench of broken sewers. The hedges are full of bright flashing fireflies.

'It was back to the paddyfields for the Philippines,' Rafael is saying. His voice is low and rasping. His narrowed eyes are hard and dull like a snake's. 'For that I never forgive the Jap.' He taps himself on the chest with a narrow brown hand.

In the Philippines, he explains to us Americans, a fresh-washed white suit is a sign of respectability. The Japs would catch a farmer going into town in his Sunday best and tear off his white suit. Back to the paddyfields, they'd tell him, a Filipino ought to be in workclothes. Then there was the slapping. When Jap officers and noncoms slapped their men's faces or boxed their ears, the soldiers bowed meekly and took it, but the Filipinos were different.

'We are very sensitive to slapping,' says Rafael with a bitter little laugh.

The Long Toms shooting into the walled city from a battery somewhere behind us box our ears and shake the house with the blast from their muzzles. When the quiet has settled down again, Rafael goes on to explain that the young Filipinos, except a few who made money selling out their own people to the invaders, found themselves trapped under the Japanese. They had studied in American schools or served in the Army or the Constabulary. They had studied law and medicine with the Americans. Careers were opening for them. None of that under the Japs. Back to the paddyfields. His English is drowned out in a rattle of Tagálog from his friends.

'Thees house was guerrilla headquarters. Yes, yes, under the Jap,' a frogfaced man says, leaning forward excitedly in his chair.

'I,' says Rafael, with his bitter thinlipped smile, 'I join the guerrillas as an Intelligence man in Baguio. Always I go there with women, always different women. They think I am a good-for-nothing boy. I make love to a Japanese woman: she is the assistant hotel manager. I am her lover, she loves me very much. Only the assistant manager can go to clean Jap commander's room. I say she must take me in his room to make love, only there we cannot be seen. I read the maps, I see all their plans and go away to give intelligence. The Jap very stupid, we Filipinos are too quick for him.'

There's a ping of a rifle somewhere in the alleys back of the house. Then another. Rafael blows out the candle. Nobody moves. 'Settling scores,' he says after a tense listening pause. His voice lingers over the words. 'In the Philippines we have many scores to settle . . . Private war.' His dry laugh creaks. 'I like the private war . . . During the occupation we kill a Jap in this house. We bury him alive in the garden.' His friends interrupt with a shrill barrage of Tagálog. The guns drown everything in another punishing salvo.

The night is quiet again. Rafael has struck a match. The ruddy light glints in the narrowed eyes, on the small bared teeth, the taut round faces in a ring round the candle. The candle flame trembles primrose color in the still air. From several of the houses in the block comes the sound of pianos tinkling oldfashioned tunes. For some reason the flashing fireflies have all gathered in one tall tree that stands out like a Christmas tree full of sparkle against the starry sky.

'Three years they kill us,' says Rafael in a low hissing tone. 'Now we begin to kill.'

A single big gun punches a last hole in the drowsy quiet of the night.

4

Conversations in Santo Tomas

Recapitulation

KIDS, looking more American than you can imagine, were playing among the parked cars outside of the tall dark doorway of Santo Tomas. The morning was still fresh. There was the sound of gunfire, but it came from far away across the river. No mortar shells were coming in. Everybody had a smiling look. A soldier, who had just taken some of the kids for a drive around the compound in his weapons carrier, waited with his hand on the gearshift for a new batch to crowd aboard. A little girl with pigtails came up to me and told me her name was Judy. She was from Cleveland. No, she'd never been to Cleveland, but she was going to go there now. Her mother had made her a red, white, and blue dress for the steamer trip. She pulled me over by the hand to where two other little girls were playing with her small sister. They were sitting on the steps playing black market with a pile of Mickey Mouse. While I was talking to them I saw a tall chalkyfaced skin and bones civilian who stood in the shade at the corner of the banana grove suddenly raise his hand to wave at a truck grinding in from the outside gate.

The truck slowed down and a dusty young man in greens jumped down and walked slowly toward the civilian with a puzzled look on his face. The puzzled look changed to recognition. They ran toward each other with their arms stretched out. 'That's his daddy,' said Judy seriously.

Two tiny American boys who couldn't be more than five years old were very busy about something on the ground beside the OWI's dusty Chevrolet. A small pile of rice had run out of a torn gunnysack in the back of the car and onto the running-board. With pursed lips and anxious eyes the two little boys were scraping the rice grain by grain onto a handkerchief. Inside, the dark vestibule was comparatively free of people. A man stood in the middle of the marble floor blinking his eyes to make out the wan faces about him after the dazzling sunlight. In his hand he held an immense bunch of small green and purple orchids. I recognized him as one of the war correspondents. His wife had been interned here. He hadn't seen her for three years. He must be bringing her the flowers. He had the happiest half-crying, half-laughing look I ever saw on a man's face.

In front of the scales in the corner of the vestibule there was quite a queue of people waiting to weigh their children. Women sat in a group sewing children's dresses out of cotton materials at sewing machines. The machines made a hurried merry clicking hum. People were exchanging addresses. In a recess two hollowfaced women were copying out each other's kitchen receipts into their notebooks. Upstairs men sprawled relaxed on their cots reading last fall's American magazines. Everybody had begun to pack up. The place had a little of the air of a college dormitory after the final exams.

In the Administration Building lines of men and women filed slowly past the desks asking questions about friends and relatives in other camps, asking when they could go to their houses or their places of business or their bodegas in Manila, asking when the Government would send them home. I stood behind the desk of Earl Carroll, a member of the executive committee, until there was a gap in his particular line and he could tear himself loose. He led the way into a small inside room.

'It's been like this for three years,' he said, with a tired grin. 'I was in the insurance business. My home's in Honolulu. I came out here in connection with the consolidation of two insurance companies and arrived three days before the war started. When the Japs took the city, I was appointed leader of the American committee for South Malate. That was the first section interned. So I was put in charge and told to organize and operate the camp. I didn't pull off my shoes for three days.'

He paused and drew a deep breath. He was a youngish man with a round face you could find in almost any business office in the States. His voice was crisp and businesslike. He didn't have the starved look many of the people had, but he looked worn and tired. As he sat there looking straight ahead of him trying to remember how it had been at first, the lines from his wide nostrils to the ends of his mouth deepened and hardened.

He straightened his shoulders and went on. People were told to come with food and clothing for three days, he explained. The Filipino employees had been great. Right away they started handing food through the iron palings at the gate. They'd write out a placard with the name of the person they wanted to see. The Jap guards tried to scatter them with the flats of their swords, but they kept coming back. Finally the Japs allowed the crowd to be organized

into a regular package line which they supervised. That
package line lasted two years.

'The Japs expected and intended to starve the internees,' he
said flatly, glancing in my face with a set look on his jaw.
'They systematically looted Red Cross stores of canned milk.
Then they had the nerve to donate a hundred cases of milk to
the interned children and to make a great hullabaloo in the
Manila papers about how generous they were. The committee decided early in the game that the children would have to
be taken care of first. The kids had their lives before them.
This war was no responsibility of theirs.'

He yawned. His face crumpled with fatigue. 'During the
early days we managed to get the Japs to recognize the Red
Cross as the agency to handle supplies,' he went on in even
tones as if he were discussing a business deal back home.
'They respected our camp organization. Couldn't imagine
how we had worked it out so fast. A constant stream of Jap
gold braid came to the office to see how we did it. One day
three or four goldbraiders waited twenty minutes in the outer
office to compliment us on our organization. But they soon
began to realize that they were boss and we were the enemy.'

'How did you finance the camp?'

He smiled. 'The Japs never got over it. They handicapped
all our efforts to get funds. The Japanese military agreed to
appropriate seventy centavos a day per person and to turn it
over to us. We were able to buy cheaper from the Chinese
merchants than they could. The Chinese jumped their prices
for the Japs. As the inflation increased, the Japs upped their
appropriation to one peso fifty and still it wasn't enough. If
the camp had been confined to their appropriation we'd have
all starved to death. The various big American companies
sent in drafts. People borrowed money on personal notes at

fantastic rates. We had to take all sorts of risks to smuggle drafts out and to smuggle cash in. There was a little cripple whom the Japs allowed to stay on in his own home for a while who smuggled notes out in his braces. You'll have to talk to him.'

'I've met him,' I said, 'isn't that Dave Sternberg?'

'Yes,' he said, and hurried on breathless with his story. 'The Red Cross was sending in twenty-five thousand dollars a month through Switzerland, but the Japs used that to build themselves up a dollar balance. We never knew what the rate of exchange was and we had to spend the currency they did turn over to us through a Jap buyer who grafted. He grafted all right. We quit buying eggs at twenty-five pesos apiece . . . The real pinch came last September. Our small reserves were depleted. The Japs cut off all communication with the outside world. We'd have been through then if it hadn't been for Luis de Alcuaz.'

'Who is he?'

'He's a young Spanish Filipino who represented the university. He was able to smuggle in seven thousand tins of meat and a ton of beans, and a hundred thousand pesos in money through a hole in the wall. He took a great risk. You better go talk to him . . . I've got to go back to my desk.'

The Secretary

I found Luis de Alcuaz in an office with whitewashed walls and dark furniture. The tall narrow room had the monastic Spanish look like the background of a painting by Zurbaran. He was a small oliveskinned young man with clear features and coffee-brown eyes. He showed very white regular teeth when he smiled.

'This is the study of the Provincial,' he explained. 'It was through my position as secretary to the university, I was able to help the interned Americans. I offered it to God,' he said with abrupt intensity. 'If I get killed, I said to myself, I am doing something I think right . . . Now I can talk about it. I passed terrible days.' His smile broke out again in the half-light of the room. 'You see, I graduated at Santo Tomas University and stayed on to take the chair of Chemistry . . . the youngest Professor of Chemistry they ever had. The university belongs to the Dominican Order. When the Japanese came, the Dominican padres were anxious not to have their university used for an internment camp, but the Americans wanted it because it was much the best place. The American committee had picked it out before the city fell. On January 2, 1942, I was already working to get the Americans interned in Santo Tomas. That day I remember going to the Jai Alai to see the Commander in charge, a big fat Jap in a geestring. He said all right he'd send the Americans into Santo Tomas. Mr. Carroll went to work to convert the university into a big hotel.' Young Alcuaz's voice dropped and his words came slowly. 'The sixteenth of that January I remember was the first time I was beaten and slapped around by a Jap. It has happened so many times since. This Jap sergeant wanted a room for some women in the university and one of the padres was expostulating with him. The sergeant started pushing the padre and I interfered. Then he slapped and beat me.'

The office was very quiet hidden away in the great stone pile of buildings. From the distance came the hollow thump of big guns battering down the old Spanish city. He started talking again.

'I passed terrible days. There were many difficulties. The Spanish consul was my continual enemy because I was helping the Americans . . . Gradually I came to be on bad terms with the padres and ceased eating and living in the seminary. I had to give up my teaching . . . Well, at Christmas, 1943, the package line was stopped. Some way had to be found of taking drafts out to the Chinese and bringing money back. I can well remember the first time I smuggled drafts out. I put them in the Father Provincial's briefcase and the money came back in the rear of the Japanese commander's car.'

He burst out laughing. Quickly his face froze into an expression of strain.

'I passed terrible days,' he said for the third time. 'I was cut off from all contact with the Americans, except *sub rosa*. Only through my fiancée was I able to communicate. She was a young lady who worked for the American committee. It became necessary to smuggle in food. My office was in a temporary building against the wall of the gymnasium. At one place I made a hole in the suwali . . . that's matting . . . that covered the iron-grilled window and I was able to pass things through the grille, but the bags had to be long and very narrow. I had special bags made very long and narrow. I told people I needed them for a chemical experiment. With these I was able to pass in forty to sixty kilos of beans a day. I had to fill them by hand in my office. I passed food in every evening from seven to eight-thirty. I poured rum over my clothes so that if the Jap sergeant who was always checking on me came in, he'd think I was drunk . . . I tell you I prayed to the Virgin of Lourdes . . . After Christmas . . . last Christmas, forty-four . . . the Japanese were frantic. I never slept at home. I carried a passport of a friend who was killed in the American bombings when I was away from my office because I had to go to arrange purchases.

'Some of the Swiss were very helpful. I was smuggling in a

radio receiving set piece by piece. Once I borrowed a wooden leg to bring in food. Only last Saturday, the day the Americans came, a Jap lieutenant questioned me. He slapped me, but it was for the last time . . . Saturday I was out after food. I tore my wrist ducking machinegun fire at the corner of Estarraga Street. I went to the office and locked everything up to keep the Japs from getting it. I was so nervous I passed out in my office. My heart became weak. Sunday morning I walked out and now it is over.'

A pleasant-faced young woman with prominent eyes and ebony black hair had come into the office by a back door. We got to our feet. Alcuaz's smile lit up his whole face.

'This,' he said, 'is my fiancée . . . We talked through the grille to fool the Japanese and now we are going to be married. There is nothing more to tell except that I have resigned as secretary of the university and the Provincial has accepted my resignation.'

Relaxation

On the roof people are strolling about looking out at the steaming city with the air of passengers on a ship that has come into port after a long and stormy voyage. A few men are stretched out in deckchairs toasting their skinny bodies in the morning sun. Two mildmannered Dutchmen are pointing out landmarks through the shimmering haze of smoke. A tall holloweyed hollowchested man edges up to me as I stand leaning on the parapet listening to them.

'I suppose you think you are getting the truth,' he says suddenly and gruffly, pushing his mouth close to my ear. 'They haven't told you of the lust for power of the man who dominated the internees because he thought he was a big shot,

and the only one who understood Jap psychology. They
haven't told you about the summary jail sentences meted out
by the court he set up where the accused was neither represented nor heard. They haven't told you about the curious
morals regulations by which people were not allowed to sleep
with their wives. They haven't told you about the people
who made money out of the internees right here in camp. No,
no, they haven't told you about that. They won't either.
You won't find out the truth. You needn't think you will.'
He turns his back and strides away with his head sunk between his shoulders.

Beside me is an elderly skeleton with drooping white mustache and very clear bright blue eyes. He's looking out, smiling vaguely, into the scorched empty shells of business buildings between us and the river.

'We know our boys are doing the best they can to clear the
Japs out of the city,' he says, in a gentle deprecating tone.
'But we can't help wishing they'd hurry. Some of us have
plans. Some of us want to get our businesses started up again.
Some of us haven't much time to lose.'

Life under the Japanese

Down in a hut among the rows of nipa huts in the compound where in each small livingroom men sat in wicker
chairs smoking their pipes with a proprietory air, or women
were busy with housework, or children were playing, I sat
talking with Dave Sternberg, trying to get him to tell me
about smuggling out the drafts. He was a cripple, a tiny
little creature with dark doe eyes and a gentle thoughtful face.
He sat in a wheelchair at the head of the board table drinking
coffee, while his darkhaired sister, who looked very much

like him around the eyes, hung wearily over the coffeepot on the stove. Several people sat on the cots with coffeecups on the table in front of them. The Sternbergs' ménage in the crowded thatched hut was evidently the center of quite a circle of friends.

He had worked on radio production, he said, before the Japanese came to Manila. Various members of his family had businesses in the city.

'The Japs let me stay out on a conditional pass because they didn't think I could do them any harm,' he said with a rueful smile. 'So there I was all alone in our big house in the barrio. That's the Barrio Basilan about ten miles out. Well, I had all these Filipino boys out there who had been employed in our business, so to give them some way of making a living I set them up in the caratella business. The caratellas are these little covered pony carts. They are the oldfashioned taxis of Manila. They go all over town picking people up at so much a ride. Well, I was in touch with a receiving set and with some guerrilla outfits and I used my cocheros for counter-propaganda. The cochero in a caratella is quite a talker usually, so my boys, when they had people in the carts who looked like they wouldn't turn them in, would give the American version of the news instead of the Japanese version. I would get the news in the night and tell it to my boys and to some garrulous people and it would spread in an unending circle, but nobody ever knew where the center was. We even distributed leaflets in English and Tagálog, but gradually the Japanese informers closed in on us until there was nobody left but me and one cochero. I sent news into Santo Tomas, too, when I sent in packages of food for my family. Mostly I'd slip a bulletin into a cigarette package. But finally in May '43. the Japanese picked me up and brought me into Santo

Tomas, and here I am,' he said.   He showed all his teeth in a broad grin.

While he was talking, a pair of grayhaired Americans had come into the hut and we had made room for them to sit down.

'They left us out longer than they did you,' Mrs. Walker took up the story in a sprightly tone.   'My husband had chronic rheumatism and we made out it was awful bad,' she said.   Her husband nodded glumly.

'We had a little plant for extracting the honey from coconuts and for a while they didn't bother us, because we were over sixty.   They sure gave us some scares, though.   We put up guerrillas in our house and for a while we took care of Yay Panlillo's little children . . . But the worst of it was when the man came and asked us to hide a machinegun.   Radio parts are so little you can tuck them away anywhere, but a machinegun's a different matter.   We shoved it under a culvert . . . I always say we owe our lives to the chickens,' she laughed quite merrily.   'I had a brood of Rhode Island Reds, and when the Japs came I was trying to give them sulfathiazol for croup with a medicine dropper.   I ran out with a chicken under my arm and the Japs got interested in our dosing the chickens.   I asked the Jap officer to hold the chicken so I could dose her. He held the chicken while I opened her mouth and Mr. Walker put the drops in with a medicine dropper.   It made things kind of human.   Even a Jap'll get human over a chicken.'

We all got to laughing.   Other people told other stories.   I never could get Dave Sternberg to tell about smuggling out the notes.

Liberation

Harry Evans had asked me to lunch. I found him setting out china plates on embroidered doilies on a cardtable. The thinfaced darkhaired man who lived with him had gone off to the kitchen to stand in line for the food. Harry Evans saw me looking at the daintily set table.

'When this happened,' he explained, 'I decided I'd take it easy and sit back and enjoy it as an extraordinary experience. I found that trying to live as pleasantly as possible made things a great deal more bearable. Even having some nice china and cutlery to wash helped. Building this nipa hut was an important experience. I had come out as an adviser to the Philippine Government in tax matters. Suddenly I found myself in one of those rare situations where a man is measured by his worth and by that alone. I did a great deal of very valuable reading. We had the good luck to be imprisoned in one of the best libraries in the East.'

His roommate had come back with a tin dinnerpail full of cooked-up army rations from the kitchen. They brought out a few odds and ends of condiments and we settled down to a leisurely lunch.

'We all had observation holes in our huts,' said Harry Evans slowly, setting down his knife and fork and twisting his chair around. 'From where I sit now I can take a bead on the road in from the main gate. It was so that we could take cover when the Japs came around. Whoever saw one called Tallyho. You would call ten centavos for a soldier and a peso for an officer. There was a rollcall at five-thirty every day. Curfew was at six-thirty. We were allowed to sit out a little between rollcall and curfew. At six-forty-five orders for the next day were broadcast over the public address system. That night the first intimation we had was that I caught sight through my peephole of the military officer Abako all dressed up in a white shirt and shined-up boots. That gave me the notion something must be going on. Then at six-forty-five came the announcement that American troops were in the city and that internees should go to the main building. I thought I'd better stay where I was and await developments . . . The first thing I heard — there had been distant firing all afternoon — was the sound of a smoothrunning motor. I said to myself no Jap motor would run as smooth as that. It must be an American motor. Then there was definitely the sound of a tank turning round and through my observation hole I could see the tank's searchlight shining on the buildings. I had an idea that the Japs would defend the place from the inside, so I lay low until the tank drew up abreast of the hut. I could see lights shining through the suwali. Then I stepped out and found Carl Mydans taking pictures . . . And that was all so few days ago.' Harry Evans's voice dropped to a whisper and he stopped talking.

It was pleasant to sit eating in silence at the nicely set table in the cool shade of the neatly kept hut. The sound of gunfire from the other side of town, and the drone of formations of planes going in to dive-bomb seemed as regular and customary as the roar of city traffic. There was still a slight smell of burning in the air.

'Well,' said the thinfaced man, 'that operation's over. The Japs didn't accomplish much . . . a little looting, a few natives shot, and villages burned. They printed a lot of money, but they weren't capable of accomplishing much.' He leaned back slowly in his chair and yawned and stretched his arms out behind him in an easy gesture of relaxation.

5

The Oldtime Americans

Resistance

WE ARE SITTING ON A COT in one of the grim, highceilinged, gray dormitories in the main building at Santo Tomas.

'Guerrillas — I know a little about guerrillas,' the man in the next cot says with a thin smile. He is a slender gray man with the shriveled caved-in look so many of the prisoners still have, even after two weeks of normal feeding. He starts talking in a low, quiet, expressionless voice. Sometimes he pauses to think up the right word.

His name is Charles J. Cushing. He's from Los Angeles. He came out to the Philippines in 1933, and married a Manila girl and had two children. When war broke out he was working at a gold mine in southern Luzon. As the Japs were landing in Legaspi, he herded a party of American families through the mountains to Lucena de Tayabas. The Japs were bombing the railroads, so the Army sent trucks to haul them to Lopez where they could take the train into Manila. They had the usual experiences of hiding in ditches while the Japs strafed and bombed, but they got to Manila.

He reported right away to USAFFE Headquarters. They

set him to blowing oil supplies and dumps of explosives. During that time he enlisted in the 302d Engineer Regiment. They were sent to Bataan, where they got busy hauling sand and gravel and building dummy airfields and dummy guns to fool the Nips, and loading the bridges to blow up when the time came to retreat. The Japs were bombing day and night. At the end of January he was picked out along with a lumberman named McGuire, since they both spoke the dialects, to lead a party across the Jap lines. There were ten Americans and ten Filipinos. They were given commissions. He was sworn in as a second lieutenant. Their mission was to scatter in the hills and to stir up what guerrilla activity they could against the Japanese. Frankly the chances of getting by looked pretty slim.

Cushing had been staring down between his knees as he talked. He looked up. 'My wife was in Manila. Maybe that's why I was willing to take a chance,' he said.

They set out at night. They had to crawl by ones and twos past the sentry posts. What saved them was that these particular Jap troops weren't used to jungle fighting and made a lot of noise crashing through the dry bamboo as they walked their posts. The Americans could always tell where they were and wait for them to pass. It was a slow business. They had only rice and water to eat, and the hearts they cut out of the swamp palm.

When they got to the Olongapo road, they camped two kilometers the other side of it and hung around to see what the Japs were up to. They used to watch the trucks go by loaded with foodstuffs, and decided to hold one of them up. The trouble was that the truck they held up was loaded with troops instead of food, and that wasn't so good. The Nips all piled out at the bend in the road and there was quite a battle for three quarters of an hour. Cushing finally managed to fix up some sticks of dynamite with a fuse. They tossed them into the truck from the steep hillside above. The Japs all looked up. They thought it was a bomb from an airplane. That gave the Americans a chance to get away.

Naturally, the Japs killed all the people they caught and burned every house along the road in reprisal. Meanwhile the Americans escaped up into the Zambales Range that runs north along the west coast of Luzon. There they ran into a Negrito named Caballero. The Negritos, Cushing explained, were a pigmy black people you still found in odd corners of the Philippines. They shot with bows and arrows, and lived in the jungles and forests, and were very keensighted at night. There was a King Tom of the Negritos back up in there who liked Americans because they used to send him 'a little rice sometimes from Fort Stotzenberg. This little fellow Caballero knew all the trails, and led them up to Camp Sanchez on Penatuba Mountain. On the road they picked up an Igorot named Sergeant Smith. The Igorots and the Negritos got on all right.

'In fact,' said Cushing, 'I found all the pagan aborigines thoroughly reliable.' His voice became deeper and firmer as he got into his story. 'They are not all pagans by a long shot,' he said, laughing; 'a lot of them have American names because a colored American evangelist, named Bishop Brown, traveled back and forth in the mountains for years, baptizing them and giving them American names. He died a few years before the war. Sergeant Smith was one of Bishop Brown's boys . . . Well, through this Sergeant Smith we managed to get a message back to Headquarters on Bataan, so that an officer was sent across the bay in a mosquito boat to us with a walkie-talkie set. We made big plans, assigned areas, laid out

work, but the fall of Singapore and of Bataan took the heart
out of us. Jap raids began to be troublesome. We were kept
up for a while by the story of the six-hundred-mile convoy
that never came . . .'

Meanwhile Charles Cushing's wife and children were being
held as hostages by the Jap military police in Manila. He had
made his way by trail through the densely forested hills up
into the mountain province. He had heard that his kid brother Walter, who had been raising guerrillas up north, was
dead. Everything seemed to be falling to pieces. He had a
right good band of guerrillas armed with rifles, but he spent
most of his time trying to keep the Igorots from slaughtering
the lowland Christians who had come up into the mountains
as settlers. The Igorots suspected any Filipino of being a
Japanese informer. The Japs kept dropping leaflets telling
him that if he surrendered he would be given amnesty; if he
didn't they would behead his wife and both children. They
made his wife write him from Dagupan. Finally they broke
him down, and on March 7, 1943, he surrendered at a place
called Taiug.

While Cushing was talking, his wife had walked in and
stood listening at the foot of the cot. She was a cool, oval-
faced girl with a somewhat Spanish look about her face.
'Dear,' he said, when he'd introduced her to us, 'suppose you
go ride herd on the children. They are running wild today.'

When she had gone he started to speak again in a gruff
whisper. He paused to swallow, then he continued in an expressionless tone, talking low, with his eyes fixed on the floor.

'In the company of the presidente of Natividad, I walked
into Taiug and handed my pistol to Colonel Mori. The garri-
son presented arms, the officer saluted, and I bowed in the
Japanese style. Then they had me.'

They made him write letters to other guerrillas telling them to surrender. They made him make a speech at the Taiug fiesta telling the Filipinos about the co-prosperity sphere. They took him to Dagupan and beat hell out of him to get him to tell the strength and position of his troops. They already knew all about it. There were plenty of Filipinos playing both sides, who told them. They beat him for days and knocked out some of his teeth. They strapped him down and gave him the water cure . . . that was the worst. They tie you down and pour water down your throat until every cavity is distended and then they jump on your stomach. The Filipino boy who cleaned up the mess told him afterwards that the water spurted up fifteen feet. What was left of him they shut up in the execution chamber in Bilibid Prison. There he got a little quinine for his malaria from a United States Army doctor.

His kidneys were injured so that he couldn't hold his water. He was just about dead. He was helpless in the hands of the Japs. They took him down to Cebu by plane, and made him write a letter to his third brother, Jimmy, who had been raising guerrillas in the Visayan Islands, begging him to surrender. He fooled them by writing 'Dear James,' instead of 'Dear Jimmy.' He'd never called him James in his life. Jimmy held out to this day and had just turned up in Tacloban. They took Charles Cushing back to the old Spanish dungeons of Fort Santiago down in the old town in Manila. 'They kept me in with a lot of Filipinos that they beat up every morning,' he said; 'you get used to that stuff after a while.'

Then they sent him out to work as a servant for some Jap Intelligence officers living in Mr. Hill's house in the American residential district of Manila. The Japs were Intelligence officers, but they wore civilian clothes. They let him have his wife and children along. His wife acted as housekeeper and did the cooking. He did the gardening and helped around the kitchen. The Japs made them assume Spanish names, and his wife had to wear dark glasses when she went out to do the marketing. They were never allowed to speak to any white people. Once a month he was sent out under guard to get a haircut.

'Then last summer they put us all back in Santo Tomas, and here we are. Of all the men that went out with me, I don't know of any other that is alive today.'

His wife had come back leading a sallowfaced little boy by the hand. She sat down quietly on the end of the cot. The little boy stood beside her, looking with dark inquiring eyes from one face to the other. 'This is Charley,' said Cushing. He put his gray hand on the little boy's shoulder.

'Girl all right?' he asked. His wife nodded. 'Well, here we are,' he said again. They looked at each other and exchanged a tired private smile.

'At first I wasn't so worried about them,' he said, in an explaining tone, 'because I had taken out considerable insurance and I figured they would get that if I was killed. But after the summer of '43, the Japs started burning the houses of people who had even a distant cousin in the guerrillas. . . . They lived off the country like locusts, slaughtering carabao, extorting rice, maybe they'd pay ten centavos for a chicken. When the people ran off to the hills, they burned and looted their houses. Most of the pro-Japs were educated boys who thought they could gain something for themselves. They sent out a lot of Tagálog gangsters from Manila to play the informer. If they took off their hat to somebody in the marketplace, that would be putting the finger on him, or sometimes they'd just stand behind a man. The Igorots got so suspicious they'd behead any stranger they saw. I guess they kinda wanted an excuse to get a few heads anyway.'

He paused and looked thoughtfully down at his little son's round brown head.

'At first we were getting away with it all right. Here and there we'd give a kind of a big brother talk. But we didn't have anything to back up our propaganda with. The morale of the Filipinos held up as long as they had Americans with them. They'd give us anything they had. They'd even kill their fighting cocks for us to eat. You know how much a Filipino thinks of his fighting cock. I remember all the people standing around in one village started crying when they saw that the rice we had was moldy. Somebody would always turn up to carry our packs. When my boys didn't have any shirts to wear, all I had to do was go into a barrio without any shirt on. People would give me their best. The same thing with shoes. . . . There were even racketeers going around collecting money, pretending it was for Americans. The trouble with us was we didn't have anything to back our propaganda up with. And after that notice the Japs published in '43, anybody who stayed out in Luzon was as good as dead . . . Well they didn't get Jimmy. You better go down to Leyte and talk to Jimmy.'

College Boy

Down in the wellswept offices set out in the broad wooden headquarters buildings among the steaming palm groves at Tolosa on Leyte, a few days later, I asked about Jimmy Cushing.

'He's a Colonel Cushing now,' the young officers told me. 'He's a wonderful fellow. He stayed on in Cebu right along in spite of the fact that there isn't much cover on the island. Part of the time he had to travel around disguised as a Spanish priest with a long black beard and colored glasses. They've killed more Japs over there than on any other island. Planes fly over there twice a week. There's a hut at the airfield where the Ladies' Aid serves you coffee and doughnuts when the plane comes in. He was over here a couple of days ago. Would you like to go over and call on him? We might be able to fix it up.'

While we were talking, a straightbacked young man in new suntans walked into the office. This was Captain Lorenzo Teves who had just hopped over from the island of Negros. He had neatly parted black hair and very white teeth he kept showing as he smilingly explained that this was the first time he'd met Americans since the war began.

Captain Teves had been in the Reserve Officers' Training Corps of Silliman University, the missionary college the Presbyterian Board of Foreign Missions has run for years over on Negros. He was in college preparing to study law when the USAFFE surrenders came in May, 1942. He explained that he didn't think the majority of the troops had wanted to surrender. The American commanding officer had threatened all officers and men who disobeyed the surrender order with courtmartial, loss of pay and allowances. He'd said they would be treated as bandits. About eighty-five per cent of the officers surrendered to the Japanese and only about forty per cent of the troops. Right away, the Japs, under Colonel Ota, began a reign of terror, slapping people right and left and confiscating American and Philippine currency. Small units began to band together to fight them. Colonel Abcede had been commandant of the training corps at Silliman. He was the only battalion commander who refused to surrender and who didn't order his officers and men to surrender. On August 3 he struck at Buenavista. His men ambushed seventeen Japs on a truck.

'We heard about it,' said Captain Teves with a quiet smile, 'in the concentration camp. We cadets were concentrated in the elementary school at Bacolod. Right away nine of us decided to escape. It was the night of September 10. It was raining hard and the rivers were flooded. An enlisted man watched the sentry while we went to the toilet. When the sentry went away, we jumped the barbed wire and ran for our lives through the banana groves. Some ran north and some ran south. It was difficult at first because the guerrillas didn't trust us. We were in double danger. We had to prove to the guerrillas that we were sincere. They were mostly led by sergeants. They recognized no officers. Some of the bands were looting . . . We had to teach them to protect the people instead . . . I had felt a moral obligation to escape and lead men.'

He was sitting bolt upright on the edge of his chair, talking in a low voice. He pronounced his English correctly and precisely. 'After we had run off, the Japanese threw a cordon of troops around the town. They didn't catch any of us.' He gave a low abrupt laugh. 'Some of us were arrested by the guerrillas. We had to prove ourselves. We have all vindicated ourselves and received responsible positions. Since then our life has been in the mountains. Sometimes for as long as two months we would eat only once a day a little parched corn. Once I nearly died from the colic, but was saved by my last ampoule of morphine. One platoon with thirty rifles held three hundred Japanese off for three days, but always eventually we had to run. No ammunition. How happy we were when in June of '43 the first shipment of supplies came in by submarine from General MacArthur. Meanwhile the Japs were attempting to conciliate the people. There were no reprisals against the families of those in the mountains. They distributed matches, soap, and clothing. It had an effect on the poor people who had no way of living in the mountains. They went back to their fields, but still they helped us. We determined to stay in the mountains forever if need be. Many officers married and had children for immortality's sake. My boy was born in a hut at three thousand feet.'

He sat straight on the edge of his chair looking thoughtfully out the window at the gray curving boles of the coconut palms. Around us typewriters chirruped. From the highway, cut through the immense plantation of palms, came the grind of trucks and jeeps and weapons-carriers. 'Our most important work,' he said after a pause, 'was Intelligence. We sent out coast watchers and organized radio stations. It was our coast watchers who reported the Japanese fleet and made possible the American victory in the first battle of the Philippine Sea. The fleet was reported ten times. Admiral Nimitz sent us his commendation. All over the island we had watchers who sent signals with the tultugan. The tultugan is the bamboo drum. It can be heard two miles. Then another tultugan takes it up. The Japanese killed many of them, but always new men volunteered. . . . Now we are impatiently awaiting the arrival of American troops so that we can finish up the Japanese. In their turn they are digging themselves in up in the mountains. But we know the mountains better. Already we are arresting collaborators and sending them to detention compounds.'

'What happened to Silliman University?' I asked him.

His eyes snapped. 'The Japanese hate Silliman more than anything. A large proportion of our officers come from Silliman cadets. Most of the American teachers were evacuated. They were respected and trusted by the people. The Japanese burned the president's house and used Hibbard Hall for a stable and burned all the books in the library. It was the finest library south of Manila. The Japanese tried to start schools, but very few people went.' He wrinkled up his nose and made a little gesture of disgust with one hand.

'Now we stand our ground, but before when the Japanese came we had to run for it. One night I remember so well the Japanese surprised our bivouac area. I had to jump for it in the middle of the night. I had fifty thousand pesos for Intelligence work. The outposts all started firing at once. I jumped out of the window. The man who had the money was so terrified he couldn't move. We ran up the hill. By sheer luck we missed another column that was coming down the road. We were swimming in the cogon grass all night. It's very tall, you know. It was a bright moonlight night. But the spirit is very good. When the bombings came in September, people ran up in the hills to get the best view shouting and jumping with joy. Their homes were wrecked, but they didn't care. Now people think we are heroes. People who come up from the lowlands have an inferiority complex.' He laughed. 'The girls don't want to dance with them.

'We have even a song of the guerrillas. It was composed by Sergeant Cristobal Hofileña at our general headquarters in the mountains, composed and sung to a guitar. I will tell you the words:

> 'From up the mountains
> We view the lowlands . . .'

He started to hum the tune. He was sitting there singing softly in the crowded busy office, then he caught himself, gave an apologetic look around and recited the words of the final verses slowly and clearly so that I could put them down.

> If the hills could tell a story
> They would speak of our privation,
> How we struggled with starvation
>   On the lonely mountainside;
> How with scanty arms and weapons
> We defied the haughty Nippons,
> How we groaned with cold and sickness,
>   Everything to us denied.
>
> Yet we laugh at all these hardships,
> We can sing away our trouble;
> For we'll carry on the struggle
>   Though we perish in the strife
> For we are decided and united
>   To fight for freedom and our way of life.

When he had finished he gave me a quick smile. 'It is time for me to go,' he said. He got to his feet, shook hands silently, and walked out.

Intelligence

Two young officers who had been working at their desks with the air of graduate students cramming for a Ph.D. came over to the table where I was sitting. The lighthaired officer had an envelope with some snapshots of lateensailed bancas and outrigger schooners and of a small white powerboat.

'These were the guerrilla navy,' he said, grinning broadly. 'The flagship was the *Athena*. They made a cannon for it out of a piece of iron pipe. It would fire one shot and then it had to be rebuilt. She had to be burned to keep her from falling into the hands of the enemy, but she shot down a Betty one day. . . .' He went on talking while I looked through the photographs. 'This has been a strange life for us. Ever since that first weak signal from Panay was heard by an amateur in the States and relayed to the War Department and from the War Department back to General Headquarters in Australia, we have been up to our necks in this eighteen hours a day. . . .'

'But all we ever do is polish our pants on office chairs,' the darkhaired officer interrupted.

'We sweated at our desks in Brisbane and we sweat at our desks in Leyte and soon we'll be sweating at our desks in Manila.'

'We are the chairborne infantry,' said the darkhaired officer with a bitter laugh.

'A submarine lands someplace,' said the lighthaired officer. 'The guerrillas come out with a brass band to take the ammo and guns ashore. A político makes a speech. The submarine's cooks serve coffee and doughnuts to all hands. She sails away to the tune of the "Star-Spangled Banner." We put it all down. We classify it and tabulate it, but do we get to see it? Never.'

'Somebody's got to do the paperwork,' growled the darkhaired officer.

'I'm going to try to get a day off to go over with you to call on Jimmy Cushing in Cebu tomorrow, but dollars to doughnuts I shan't get to go,' said the lighthaired officer cheerfully.

Farm Eight

When I met Major Telesco for breakfast long before day next morning, the lighthaired officer wasn't there, so it was obvious he hadn't managed to get away. It turned out that the plane wasn't going over to Cebu that day. It was going over to a place in northern Mindanao known as Farm Eight. Full of hot coffee and toast and fried eggs, we drove in a jeep down the empty road through the bland stale air of the Leyte night to the airfield. There was a red alert on that held us up a little. People were sitting on the edges of foxholes back of the operations hut, slapping at mosquitoes, and exchanging snatches of whispered talk while the irregular motors of strange-sounding planes bumbled and stuttered somewhere above the low overcast. There was no antiaircraft fire. People went on talking in a desultory way, but answers didn't fit questions very well. Everybody had one ear cocked for the screech of a bomb. Gradually the rumble overhead subsided. The all clear signal came. Very gradually the grayness of early dawn was diluting the dense steamy dark.

While we waited for the field to get light enough for the takeoff, we fell to talking with two wanlooking men in white woolen skullcaps who sat on the ground against the wall of the hut with their knees drawn up to their chins. As the light grew, we could see that their faces were thin and drawn and pointed with pain. We asked them which way they were headed.

'Out,' one said vaguely.

'Air-evac,' the other explained.

'Where were you hurt?' asked the Major in a fatherly tone.

The man nearest to us pulled off his skullcap. The top of his head was gone. Instead there was a depression like the crater of a volcano. 'Shrapnel on top of Zigzag Pass,' he said.

'You neglected to keep your helmet on,' said the Major, with a touch of rank in his voice.

'We was so dead by the time we got up there, and the Japs was shellin' us so, we juss dropped everythin' an' started to dig in. Then I got it. I'm afraid I ain't goin' to be much good after this.'

'Sure you will,' said the Major. 'They'll put a silver plate in your head and you'll be better than ever.'

'I guess it means a long time in hospital,' the man insisted drearily, 'and I'm afraid I won't be much good afterwards.'

An olive-drab C47 had appeared on the runway opposite.

'Here we are!' cried the Major cheerily as he closed up the briefcase he'd opened to show us the matchboxes and chewing gum and chocolate and sewing kits with MacArthur's photograph on them he was taking along for distribution among the guerrillas. 'Best of luck, boys.'

The overcast was breaking up in pools of pearly light when we took off. Everybody sat around smoking cigars on the ammunition boxes that filled the center of the cabin. Out over the gulf it was clear. The clouds were white and the still water was a misty plum-blue. The rising sun lit up with amber and gold clouds piled against lushgreen hills back of the headlands and the empty bays and inlets of the coast of Leyte. We were in the company of a second C47. It was pleasant to see the dragonfly shapes of our fighter escorts flanking us on either side. The fighters gilded with morning light skimmed and dove and soared around us like porpoises playing round the bow of a sailing ship.

After about an hour Major Telesco, his round dark face a wreath of smiles, came back from the front of the plane with a map in his hand. 'Map's no good . . . Nobody knows where it is . . . Nobody's ever been in there before,' he shouted in my ear. 'In a few minutes we'll be over the island where the beautiful Chinese girl lives. She's the most beautiful Chinese girl I ever saw, the wife of a Chinese diplomat. We always give her a buzz.'

He vigorously winked one eye and sat down beside me. We sat looking out through the murky plexiglass of the window at distant islands vanishing into cloud across a sea lacy with whitecaps. Skimming low over the water, the plane rode the airwaves like a boat in a heavy swell. Suddenly there were palm groves beneath us, a curve of beach, a pink stucco house, cultivated fields, and behind a hillside rising abruptly into cloud.

'There she is!' shouted the major, his brown eyes swimming. He jumped to his feet. 'Too bad we can't stop to call.' Already the plane was bucking into the choppy aircurrents in the island's lee.

A little later, from the nose of the plane, stooping to look over the shoulders of the pilot and co-pilot, we began to make out ahead the rolling coast of Mindanao, hazy with heat. Inland, dim mountains hovered above strings of white clouds. 'Where are the Japs?' I asked Major Telesco with my mouth to his ear. Grinning, he pointed directly downward. Then his face went serious as he started to study the map again. We crossed the forested lowlands of the coastal plain. Soon we were following the sheen of a snaky river inland. The map was laid out on the pilot's knee. Every face was intent on it. As we climbed, the valley deepened. Slopes dense with foliage became steeper. We were winding up a deep trench of green. The plane twisted and turned between steep hillsides where patches of morning clouds still clung to the huge trees. Ahead a great waterfall was tumbling into the canyon. The plane leapt a jagged ridge like a horse taking a jump. Major Telesco was shaking his head over the map. 'No damn good,' he shouted. We were headed toward a blue pile of mountains far inland.

Now we were crossing a tangle of deep glens. We

skimmed the foothill country in a halfcircle and headed toward the mountains. Major Telesco burst out laughing. 'There it is,' he shouted, pointing out through the nose of the plane at a section of grassy plateau country. He turned back to give me the wink. 'It's not very smooth, but there it is.'

We buzzed low across a long meadow that still kept some of the checkerboard pattern of the original corn and camote fields. The pilot circled and buzzed again to take another look, and then brought us down without a jar. We stepped out into a broad upland valley flanked by deep gulches and spiny ridges on one side, and on the other by a great distant pile of mountains. The air was cold and sweet. It was like the high grazing country in the Rockies. For a moment the strip was clear, but immediately ragged little barefoot men with rifles began to spring up everywhere out of the grass and from under clumps of trees. They swarmed round the plane laughing and shouting. The officers managed to look quite natty in their frayed but wellwashed suntans. Before five minutes were up, they had their troops at work with much hurly-burly unloading the ammunition boxes.

'Our colonel is on his way,' the officers told us proudly, as they shook hands. 'Yesterday Colonel Fertig was here.' It was the third time planes had come in to this particular field, they said.

We passengers who had come in on the plane stood around in the bright sunlight in the middle of the bustle and din looking about us with blinking eyes at the soaring blue mountains and the hedgerows of great trees and the northerlylooking meadows and cornfields. It was good to sniff the clean upland air. The major's short energetic figure was everywhere. As he went he looked about him out of large brown eyes with the air of a man near to bursting with pride and delight. 'Here it's a nice war,' he whispered confidentially, as he hustled past me.

From up the valley comes the rumble of a motor. People start to run for cover in the ditches, but it turns out not to be a hostile plane, so immediately they crowd back laughing. It is the local interurban bus, an ancient, lumbering, rattletrap yellow vehicle with open sides and benches across it like a horsecar, which advances roaring and spluttering up the dusty track along the edge of the airstrip. An American flag flies from the cracked windshield, and three pretty girls sit smiling beside the driver. 'Buknidon bus No. 2' reads in red a splattered sign across the front. Dusty clusters of thread-bare guerrillas hang from the uprights that support the roof. Naked little boys run along behind. The bus parks on the field and the troops begin to load it up with the boxes out of the plane.

Saddlehorses for us to ride are produced out of the shade of a grove of trees at the edge of the airstrip and it is suggested that we might want to ride toward the village to meet Colonel Grinstead, who is on his way down from his headquarters a couple of miles away in the hills. We set out at a trot along an old country road with clayey red ruts like a Virginia road that cuts straight through the fat green lands of the upland valley. On the way we meet a group of people coming toward us. In the middle of them walks a tall man, head and shoulders taller than the Filipinos around him. He walks with long springy strides swinging a heavy cane. He has clear gray eyes and a bushy grizzled beard. His overseas cap is set jauntily on the side of his head.

We scramble down off our ponies to shake hands. There's something easy and genial and completely selfreliant about James Grinstead's manner when you meet him that's very oldtime American. You think at once of a locomotive engineer or the captain of a riverboat. He's from Oklahoma. He has that air of innate culture about him you often find in western prospectors and pioneers, the look of a man capable of sitting back and being entertained by the spectacle of his own life. His story about his beard is that he isn't going to shave it off till the Big Chief lands on Mindanao. His troops call him Santa Claus on account of it. He's an oldtimer on Mindanao, he tells us. A number of years back he retired as a sergeant from the Philippine Constabulary and set himself up near Cotogato as a coconut planter.

'A lazy man's life,' he explains; 'that's why I like it.'

We have turned back toward the airfield and are talking as we walk along. He has a deep, resonant voice with a southwestern drawl, and the amused, half-deprecatory manner of a good storyteller. His eyes, under a square forehead and bushy eyebrows, twinkle as he talks.

'It's a funny war,' he says; 'at least I've found it so. When the Jap first came, I hid out for two months on my own place without his ever findin' me. Then I took to the hills. I haven't led such a bad life as you'd think.'

While we walk along, leading our horses and talking, a formation of planes drones across the dark-blue sky overhead. The Filipinos around us look up nervously from under their big hats. 'They are ours,' says Colonel Grinstead, laughing, 'even I can tell that . . . I'm afraid you won't find us much on the military side up here. We are so used to thinkin' any plane is a Jap that it's goin' to take us a little while to get over the habit of crawlin' in ditches.'

One of the Corsairs of our fighter escort is circling to come in. We all follow the dark slender plane with our eyes as it speeds across the grass. All at once the nose digs in and the tail shoots up. The Corsair has crashed.

Major Telesco jumps into the saddle, kicks his heels into his pony, and gallops off. Somebody offers the colonel a horse. 'No, thanks, I find I can get there just as fast walkin',' he drawls. We all ride after the major as fast as we can get our horses to go. When we reach the plane we see that the propeller and nose are dug into the soft dirt. Sweating and redfaced, the pilot unhurt but sore is climbing down out of his seat. 'A nice target for the Japs,' whispers the major. 'Their Del Monte strip is only twelve miles away.'

Guerrillas come running with ropes. Several of them are fetching a bamboo ladder from the staging where they fasten the sleeve to show the wind direction. Two ropes of home-made hempen fiber are fastened to the tail of the plane. Bunches of little guerrillas hang from them. The plane's tail is pulled down. Up comes its twisted propeller out of the dirt. A carabao cart is backed up to the tail, and with much pulling and hauling and sweating the Corsair is towed tail-first off the field.

Colonel Grinstead has caught up with us and stands looking quietly at the humming swarm of his ragged troops.

'That must be one of the soft places where the Japs dropped their bombs last week,' he says in an untroubled ruminative tone. 'We just have these rollers made of palm trunks and it's hard to get the places hard enough when we fill them in.' He looks up at me with a twinkle in his eye. 'Of course, we've got our tractor, which I understand is now world-famous, and its roller, but that's only workin' some of the time. It's more somethin' to boast about.'

The major has come up, drenched and breathless, to say that he is sending for mechanics and spare parts to come in with the C47's when they return to pick us up in the after-noon. There's a chance they can patch the plane up and fly it out.

'If the Jap don't pay us his regular afternoon visit,' drawls Colonel Grinstead with his leisurely smile. 'They usually fly over just at dusk; but meanwhile,' he adds in his amused and genial tone of voice, 'my boys will turn that plane into a nice haystack. They are good at that. Now if you gentlemen would like to come along, I think the Rodriguezes are expectin' us for lunch.'

He leads the way down a path that winds through the tall grass from the airstrip down into a leafy valley. From the edge overlooking some cornfields and a treepacked riverbank, he points out the ravine where five miles away his troops are holding back the Jap. 'We had about five hundred of them cornered when they pulled out of here last week, but we had to let them go. Not enough ammo. Not enough chow. Boys too sick. In the trenches they live on dog and raw bananas, but they don't often get the dog. They need clothes and medicine. They are full of malaria and amoebic and bacterial dysentery. So all we can do with the Jap is kinda get in his way.' He laughs his deliberate laugh.

'When he was up here, a week ago tomorrow,' he says, 'we held him for three days, but then the only thing we could do was get out. We went up in those hills.' He turns back to point out the green ridge the other side of the airstrip. 'A little way beyond that ridge is the Moro country. We stayed partway up. The Jap dug up the airstrip a little and then he pulled out and ran. Out of chow, I guess. He went back to report he'd killed a thousand guerrillas and destroyed the airstrip.'

He is leading the way down the path again, turning back toward us from time to time as he talks. 'We patched things up as best we could. It took us only seventeen days to build the strip in the first place. Men, women, and children worked on it with rollers made of coconut logs and those rough wooden tampers you see layin' around. We had to run the tractor on coconut oil. Why not? We've run generators for radio sets with alcohol made from tuba. We finished the field about a month ago, and as soon as planes started to come in with supplies the Jap got curious and began to give us a daily workover. It is always surprisin' to me what a lot of bombin' and strafin' he can do without real damage. He came mornin' and evenin' just at dusk and made a hell of a racket, but all he did was wound one old tomcat in the leg. The tomcat got well in time to sire a litter of kittens. . . . But last week he moved in on us all right. When he left, we followed him up and cut off that party of about five hundred I was tellin' you about down at the fork of the river. We just didn't have the men or the ammo to clean 'em up. If he knew how thinly my men were strung out along their perimeter, I bet a dollar he'd be back this afternoon.'

The noon sun was burning hot. We arrived sweating and thirsty at a group of pomolo trees in the corner of a field densely grown with tall shimmering corn. Behind the trees was a barn with a high porch under a galvanized-iron roof. The Rodriguez family was waiting for us in a group in the shade of the porch. They looked very Spanish. There was the grayhaired man, and his wife, and the blackeyed daughters and the uncles and cousins and nephews. In the background stood friends and servants. All greeted us with warm hospitality. The girls offered us fresh water to drink and pomolos, which are a primitive type of grapefruit, and brought out the few chairs the Japs had left them for us to sit on. Mr. Rodriguez explained apologetically that this barn was his home since the Japs had burned his house in the valley. He was proud to welcome us to it. He had five sons in the Army.

'They call it guerrillas, but we call it the Army of the Philippines.'

After we had cooled off a little in the shade, they made us sit in the middle of the long table with a white tablecloth that was set the length of the porch. There was a glass for the colonel, but the rest of us drank out of green sections of bamboo. The girls, smiling and laughing, kept passing around the table pouring out the milky fresh tuba, which is the fermented sap of the coconut palm. The air was cool and streaked with heavy fragrance from the blossoms of the pomolos and from the roses that bloomed along the fence. Americans and Filipinos sat there cooling off, talking in low voices while our host's pretty daughters passed the tuba and ran softly back and forth with dishes from the kitchen.

Only when a rumble of planes was heard overhead was there any stir. The girls and old women started to move toward the shelter down in the creekbed. The children bolted. They weren't yet used to having planes turn out friendly. Colonel Grinstead stepped out into the path and shaded his eyes to look up. 'It's that same formation of ours coming back from its mission,' he said. As soon as they heard his quiet confident voice, the people started coming back into the house.

We sat in a row looking out from the dense shade, through the branches of pomolo trees full of white flowers and yellow green fruit, at the cornfields shimmering in the heat while the girls brought out a magnificent meal of upland rice and chicken broth, and stewed chicken and dumplings, and suckling pig roasted on a spit, and pork chops cooked in coconut oil, and green beans, and fruit pudding.

While we ate we talked. Mr. Luminarias, the young deputy governor of the province, was telling about the beginning of the guerrilla movement in Mindanao. In October,

1942, he said, there had been the first rising against the Japanese-controlled police. The Filipinos had used ripe bananas, pretending they were hand grenades, and the police had surrendered and joined the guerrillas. Then in March, 1943, a government had been set up in a meeting at a school. 'Since then we have complete civil government.'

At first the Americans had to hide out. They were taken in by the country people, Colonel Grinstead explained. The Jap never controlled any more of Mindanao than he could see in front of his nose. Mr. Kuder, the superintendent of schools, did a great deal to influence the Moros. He stayed right on until he had to be evacuated home on account of illness.

The Colonel laughed. Of course, the Americans had to keep their wits about them. Maybe the fate of those that fell into the hands of the Jap sharpened the wits of the survivors. Several Americans had been pretty badly hashed up before they were killed. . . . Well, gradually with the help of young officers of the Philippine Army they built an organization. In the course of time the whole works came under the command of Colonel Fertig. Colonel Fertig was a mining engineer who had come over to Mindanao to build airstrips and gotten caught here. He'd proved a grand organizer. 'Of course,' added Grinstead, 'we don't any of us think much of ourselves as military men. We've had to put up with certain geographical limitations. . . . How far do you think we are from Colonel Fertig's headquarters right now?' he asked.

None of us could answer.

He stretched his broad mouth in a grin. 'Twenty-four days of the hardest kind of hikin'. We communicate by radio. I consider Fertig one of my best friends, but in three years I don't think I've seen him three times.'

I had met Colonel Fertig at headquarters in Tolosa a few

days before. I had a vivid recollection of a quiet man with forceful gray eyes and a small goatee, who looked rather like a country doctor. He wouldn't hear of any talk of the privation and danger of his life any more than Grinstead would. Now Grinstead was explaining how Fertig never had a headquarters without electric light. Sometimes they had to use a waterwheel to turn over the generator. In Misamis Occidental they'd had street lights up to June, 1943. Lanao under Colonel Hedges had been more peaceful for the last three years than in any three years in its history. There had been remarkably little crime in guerrilla territory. Things had run surprisingly smoothly. 'Of course, when the Jap came in force we had to get out the back way. We always kept the back door open. One reason we never could oppose the Jap was that we could never concentrate our troops. The country couldn't feed more than a smatterin' at a time. The supplies that came in by submarine were ammunition and radio parts and medicine. Never any room for food. . . . About all we've been able to do is move in when the Jap moves out. . . . Wherever he goes the fabric of society breaks down. When we go back we patch things up again as best we can.'

We were drinking remarkably good coffee. It was grown in the province, they told us. Mr. Rodriguez and the deputy governor talked reminiscently of last week's scare. They had had three days' notice. But they had lingered hoping the Japs would be stopped at the river. Then they had to run for it. The Japanese soldiers had set fire to the barn we were sitting in and smashed up most of the furniture, but fortunately they hadn't done a good job. The fire had gone out after burning a corner of the floor.

'We were lucky,' one of the slanteyed girls said in her soft voice. 'Where we crossed the river we found some nipa huts and were able to get out of the rain. Up here it's cold at night, you know. And how your heart beats when your horse gets stuck in the mud, and you think the Japanese will catch you.'

After lunch we walked slowly through the still afternoon, shrill with cicadas and dryflies, into the village. There was a pretty green plaza shaded by huge trees under which a few vendors squatted. Most of them were sourfaced Moros in turbans who had brought in bolts of homespun cloth for sale. There were bags of nuts and dried fruits and a few handfuls of the inevitable tiny desiccated shrimps. Quite unharmed in the middle of the grassy central square stood a stiff cement statue of Rizal. Around the plaza were hedges of flowering shrubs with vineclad bamboo arches and gates in them which opened into nicely laid-out gardens. Not a house was standing. The Japs had burned every one.

While we were in the plaza we heard the distant growl of a formation of planes. We set out walking fast down the road toward the airstrip. 'You never can tell what the Jap'll do, he might pay us a call,' Grinstead was saying.

Soon we could make out our own olive-drab transports circling the strip. When we got back to it the airfield looked like a fairground. Men, women, and children had trooped in from far and near. The guerrilla officers were having a hard time keeping a runway clear for the planes to land on. The Colonel shook his head. 'A lot of them have never seen a friendly plane in their lives,' he said. 'I'll be nervous as a flea on a hot griddle until those planes get out of here. . . . It's gettin' near the time when the Jap likes to come callin'.'

There was a dense shouting crowd around the open side doors of the C47's. The crews were throwing out candy and cigarettes and distributing souvenirs and knickknacks with the Commanding General's 'I shall return' picture on them. There were Moros in the throng and the boys off the transports were carrying on a brisk trade with them for their engraved bolos and krisses. In the outskirts of the crowd all the girls in the neighborhood, in their best clothes and with flowers in their hair, were strolling briskly about in twos and threes, Spanish fashion. Here and there among the people serious-looking fellows stood guard leaning on their long spears. If a guerrilla didn't have a gun he had a spear. If he didn't have a spear he had a bolo or a knife.

The afternoon dragged on. More and more souvenirs appeared for sale and barter. A fresh meal had been set out on their porch by the Rodriguez family for the newly arrived plane crews to eat before they took off. Colonel Grinstead kept looking at his watch. The afternoon began to drag.

One of the pretty little Rodriguez girls came running across the field to where we stood under a broadspreading mango. She was carrying a plate covered with a napkin. 'It is a squash pie made with cassava flour,' she said, smiling. 'Mother says you must taste it.' She held it up under the Colonel's nose.

'As if she hadn't stuffed us already,' he said. 'It's a funny war,' he added as he pulled out his claspknife and started dividing up the pie.

While we stood in the shade munching on the pie, I asked him why in his opinion the resistance seemed to go so much better in places where a few Americans were back of it. 'Well, in Mindanao the oldtime Americans have always had a pretty good reputation,' he replied with his slow judicial drawl. 'Not too many bastards have come in yet to ruin it. The people have confidence that we'll treat 'em square. They'd rather have an American in command than their own leaders.

I'll tell you why. Whenever a Filipino gets to some position, he's assailed by a mob of relatives who want soft jobs. He'd be socially ostracized if he turned 'em down. Americans don't have such big families and they expect to support themselves by their own efforts. People respect their independence.'

As we talked, we couldn't help occasionally scanning the sky with a certain apprehension. 'If they come,' said the Colonel, 'they'll make a killin'.'

At last the Major was beckoning to us from the door of our C47. Already the escort planes were taking off amid clouds of red dust. We shook hands all around and set off at a dog-trot toward our plane. As we were climbing the little ladder, Mr. Luminarias, the brighteyed young man in the linen suit who was deputy governor of the Province of Buknidon, came running after us and asked us please not to forget to send in books and newspapers and magazines next time.

'You do not know what it means to be out of the world,' he said breathlessly. 'For three years we have been cut off from the civilized world.'

The boys of the crew lifted in their last souvenirs, a bundle of spears, an armful of big straw hats, and then the steps. Over the hats and bobbing heads of the crowd we had a last glimpse of Grinstead's broad forehead and gray eyes and bushy beard as he gently waved the people back from under the wings of the plane. The doors were pulled to and we settled back into the bucket seats for the takeoff.

Leyte, March 3, 1945

PART THREE

In the Year of Our Defeat

1

Land of the Fragebogen

Headquarters in Frankfurt

'THERE SEEMS to have been a little trouble here,' the young aviator in a fifty mission cap opposite me whispers in a soft drawl as the train slows down. I wake up with red rays stinging through the film of sleep in my eyes. A streak of dawn oozes through a row of windows in an empty wall and washes the cracks in upended masonry with bloody light, and picks out tilting girders and steel rods of smashed concrete twisted like stems of weeds in a pond. The train is moving slowly through the wreckage of some industrial plant. Further on the glare out of the east pours through a crazily toppling sky sign: WEST WAGGON GEZELLSCHAFT.

'The Germans must take a dim view of us,' says the aviator, making an ironical clucking noise with his tongue.

We all crane our necks to look out of the grimy window of our compartment at the tumbled desolation of battered buildings that stretches as far as you can see in the tawny light under a sky closepacked with dirty clouds.

'The more I see the more I hate the krauts for having made us do it,' shouts a man from the far corner.

The train crosses the Rhine slowly beside the ponderous zigzag of a blown railroad bridge. Out in the olivecolored river a piledriver on a tiny black barge is at work on an abutment for a new bridge. Whang! Whang! Whang! There's something cheerful and busy about its metallic ring in the early morning air.

Through flattened suburbs where the russet leaves are still on the trees the train glides gently into the Frankfurt Station.

Frankfurt resembles a city as much as a pile of bones and a smashed skull on the prairies resembles a prize Hereford steer, but white enameled streetcars packed with people jingle purposefully as they run along the cleared asphalt streets. People in city clothes with city faces and briefcases under their arms trot busily about among the high rubbish piles, dart into punched-out doorways under tottering walls. They behave horribly like ants when you have kicked over an anthill.

Here and there on a scrap of blackened façade a clock has survived. The clocks are all going. They all tell the right time.

A tall spare elderly Frankfurter with a close-clipped banker's mustache takes us around to see the sights. The shells of great ruined stone houses stretch all along the riverbank. There is the old mansion of the Rothschilds, the eighteenth-century palace where Schopenhauer lived. White columns still stand in front of the seared husk of the Public Library under a Latin inscription to the effect that knowledge insures the freedom of the state. There are squares among the ruins full of trees from which the last yellow leaves are falling. Where the houses have been blown away, you can look into rows of autumnal gardens. At every intersection there's a traffic cop in a blue uniform with a long warm overcoat. The traffic cops are the happiest-looking people in Frankfurt. They are warm. They are fed. Their uniforms are clean. And they can order the other Germans around.

Our guide is taking us around to see the sights as if they were still there. 'Here,' he says, pointing to a trace of a medieval building faint as a picture on a burned postal card blown out of an ashcan, 'is the famous Roemer where the Emperors of the Holy Roman Empire were crowned. The foundations were laid by Charlemagne, King of the Franks. On this balcony' — he pointed vaguely upward — 'they came out to show themselves to the people and pavilions were pitched on the square and the fountains ran with wine, this side white wine and the other side red, and oxen were roasted whole and the people scrambled in a merry scrimmage for the meat.'

Our feet were sore from stumbling over heaps of broken stones and our noses were full of the smell of cold ashes by the time we got to the zoo.

The director met us at the gate. He was a wellbuilt young-ish man in a buttoned-up raincoat with a rather rakish felt hat. He had a way of smiling while he talked. He fumbled a little for his English, but he spoke it with a humorous turn.

'It has been very difficult,' he said. 'I have been interested in the pseechological scientific study of the man-apes, pri-mates, you say. The grown males are very furious, you know, but in the bombings, all through the bad time they were humble and clung to each other and sobbed. The gorilla died, it was too cold. Scientific work has been difficult.'

We followed him around the muddy paths that skirted shellholes. 'And now all this I have to repair,' he kept say-ing as he showed us around the wrecked enclosures and the mudsplattered little shelters patched with tarpaper and tin and raw boards. 'The only building undamaged was the worst one I wanted to tear down. . . . See, my elephants are from a circus which was scattered in the retreat. My camels come from another place. My main building' — he pointed to a mass of pink stucco with big windows ornamented with weary classical orders that rose behind us hollow and shattered as a layercake that has been stepped on — 'must very much be repaired. It was from restaurants and entertainments that the tiergarden derived its income. Now I must make circus acts and variété and dancing for American soldiers. Two weeks ago I make firework . . .' He laughed. He motioned us into a smelly little building. 'Here,' he said proudly, 'is the last two chimpanzee. The male is very furious. The female is five years old. She should be larger, but her nourishment is insufficient.'

In the cage next to the woebegone primates was a furry tumble of lion cubs. He looked at them and laughed. 'They look well, no? I liberated them from Leipzig in the last days of the collapse, although I was very bad from bloodpoisoning by being in the hand by the man-ape bitten. I drove from Leipzig very quickly in a little car to save them from the Russians, with the five cubs and a box of alligators.'

American Military Government is set up in the ponderous building back of the opera that used to house the light metals trust. In the entrance stairway stands the bronze statue of Justice that Longfellow once wrote a poem about. Every morning the young officers of the detachment meet round a doughnutshaped table in a big bright conference room on the upper floor. Each officer reads a report on the progress of the particular section of city government he has charge of. The reports are in terse military style. The officers try to read them snappily, but something lugubrious gets into their voices as if their hearts weren't in the work. From the reports you learn what it is like for a people to be beaten in war in the year nineteen hundred and forty-five of the Christian era.

This morning we start on a cheerful note. The officer in charge of housing reads off that twenty-two thousand units, apartments mostly, have been rehabilitated and winterized. Frankfurt's population, however, due to arrivals of refugees from the east, is mounting by two thousand a week. . . . Public safety announces that there have been no crimes to report against military personnel. A raid on a crowded street netted only five arrests for blackmarket activities. The cameramen got some action pictures. A large number of persons were held for failing to report for forced labor. . . . Walls of ruined houses collapsing in the recent high winds killed one woman and injured two. . . . The city's bombdisposal unit had been severely crippled when a bomb they were attempting to render harmless went off with rather bad results for the German personnel. . . . Food: arrangements had been made to allow a certain distribution of white flour for Christmas. In this we were following a local custom. Fish was beginning to come in from Bremen. However, at the present writing the American zone as a whole still had only enough food on hand to furnish eleven hundred calories a day per person. In many places they weren't getting that. People in the heavyworker category received a little more, but in Frankfurt only two and one tenth per cent of the people had qualified for the heavyworker category. . . . There was some cause for gratification in the fact that the stock market, except for I.G. Farben shares, had been going up steadily since it had been allowed to reopen. . . . Public health remained surprisingly good. Out of the four thousand hospital beds available for the city seven hundred and thirty-five were vacant. . . . There had been a cut in electric power. Electric heating appliances had been removed from homes. The people of Frankfurt were allowed to use for cooking one hot plate for one hour three times a day for every five persons. Where there was gas the situation was a little better. . . . Coal was still critical, but the first barge had come in by river from the Ruhr. The city had on hand eight hundred tons of briquettes, four hundred tons of coke, and two hundred and forty tons of coal. . . . Travel on street-cars showed an increase every week over the preceding week. Sixty-three per cent of the total trackage was back in operation. . . . Two hundred and three physicians had been licensed to practice. . . . Eighty lawyers were defending clients before the military courts. . . . After questioning by the War Crimes Commission a prisoner had hanged himself with his shoelaces in his cell.

Driving away from the battered hulk of the main railroad station down one of the broad ruined shopping streets, you come to a barbed-wire barricade. All cars are stopped. At the gate are snappy young American guards with pink faces and white mufflers and white gloves. Inside the barricade you look with unaccustomed eyes on buildings that are standing intact, that have windows in them. There are green lawns and trees, back of immense parking places for military vehicles. Across the background stretch the long sleek lines of the I.G. Farben office building that houses the offices of Headquarters of the United States Forces in Europe. On either side are rows of modern apartment houses and dwellings where the officers are quartered. This is the conqueror's part of the city where none of the conquered may come except with a special pass.

Today an officer is driving me home with him to lunch. The car leaves us on the steps of an undamaged modern residence in a corner of the compound. Beyond the barbed wire at the end of the street the ruin begins again. We walk through a library and sit down in a big sunny drawingroom with Chinese rugs. The place is neat and clean and warm. All the knickknacks are carefully dusted. The barbed wire outside the windows cuts the compound off from the suffering city. The double windows cut the drawingroom off from the wintry day. Not a sound comes in to us as we sit in the brocaded chairs. You don't even have the feeling of being in Germany. Something about the way the Louis XVI furniture is arranged reminds me of the drawingroom of a house I've occasionally visited in Grosse Point near Detroit. It might be the home of a twenty-five-thousand-dollar-a-year man anywhere.

'This is really a general's house,' my friend explains. 'I was here with several other officers, but they've all gone home, and the billeting office seems to have forgotten me here.'

A middle-aged German woman with crinkly blond hair in a maid's cap and uniform announces lunch. We sit at either end of an acre of white tablecloth piled with polished silverware and eat venison steak washed down by firstrate burgundy.

'It's funny,' my friend is saying, 'but I don't have any appetite.' Here he was, he explained with a shake of the head, all alone with a pack of servants. He couldn't get rid of them even when he stopped paying them. He guessed they came just for the heat and to smell the good food. He had one of the best cooks in Frankfurt, but he couldn't seem to eat.

My friend came from the Great Lakes region back home. He was in the insurance business, but he had always been interested in the National Guard. Although he was over age he gave up his business and left his wife and children because he thought he might be useful to the Army in Military Government. He'd had experience in municipal affairs at home. He'd gone to Charlottesville and Leavenworth and worked his head off. Well, they had kept him cooped up in England until a month after D–day and then he'd gotten over to France and had been put in charge of a detail moving dead horses off the streets. He didn't mind that, he explained. He'd been crazy to do anything that got him within sound of gunfire, but the way he thought he really could be useful was as an expert in municipal finance.

'Well, now I'm in Military Government,' he said as we were eating our dessert, 'but I haven't any authority. In a place where there's a headquarters like this stuffed with stars and chicken colonels, I just haven't got the rank to accomplish anything. . . . A man gets fed up with being kicked around by USFET . . . so here I am.' He pushed the untasted apple tartlet away from him and got to his feet. 'Like all the rest of 'em . . . waiting to go home . . . and just drifting.'

Driving back to town in the tailend of a raw afternoon had been like driving through one of Dante's icy hells. In the freezing fog, along the road, we had passed crowds of men and women bowed under knapsacks and bundles of sticks, pulling baby carriages and carts full of wood, pushing heavily loaded bicycles. We went along honking and blinking the lights of the jeep to try to get them to move out of the way. 'Damn krauts,' the driver kept muttering. 'They git themselves run over just on purpose . . . I'd just as soon run 'em down as not.'

We passed some trucks crowded tight with grayfaced young men in gray. 'At least the military prisoners get to ride,' said the lieutenant. 'The lesson of this war to me is, don't ever be a civilian.'

At last we made it through the crowded foggy unlit streets back to the correspondents' hotel and dragged our stiff limbs out of the open jeep. The bar wasn't functioning yet, so the lieutenant and I went up to the bedroom to thaw ourselves out over the radiator. We stood at the window a moment pulling the drenched gloves off our icy fingers and looking down the shaft of light from the window through a gap in the wall of the hotel next door into an emptiness of dangling plumbing where a piece of a stairway with red flowered carpeting on it stopped abruptly at nothing. Turning back into the warm, well-lighted, perfectly standardized hotel bedroom, we found that we had both felt the same momentary sense of surprise that it was us in here with the warm conquerors instead of out there with the dead jerries.

The lieutenant worked in Intelligence. He was a young man from Brooklyn with a thoughtful ruddy face and full lips.

Suddenly he sat down on the edge of the bed and started to talk. 'My people are Jewish,' he began, 'so don't think I'm not bitter against the krauts. I'm for shooting the war criminals wherever we can prove they are guilty and getting it over with. But for God's sake, tell me what we are trying to do.'

He got up and began to walk back and forth. 'Well, they tell you it's like the fire department . . . the fire department has to do a certain amount of damage, even blow up buildings, to put the fire out. Sure, but you don't see the fire department starting new fires all over town just because one block is burning. Or do you? Hatred is like a fire. You've got to put it

out. I've been interrogating German officers for the War
Crimes Commission, and when I find them half-starved to
death right in our own P.W. cages and being treated like you
wouldn't treat a dog, I ask myself some questions. Sometimes I have to get them fed up and hospitalized before I can
get a coherent story out of them. Brutality is more contagious
than typhus and a hell of a lot more difficult to stamp out. . . .
Right here at USFET in Frankfurt we countenance things that
would have given us cold chills back home. . . . I'm not blam-
ing the Regular Army men for all of it, either. Regular Army
men are a hell of a fine bunch of men and I've come to admire
them very much, but the trouble is they have no training in
political things. They are trained to follow directives from
Washington. They do, and slavishly. . . . I do blame them
for not having the courage to follow their own decent instincts. That's how General Patton got into trouble. . . .
Patton is one of those men who never opens his mouth without putting his foot in it, and God knows he's a tough baby,
but his instincts were all right. Throwing him overboard
was cowardice. All these directives about don't coddle the
German have thrown open the gates for every criminal tend-
ency we've got in us. Just because the Germans did these
things is no reason for us to do them. Well, I know war isn't
a pretty business, but this isn't war. This is peace. . . . Hell,
let's go down and get a drink before I blow my top and start
talking.'

Denazification

It was a raw rainy Germany morning. We had been driving
through woods of regularly spaced pine trees all the same size
that alternated with square patches of green meadowland.

Along the edges of the road trudged the inevitable file of men and women bundled up in heavy clothes and bowed under rucksacks. Across their shoulders each one of them carried the inevitable bundle of sticks. Many of them pulled or pushed before them the inevitable small carts stacked with cut logs.

'Their forests ought to be the saving of them this winter,' I was saying to the Military Government officer who was driving the jeep. 'If they can't get coal, they'll at least have wood.'

'It's hard to get the stuff into the cities . . . Law Number Eight.'

'What's that?'

'Denazification. The trouble is all the foresters turn out to be Nazis. . . . Forestry in Germany was a favorite occupation for von This and von That, bigtime Nazis every one. A lot of them were mandatory arrest cases. We are having trouble finding anybody else who knows how to get the logs out.'

After a succession of smashed towns along a river, the road broke through into the woods again and came out suddenly on an old stone wall built around a cluster of tall gables. On the corners were round towers with conical tops. We drove through an ancient gate into a village street of half-timbered houses intact and neatly picturesque as an illustration for a volume of Grimm's *Fairy Tales*. In front of the houses were little gardens packed with fat chrysanthemums. In the yards grew solemn rows of green and purple cabbages. A few roses and dahlias were still in blossom along the fences in spite of the wintry weather. On a big pink stucco house a sign read MILITARY GOVERNMENT.

The office was heated by a white porcelain stove. The tall captain at the desk, in the center of the room, got to his feet,

and offered us chairs. We settled down near the stove to thaw
out a little in the cozy warmth. Our hands and knees and elbows were numb from the long ride in the open jeep. Meanwhile we asked the captain about himself. He came from the
California ranching country. He'd been seventeen years a
sergeant in the Regular Army and had won his commission in
France.

'Gentlemen,' he said, 'I'm glad to see some newspapermen.
We are proud of what we have done here. We are ninety
per cent denazified.'

'Ninety-two per cent,' said the thinfaced sergeant from his
desk in the corner.

'That means there are no Nazis left doing anything but
ditch-digging and heavy work?'

'That's what it means.'

'How do you do it?'

'It's the fragebogen. You don't know about the fragebogen. The fragebogen's the greatest thing in Germany.'

The sergeant came out from his desk and handed us a long
questionnaire of the type developed by United States immigra-
tion inspectors.

'If they get past this, they can hold any job they want. If
they don't, they can't have any position where they employ
labor or exercise a skilled trade or profession. They can't do
nothing but pick-and-shovel work. . . . And if they lie on
their fragebogen, we have 'em up in court and they don't get
off easy. Every man or woman who has any position of authority has got to make out a fragebogen. If it turns out they are
big Nazis, it's mandatory arrest. If they are small Nazis, they
report to the labor gang. Everybody gets fragebogened sooner
or later. Then we know what's what.'

'How about doctors?'

'If they can't be replaced, we are allowed to give them a temporary permit to practice. Suppose a man's a plumber. He's got to do his own work. He can't hire an assistant. Well, let's see what have we got to show you here. This is mostly a farming community. . . . The people are all tailors in their spare time, garment workers, they do the work at home. . . . We've got a shipyard and a wine plant. . . . We've got plans to build a new bridge. Now they have to use a ferry. . . . There's the Boy Scout movement. . . . But I was forgetting,' he added promptly, 'I think we've got the only woman burgomeister in Germany in one of our little towns.'

The captain led us back into his living quarters and offered us some German cigars. He introduced us to the slickhaired lieutenant who was his second in command. We sat down in front of the window in deep chairs of taffycolored leather. It was a highceilinged yellow room. Around the walls were photographs of some German's family, healthy-looking young men and women with knapsacks starting off on walking trips, blond men with guns standing over piles of slain deer, old men with mustaches in the uniform of the Kaiser's officers. Above them were rows and rows of the small horns of roebuck and a few stuffed heads with spreading antlers of the large European deer. From the balcony you could see a light-green valley hemmed in by hills planted with orderly ranks of pines and firs marching down to the banks of a darkgreen river. The captain poured out the thin German wine into tall crystal goblets that had some German's monogram on them.

'I was throwing shells into a town like this twenty-four hours before I was detached for Military Government. They gave us a two-hour lecture, and before I knew it I was running a place the size of Springfield, Illinois,' explained the lieutenant. 'I can't help wondering how well I'm qualified,' he added, laughing. 'It's the life of Riley,' interrupted the captain; 'look at the quarters we've got . . . a funny thing happened. One morning the kraut that owns this place comes back from a P.W. camp. I hear a little whistle outside the front door that wakes me up. I go out and there's kind of a lanky guy waiting. I guess he thought it was his wife coming to the door. He didn't know the family wasn't here any more. You oughta seen his face.'

After lunch we crossed the ferry and drove out up a broad winding valley to a scattering of houses perched on a ridge among fir trees. This was the village that had the lady burgomeister. Tiled roofs, broad eaves, barnyards piled high with manure. A few sheep. A couple of hissing flocks of geese. She wasn't at her office. We found her doing her housework in a big plain room with a stove with mustard-colored tiles filling half of one wall. There were white frilled curtains in the windows, red geraniums, and a big tinted photograph of a sternlooking man with a handlebar mustache, who must have been her father, on the wall.

Her name was Fräulein Wolff. She was a freshfaced young woman with glasses. Unmarried, she had been chief clerk in charge of rationing under the old burgomeister. She had never been a Nazi. No, she had never had anything to do with politics. Her eyes were spry and selfpossessed behind her glasses. Her dress and apron were very clean. She had the look of having just been scrubbed with strong kitchen soap and so had everything in the room. This was her father's house. She'd always lived here.

We asked her what the village produced.

'Milk,' she answered, smiling. Then she went on to explain that they weren't getting much of it to market because the farmers were drinking it themselves.

Why?

They weren't allowed to make any beer. So they drank milk. The Kaiser had tried it. The Weimar Republic had tried it, and now the Americans were trying it. No use forbidding beer. When the German farmer couldn't get beer, he just drank his milk. She looked at us with a deprecatory smile.

We asked if she knew she was the first woman in her country to hold the post of burgomeister. She didn't seem impressed. 'Somebody's got to be first,' she said flatly.

She stood there with the dustcloth in her hand looking at us attentively through her glasses, waiting for more questions. Nobody seemed to think of any, so she made an impatient little motion with the dustcloth. You could see she wanted to get back to her housework. We said goodbye and she gave us another of her doubtful smiles.

Relaxation

We drive north under a squally gray sky along the curving double ribbon of the autobahn. Again the picturebook landscape: flattened hills crowned with orderly plantations of beech and pine, castles ruined in far earlier wars than this — villages of half-timbered houses, with here and there a sharp thin steeple like an exclamation point. Very few relics of this present war. Only occasionally an old gun emplacement, a tank abandoned at the edge of a patch of woods, or a shapeless mass of twisted metal at the foot of an embankment that might have been a halftrack or a fighter-plane. After all the ruin it's a pleasure to see a string of towns that are undamaged.

We've left the autobahn and are following the windings of a secondary road paved with smooth square cobbles through medieval villages out of the backgrounds of the Brueghels. By the time we are thoroughly chilled riding through the raw autumn gale in the open jeep, we see ahead of us the fine spires and the battlements and huddled hunchbacked houses of a considerable town. We climb up through winding stone streets, come out on an open parade ground under a brownstone city wall, and turn into a court beside a gawky German barracks building of gingerbreadcolored brick. Sleet blows in our faces as we haul our legs stiffly out of the car. Inside the house it is warm. There's a parlor with overstuffed furniture, and a diningroom beyond. This was the officers' mess of the German regiment that used to be quartered here. Along the walls there are still some big silver trays bearing the regiment's crest and insignia. There are white tablecloths. The major is sitting at the end of the center table drinking cognac and water. He greets us hospitably and pours us out a drink. Several other officers are sitting around with their tunics unbuttoned, smoking and drinking. It is Saturday afternoon.

The major calls loudly for Mamma, and a Russian woman with deepset brown eyes comes in from the kitchen.

'Bring 'em some lunch, Mamma,' roars the major. 'She's our housekeeper,' he explains. 'Her people were White Russians, but the krauts had her in a concentration camp.'

With a good deal of giggling, two girls, one of them German, with her blond hair done up in a high wave, and the other French, come in to set our places for us. The French girl has little curls around her forehead. She is very young. She throws herself around like a French maid in a play. She's very pretty, but her voice is husky. The Russian woman with deepset eyes explains that it is because the Germans made her work in a sulphur plant. The fumes ruined her voice. When the girls have brought in our plates, they drop down into chairs between the officers at the table. Somebody makes a pass to grab the little French girl around the waist and she punches him in the muscle of the arm with her two small fists. They laugh and scuffle.

Every time the Russian woman comes into the room, she is followed by a tiny goldenhaired child.

'That's Mimi,' explains the major, pouring himself out another drink. 'Mamma found her in a concentration camp. Her parents had disappeared, so she adopted her. Then she adopted us.'

The little girl sees that we are talking about her. She toddles over to us bringing a painted tin candy box. She opens it to show us what is inside. It is full of cigarette butts. 'She picks them up . . . she learned that in the concentration camp,' said Mamma, with a motherly smile. 'It is her greatest treasure.'

Outside, the weather is fierce. Sleet beats against the windows. We sit all afternoon at the table in the warm diningroom drinking cognac and water and talking. The girls giggle and tease and flounce in and out of chairs, tangling now with one man, now with another. Every now and then somebody comes in from outofdoors, shaking the wet off his clothes and bringing a gust of cold in with him.

There's the young lieutenant in charge of the military police detachment. He's a husky young Pole from Pennsylvania who looks as if he might have been in the prizering at some time or other. The captain who's in charge of a small town down the line corners him to ask him if he can't do something to find the truckdriver who ran over a young German over in his territory. He's a frecklefaced young man with nice teeth and an enthusiastic salesman's manner.

'I know this boy was a careful driver. He was one hundred per cent anti-Nazi and a darn good boy. We had him slated to take over an important business and then somebody kills him on us. You know how hard it is to find a really reliable kraut.'

The military police lieutenant says he'll do his best. 'But what are you going to do,' he adds, 'if the krauts won't get off the road.'

Two Frenchmen from the United Nations' Relief have come in. One of them speaks good English. Right away the military police lieutenant is after him.

'Your DP's have been at it again,' he says, with his sleepy smile. 'Killed and stripped a young kraut down a back alley last night. . . . Boy, we've got to stop it.'

The Frenchman shrugs and gesticulates. How can they keep track of two thousand displaced persons when there are just two of them?

The third relief man is an American, a tough-looking sallow character with a hatchet face. He's from Chicago. Got out of the Army and took a relief job in Germany. This morning he resigned. He's going home and he's going to tell 'em a few things in Washington on the way. He's had it.

'The trouble with all this business,' says a mildmannered towheaded lieutenant from Utah, 'is that we didn't have enough preparation for the job.'

'I should like to handle the P.T.T. for the whole detachment,' explains the freckled captain, moving his chair up beside the major's, 'I like that. It's good fun. We've got the telephone service seventy-eight per cent restored down in

our kreiss. I like P.T.T. and I like "Political Parties" . . .'
'The captain was interested in politics back home,' the
lieutenant who came in with him interrupts teasingly. 'He
used to ride herd on the young Republicans in western
Kansas.'
The captain makes a pass toward him with the flat of his
hand, showing all his broad teeth in a grin. 'Don't tell 'em
that . . . that's old stuff. I've been getting the political
parties set up down in our kreiss. We've set up the Social
Democrats and now I've authorized the Communists. If they
do what they say they are going to do, it'll be real democratic. All their officers are to be elected in a party conven-
tion. . . . No cells taking orders from above or anything like
that. . . . The way these boys talk, it's democracy they want,
like back home. I gave 'em the green light.'
'We'll see how they work out,' said the major doubtfully.
'We ought to have more preparation,' the towheaded lieutenant was insisting. 'I work for a railroad back home. I
know something about railroading. If I say it myself, I know
something about the infantry. But I just don't have the
preparation for this job . . . I only had a highschool education . . .'
'I went to school all right at Charlottesville,' interrupted
an older man with glasses who had been a school superintendent back home, 'but most of the time I've had to throw the
book out of the window.'
'In this game you have to work by guess and by God,'
broke in a third man.
'It's surprising we do as well as we do with the conflicting
directives we get and the reports . . . my outfit sent in eighty-
seven separate reports last month . . . and redeployment takes
our best men as soon as they are broken in.'

'Everybody gets redeployed except Military Government officers.'

'We're Saturday's children all right. . . . They've got us frozen till March 2. . . . And promotion? Nix. Nobody ever heard of a promotion in Military Government.'

'And are we browned off?' They looked into each other's long faces and all burst out laughing. The girls hadn't been listening. They heard the laughter and joined in shrilly.

'And then some joker writes an article in the newspapers and calls us dregs,' said the captain who had been a school superintendent.

'Oh, my aching back.'

Mamma had brought in two more bottles of cognac. The major filled his glass and sent the bottles off round the table. The towheaded young lieutenant raised his glass.

'Hello, dregs,' he said.

We Tell the Germans

The lieutenant representing Military Government sits at his desk in a small Hessian town. Across the room is a stout German woman at a typewriter. Between them on a chair beside the telephone sits the pretty little darkhaired girl with a glum expression on her face who's the interpreter. Across the hall is an office full of German employees who keep coming to the door to ask for instructions. Beyond is an anteroom full of the local inhabitants. People don't mind waiting because here it is warm. In every other house in town it is cold.

The lieutenant is a young man with dark hair and a high forehead. The light glints on his glasses as he leans over his work. He's taught school in South Dakota and worked in a bank in a farming community in Minnesota.

'How many hats are you wearing at this moment, lieutenant?' I ask him.

He looks thoughtfully up at the ceiling which for some reason is papered with a hideous wallpaper in maple-leaf design. 'Eight, right at the moment, to be exact,' he answers. 'Let's see . . . Fiscal Matters, that's banking, Trade and Industry, Religion and Education, Transportation, Property Control, Public Utilities, Rationing and Price Control . . . Of course, all we do is supervise.'

While we are talking, a thinfaced man has been ushered in. He has three oil paintings of alpine scenes under his arm. He exhibits them indignantly to the lieutenant. American troops have been billeted in his house and have damaged these valuable paintings. A fourth artwork embroidered on silk has disappeared entirely. He points to a hole that might have been made by a bullet.

'Boys will be boys,' groans the lieutenant. 'Tell him to make his complaint in writing.'

He goes on with the paperwork on his desk. There's a man who wants to get a spare part for an Opel, the German equivalent of a Chevrolet. A requisition will have to be made out and he'll have to go over into the British zone and get it okayed by the British, because that's the only place where such parts are being manufactured. Then he can get his part and bring it back and put it in his car.

'Will the British make any difficulty?'

'No, we have good co-operation on things like that.'

'Suppose it was the French zone?'

'If anybody knows any way of getting anything out of the French zone, they haven't told me about it.'

'Or the Russian?'

'We don't talk about the Russian zone.'

There's a letter from an Evangelical minister who claims he was framed by the Nazis, who accused him of tickling the little girls in Sunday School, and placed him in jail. He wants to be reinstated.

There's a complaint from a chair factory that is all ready to reopen for business, denazified and all that, but can't get any screws.

A girl comes in bringing a handful of pure silver foil she's found in an unmarked package among the mass of lost and undeliverable packages being gone over at the postoffice. There's about fifty pounds of it. What shall she do with it?

'Send it to the Reichsbank.'

There's a man who wants to use a lot of demounted barracks buildings out at the airport, to build temporary homes for workers in an ex-war plant that's about to open to make agricultural machinery.

There's a long discussion as to whether five chairs upholstered in red velvet were or were not on the inventory of a house occupied by an outfit of engineers.

'If it weren't for the D.P.'s and the tactical units that want to occupy every house in town, I'd lead a quiet life,' said the lieutenant.

Meanwhile, a sharpfaced old German official with a long thin nose and flapping red ears has come in and sat down. He's the local banker in the denazified bank. There's a long discussion through the pretty interpreter, who looks glummer and boreder than ever, on the subject of what kind of reports must be turned in on the blocked accounts of Nazi depositors.

'Tell him every account, no matter how small, must show a separate report.'

This discussion is interrupted by a conversation over the

phone with the manager of the color and dye factory. They want to go to work, but they can't get any soda.

A ratfaced little man in a very large black overcoat with a greasy velvet collar is ushered in, trembling visibly.

'Oh, you're the man I wanted to see,' says the lieutenant cheerfully. 'We are authorized to open three movie theaters in three separate towns in the kreiss ... A kreiss is like a county,' he whispers for my benefit. 'But none of the owners is qualified, all been fragebogened out. Each theater must be placed in the hands of a trustee. I understand you only applied to run one. Well, you've been cleared. You are completely okay. At least that's the present report. You must go down to Frankfurt tomorrow to get film.'

The little man doesn't seem at all elated by the prospect. Still trembling, he backs out of the room nodding violently and saying, 'Yes sir, yes sir.'

'These people, you know, are the damnedest squealers,' said the lieutenant apropos of nothing. 'They are always turning each other in.'

The blackhaired girl looked from one to the other with the same glum pouting expression on her face and nodded gloomily.

Summary Justice

An American flag has been draped across the end of a German courtroom. In front of it sits a rosyfaced young American lieutenant with a serious look of concentration on his face, and beside him a frowsy German woman who's the interpreter. To his left on the next level down, a pompous-looking young German with a highbridged nose and tow hair stands behind a desk covered with papers. He's the prosecutor. On the other side sits the defense counsel. He is the judge of the local German court who acts as defense counsel when his court isn't sitting. He has the mane of stiff leonine irongray hair you see in engravings of the German romantics of the early nineteenth century, and a pair of flowing Bismarck mustaches, a picture of the oldtime German we would like to resurrect if we could.

The prisoner stands in the middle. From where we stand in the back of the courtroom we can't see his face, only a broad back with a head of dark hair drawn down into it in a posture of defiance. He's standing with his feet wide apart. His fists that clench and unclench slowly hang away from his body.

Through the long windows of the courtroom you can see the long greenish buildings with mossy tiled roofs that bound a pleasant market square where a few leaves still flutter on the plane trees between the peaked roofs and high pointed windows and the pinnacles of a big Gothic church beyond.

The prosecutor reads the charge in German and English. He's hardly finished when the prisoner growls out, 'Guilty.'

The young American officer, talking clearly and slowly, asks him through the interpreter if he understands the seriousness of the charge and what a plea of guilty means. He explains his rights in an American court, that it will be up to the prosecution to prove the charges against him. The prisoner exchanges a few words with his counsel in most uncordial tones. My friend the major nudges me. 'You see he's a Nazi and he thinks the judge is a collaborationist,' he whispers in my ear. The judge doesn't seem to care much for his client either.

The prisoner has changed his plea to not guilty on the first two counts and guilty on the third. He is charged with possession of firearms, including two pistols and ammunition for them, with failing to report said firearms and ammunition, and with forging his landlady's signature on the change of residence slip he turned in to the police. The arrest was made on the landlady's information. The police searched the room and found the weapons. A green young German policeman, with the look of a schoolboy reciting a lesson in class, is reciting the evidence against him.

'No use waiting for this case to be decided,' whispers the major who brought me into the courtroom. 'We can only give a year in this court. . . . This'll have to go up to the Intermediate Court that rides circuit. They'll give him plenty.'

Country Life

We're driving around Upper Hesse, the land of the Hessian mercenaries in the Revolutionary War. We visit a light and power plant that Allied aviation mysteriously spared in the bombings. The plant runs on brown coal taken from two mines, a couple of kilometers away, and supplies electricity to Frankfurt and Berlin. It's not as tidy as an American power plant, but it's running full blast.

We visit an immense Henkel plant in a group of modest-looking sheds that turned out aluminum castings for airplanes and highprecision instruments. Unfinished parts of airplane motors stand in the lathes and presses right where they were when the Americans came into town. The girl interpreter who's going around with us tells us that she was working there that day.

'Brr, it was cold in the unheated buildings,' she said. 'The nightshift worked that night, and then the Americans came and we all were sent home, and that was all.'

We begin to see Hessian peasants in their traditional dress. The women wear their hair pulled off their faces and tied up in a stiff little cylindrical knot on top of their heads. They wear embroidered blouses and black kneelength dresses flared out by innumerable petticoats. The men wear black smocks and kneebreeches over the same heavy knitted stockings the women wear. Some of them have eighteenth-century black felt hats. They all have a toyshop look of being whittled out of wood. The older people have grim nutcracker faces.

They slog along beside long wooden carts drawn by oxen or bulls or cows. Their wheelplows and heavy harrows seem antiquated. Here and there you even see a wooden plow. In every farmhouse yard, right under the front windows, you see the steaming manure piles that so intrigued Mark Twain. The long coffinshaped tanks on wheels are hauling tankage and human manure out to the fields. Like the Chinese, the Hessians can't afford to waste a thing. But the winter wheat looks good, the pasture land is dotted with little piles of manure.

Driving through one town we pick up a girl, employee of Military Government, who wants to go to the dentist in the next village. This turns out to be a village of Elizabethan half-timbered houses, with an unusually steaming and mountainous manure pile in every front yard. When we get to the dentist's, the officer who's taking me around suggests that we go in while the girl gets fixed up.

The dentist is a little ruddyfaced man with red ears and a sharp nose. His office is well equipped. He has a girl assistant. While he works on the girl's teeth, he talks to us Americans in a suave little offhand voice. His English is good. It's all about this one being a Nazi and that one being a Nazi. When we leave, the officer says to me in a tone of disgust, 'I just wanted you to take a look at this guy. He's the man who turned in his brother-in-law.'

The Worm Turns

When we get back to the inn where Military Government is lodged, we found the frecklefaced captain, up in his room, packing his bags. A droopy German woman in black, who used to live in New Jersey, is helping him. The pretty black-haired girl interpreter sits on the edge of the couch looking sour as ever.

'Well, Ed, we're moving,' the captain said to the lieutenant. 'I just got back from headquarters . . . talked to all the brass. They like what we've been doing down here. They like it so well they've given me everything I asked. I fixed up more things than you can shake a stick at. . . . First, I'm on the list to go home next month . . . I tell you I'm happy. . . . This is why' . . . he opened his wallet and handed me a photograph of a very pretty young blond girl, with a baby in her arms. 'Ain't that a good reason?' he said. 'Then for the rest of the month they told me I could either move on up to the major's with you and the rest of the boys. . . . You see, the I Detachments are coming in,' he added for my information. 'We'll just leave an office here. We'll work up where we were yesterday . . . or else I can go right to headquarters.'

He let himself drop on the couch between me and the girl, and turned to me confidentially. 'Do you know what I think I'm going to do? I've got my eye on a farm. I think maybe, instead of taking a job, I'll try raising me some chickens . . . I can buy the farm all right, but then I'll have to pay for it.'

The lieutenant was pacing up and down the room with his

lips pursed. 'Something has come up,' he said as soon as the captain stopped talking.

'What?'

'Becker.'

'What's the trouble with Becker?'

'He's been telling the girls in the office they have to clear through him if they want to keep their jobs. He's beginning to act like he was running this detachment.'

'Damn little rat. What business is it of his?' The captain jumped to his feet, 'I'll wring his neck . . . Excuse me,' he said, turning to me. 'The trouble with these krauts is if you give 'em an inch they take the whole cake . . . if you get what I mean.'

He strode out of the door into the hall. 'Hey, Karl,' we heard him calling. An obsequious elderly German voice answered from below. The captain came back into the room, showing all his teeth in a grin. 'That's our local cop. I told him to find Herr Becker and have him here in jigtime. I'll chew his ears off. . . . You see we're so shorthanded we have to give these krauts authority and then they abuse it.'

A little later, while we were eating our supper at the long polished oak table in the private diningroom downstairs, I saw through the open door into the hall a small young man wearing a belted raincoat who stood with his feet wide apart as if bracing himself for a shock. We hadn't seen him come in. He stood motionless in the hall watching us cautiously out of weasel eyes. He had a sharp little foxterrier face, light hair slicked back on his head, and protruding pink ears. When the captain caught sight of him, he gave a kind of growl and jumped up from the table. 'There's Becker,' he said, and strode toward him. Becker made a stiff bow while a smile like sugar molded his small girlish lips. They disappeared into another room. The lieutenant followed. From where I sat, I could hear their voices, the two gruff American voices laying down the law and the whining German voice winding in and out.

'Did you fire him?' I asked when the captain came back. He dropped glumly into his seat. 'Couldn't do that, he's too damned useful . . . I told him what's what. . . . What the hell, I'll be out of here in thirty days.'

We Call on the Burgomeister

After dinner the frecklefaced captain had to go to call on the burgomeister of the next town. We drove out of the dense night of the road into the denser squared-off night of an unlighted town. Feeling our way up the path to the burgomeister's door from the road, we could see by the flashlight that we were walking through solid beds of magnificent chrysanthemums. It was very gemühtlich in the burgomeister's warm well-lighted parlor. The oldtime Germany American students used to write home about forty years ago. The burgomeister was a wellset whitehaired man with granite features, an old Social Democrat, the Americans had found on the shelf somewhere and dusted off. His wife was stout and smiling. They had one plain and one goodlooking daughter. The Landrat was there, too, and his wife and son. The Landrat was a middleaged man with a keen sharp face that had an expression on it of a man accustomed to giving orders. They brought out little glasses of schnapps and a plate of tiny dry cakes.

The captain had a lot to tell them. His manner was breezy and cheerful, almost as if he were addressing a club of boosting young businessmen back home. He had arranged for some motion-picture houses to open. He had arranged that the pianist from Berlin who wanted to give concerts through the kreiss could give them; that was if he had written the right answers on his fragebogen. He was ready to open the Public Library.

Our hosts were smiling and friendly. The captain was showing his big white teeth and smiling all over his freckled face. It obviously gave him pleasure to be able to bring these good people some good news at last. We drank a toast. In German and English we pieced together a story they were trying to tell us about the books in the library. About the time of the book-burnings the people of this town had managed to make about three hundred volumes disappear. One man walled up his library with a brick wall. All these old pre-Nazi books were ready to go back into circulation.

'Well, tell the librarian to be at my office at eleven o'clock tomorrow morning,' said the captain. 'We'll fix the whole thing up then . . . Not a second later . . . if she wants to get her library open she'd better get there on time.'

The burgomeister poured out another round of schnapps.

Next morning we were calling on the same burgomeister in his office in the old town hall of the ancient walled hilltown. The captain had decided that before leaving he wanted to buy a Leica. Most of the cameras in the region had already been liberated, he told me, but the Landrat's son thought he knew where one was. While we waited in the burgomeister's office for the young man to come back, we studied the pictures of former burgomeisters on the wall. The oldest one was an etching of a splendid old fellow in a stock, with bristling hair. The next one was a photograph taken around 1880 of a benevolent-looking German official of the Bismarck period. The latest photograph was of a half-draft half-crafty-looking man with a soft sharp face.

'He was very rich,' explained the present incumbent, smiling at us from his desk. 'He died in 1936.' The Landrat's son came back into the office with a camera in his hand. While we were looking at it, a sharpfaced little German woman in a tweed suit burst into the room. She was talking fast German in a hysterical hissing voice. The gist of it was clear enough. The camera was hers. She didn't want to sell it. It was the last thing she had that was her dead husband's. The Americans had stolen everything she had in the shop, she shouted shrilly.

'I just wanted to buy it,' said the captain. 'I could take it, you know.'

She grabbed the camera off the desk and burst out through the padded doors of the burgomeister's office as fast as she came in.

'Nazi, Nazi, Nazi, Nazi,' murmured the burgomeister softly from his desk. He sat there vacantly wagging his old white head.

As we went out, the captain asked me, 'Did you notice the photograph of that last burgomeister, the one on the right? Didn't he have a little cross in his lapel?' I agreed that he had something in his lapel. 'He had something in his lapel that looked like a damn good imitation of a swastika. That picture will have to come down. That's our orders.'

German Saturday Night

It is a night of dense dripping fog. We sit drinking cognac and water at the officers' club. The club occupies the ground-floor of a hunting lodge that belonged to a wealthy German family. As we came in, we had been greeted by a grizzled stuffed bird on a pedestal that someone insisted was a specimen of the greater bustard. Every inch of wallspace was taken up by rows of small horns of roebucks with the date and place of decease carefully written out on the triangular piece of bone attached to each pair. Interspersed between them were early nineteenth-century English prints and photographs of groups of whiskered men on horseback in the uniforms of the First World War. In a back room a German orchestra was having tough sledding with 'Night and Day.' A few officers were dancing with German girls, but most of them sat on the leather couches, around the walls, staring into their cognac. The girls were fairly pretty, the officers were healthylooking freshfaced young men. There was plenty to drink. But girls and men looked hopelessly depressed. Crêpe curtains of homesickness and Saturday-night blues were settling down on the room so thick you could feel them. When the music stopped, the place was absolutely still.

All through the dancing, the plump officer who'd been a police sergeant in Brooklyn had been sitting alone at a small round table with his head in his hands. Suddenly he lifted up a round woebegone countenance, and with a voice stiff with gloom croaked out . . . 'It's not the duty . . . I don't mind it when I'm on duty. As long as I can keep busy, I feel all right . . . It's the recreation that hurts.'

Bad Wiessee, Bavaria, November 6, 1945

2

The Vienna Frontier

The Road Through the Russian Zone

ALL AFTERNOON we had been passing long strings of covered wagons. It was a captured division on its way home to Hungary. The Hungarians had been given some Wehrmacht horses, and turned loose. Dressed in scraps of uniforms from every army in Europe they sat with their feet on the tongues of the brokendown farm wagons rigged with makeshift canvas covers, and jogged along in the rain. Beside them, in a confusion of bedding and cookstoves and pots and pans and cradles, hunched their women with their heads tied up in handkerchiefs and their ragged holloweyed children. As the road wound amid thickening twilight through the ravines of the foothill country, we saw their little campfires flickering red among beechwoods carpeted with brown leaves.

By the time we reached Linz, we began to get the feeling of the frontier. Linz was a gray stony place of narrow streets choked with raw rivermist off the Danube. A few American soldiers roamed lonesomely on the edges of a long square with a weatherworn baroque fountain in the middle of it. The tall old gray buildings were just battered enough from the bombings to wear a look of unspeakable wretchedness in the chill glare of a single unshaded streetlight. The mist was beginning to freeze into sleet. We took a walk to get our feet warm.

When we tried to cross the Danube bridge a grinning military policeman hauled us back. 'Can't go over there without a pass. That's the Russian zone,' he said.

'How do you get along with the Russians?'

'We get along with 'em all right. They are kinder crude,' he said. 'They don't seem eddicated.'

Opposite the fountain there was a small hotel that had been taken over by the Army for transient officers. The bedrooms were off a narrow stone court open to the sleet and the night. My room was icily cold, with two beds in it hard as rock, with no cover except a feather bed tailored to the size of a very small dwarf. If anybody denies the Germans are barbarians, all they have to do is try to sleep in their beds. I had crawled into everything woolen I had and was composing myself shiveringly to sleep when the light flashed on and I found a fresh-faced young American captain smiling down at me. He was so tall and broad I wondered how he would ever fold himself into that other feather bed. He had black hair and black eyes and very regular white teeth. He apologized for waking me and explained that the second bed in my room was the only one left in the hotel. There was something about the way he pronounced his vowels that reminded me of the way the Pennsylvania Mennonites speak English. As he got undressed, he talked in a friendly cornbelt way. He was from Iowa, a German, he said with a flashing smile. He was with a tank destroyer outfit.

'My people are Germans' — there was a little 'b' in his 'p' when he said people — 'but they've been in Iowa eighty years. We belong to one of those religious communities. I'm one of those few farmboys who want to go back to the farm. I've got the points, but I'm only going home on leave. My outfit is up in Czechoslovakia and I'm down here on a fourday leave right now. You see there is a complication.' He let his boots drop to the floor with a thud. 'I'm going to marry a Sudeten girl. She's German. I've been going with her four months. We want to get married. She speaks very good English. She's highly educated. She's come down here to get a job in one of the American offices. They are running all the Germans out of Czechoslovakia. It's rugged. An eye for an eye, you know. . . . Anyway, she'll be safe here in Linz working for the Americans. If I could marry her right now, we could go home together, but we can't, so I've got to go home and tell the folks about it. I want to go home in the worst way and grow some corn, but there's this complication . . . Goodnight,' he said cheerfully and abruptly as he strode across the room in his underclothes to turn off the light.

Next morning after breakfast we drove out of Linz into flat brown country under a low sleety sky. At a short bridge we crossed into the Russian zone. As soon as he saw the sentry at the American end let our car by, the sentry at the Russian end swung up his bar. We drove through an empty village with a few slogans in Russian and a few fluttering red flags. After that we began to pass grimy soldiers with high cheekbones driving narrow wooden wagons. A holloweyed officer with a red band on his cap was bowling along in an ancient victoria with a yellow wicker body. Bundled up on the driver's seat was the flatfaced izvozchik of all the droshkies in Russian literature.

In the last pass before Vienna, where the road wound up in

a series of hairpin turns between high rounded hills, the sleet became heavy blobs of snow. The road was deep in slush. As the turns grew sharper, we got tangled in a convoy of American lendlease trucks with Russian markings on them. They were driven by bigeyed young Slavs who had an appealing coltish look of being right out of the isba. Every other truck was towing a truck that had broken down. As we sludged up into the pass the snow grew deeper. The Russians were slithering all over the road. Right up at the summit there was fog as well as snow. There the trucks had stalled entirely. They wallowed zigzagged every which way across the road. Here and there a truck had slid over the edge and tilted out over the void in the grip of the gnarled trees and bushes of the roadside. The Russians in their long coats stood around helplessly in groups shaking their heads and thrashing their arms to keep warm.

The driver of our car was a skinny young fellow with a hawk face and a gray eye from Louisiana, Missouri. He was a man of few words, but when he spoke, in a voice that had a raw Missouri twang to it, he liked to make it count. He was grinning as he skidded the car neatly through the deep snow round the ends of the stalled trucks. 'No use our buyin' those boys trucks,' he said finally. 'They can't maintain 'em.'

At last we shook ourselves loose from the convoy and began to loop down through the fog into the lowlands where the snow became sleet and rain again. The villages had a dead and empty look. We came to a sharp turn of the road where a group of Russian soldiers stood around a decorated arch made of firboughs strung with red and green paper festoons. The firboughs and the flat Slav faces and the red and green decorations against the broken-down houses banked with snowdrifts yellow and pitted from the rain, and the way the Rus-

sians in their high boots stood in a group under the arch as if
they were about to break into song, made me think of all the
choruses in all the Russian operas I'd ever seen. It was amazing to find yourself so deep in Russia so soon. A rednosed
sentry with a tommygun let us through another barricade.
We crossed some railroad tracks encumbered with rusting
engines and splintered freightcars. We caught a dim glimpse
of the façade of Schoenbrun through the mist and very soon
we were driving through the broad empty raindrenched
avenues of Vienna.

Filter Between East and West

Vienna is heartbreaking. The city has been dying by inches
since the collapse of the Hapsburg system in World War One
left it a capital without an empire, but even after all these
decades of slow strangulation and the Nazi butcheries and the
Allied bombings and the brutalities of the Russian armies, it
still wears a few of the airs and graces of a metropolis. Vienna
is an old musical comedy queen dying in the poorhouse, who
can still shape her cracked lips into the confident smile of a
woman whom many men have loved, when the doctor makes
his rounds of the ward. There is still a touch of Viennese grace
about the beautiful old buildings and the manners of the people. In the small hotel that's been taken over for the American press there's something about the pink chandeliers and the
lace curtains in the tall windows of the diningroom and the
half-teasing obsequiousness of the headwaiter with his tail-
coat and his dyed mustaches that you could find only in Vienna. In all the poverty and humiliations of the war years
the city has not quite forgotten that it once saw great days.
The shivering misery of the people in the streets, the burnt-

out filigree of Saint Stephen's Cathedral, the shattered baroque façades, the boarded-up shops, the grassgrown ruins, seem more touching here than in the cities of Germany proper. Perhaps it is because the destruction was not so complete. Much of the frame of the city remains.

The parks and squares have been dug up for airraid shelters. Wherever there is a patch of grass you see a scattering of the white crosses of the graves of the Russians who died in their assault on the city. The wide avenues of the Ring with their rows of trees are empty and desolate. The palaces and museums and the offices of the old imperial administration, the acres of masonry in all the styles of the eighteenth and nineteenth centuries stand burned-out and bombed-out and vacant. All that remains of the Hapsburgs is their statuary. Vast bronze groups of men and horses and symbolic figures, celebrating forgotten achievements of forgotten reigns, writhe monumentally at the end of every vista, giving the empty city the look of a half-demolished world's fair.

In spite of all the failures of the last quarter century, the life that is starting up again in the ruins takes on a semblance of the old pattern. In the stately halls of unheated government buildings groups of cadaverous men shiver in their overcoats waiting to see the minister. In the Chancellery where Dolfuss was murdered a grimfaced youngish man with a head of coarse yellow hair is making a statement of protest to the world press from the end of a long green baize table in a splendid eighteenth-century room which has lost half its ceiling, but is still ornamented with mirrors wreathed in gold cupids. He is handing out those same little booklets embellished with maps and tables of figures on slick paper illustrating the sorrows of a misplaced national minority (this time it's Carinthia) that I can remember littering the corridors of Versailles.

In a lecture hall in another building a tall man in black with a pale square scarred head is delivering an address on the position of Austria in foreign affairs. He is saying that Vienna as the capital of a new Austrian republic will find new life as an interpreter and filter between the eastern Europe that will grow up with its face turned toward Moscow and the western Europe that will grow up with its face turned toward Washington.

In the small Gothic chapel hung with crimson damask in the royal palace the famous boys' choir that sang Mass for so many centuries Sunday mornings for the Hapsburgs and the dignitaries of their court still sings the cheerful Schubert Masses. The only difference is that now it's American and English and French gold braid that the aged beadles obsequiously seat in the gallery.

Though many of the auditoriums are ruined, all the theaters are open. Concert programs offer more good music in a week than you could hear in a month in New York. 'Nightclubs,' operating from six to eight-thirty in the evening, put on songs and political skits that people crowd in to see even if there is nothing to eat and nothing to drink. In cafés, uncleaned and unheated, people sit reading the newspapers over cups of the moldy-tasting dark gruel called coffee that has become truly the national drink of the European Continent.

'What do you eat?' you ask people.

'Bread and dried peas,' they answer.

'How do you get the money to buy the rations?'

By selling furniture or extra clothes or themselves, they answer. When things get too bad, they say the Americans will feed them. There's no business or industry. Outside of bakeries you can count on your fingers the stores that are open. The black market which the M.P.'s of four nations vie with

each other in harrying out of existence in the Nachmarkt is
pathetically small for a city the size of Vienna. At night the
unlit streets, encumbered by great squared-off heaps of brick
and stone from ruined buildings, are full of robbery and violence variously attributed to deserters, to Russians, and to
displaced persons in general. After dark as in medieval days a
man goes out at his own risk. If you wander off your beat,
poking around the rubbish of Beethoven's and Mozart's city,
you are pretty sure eventually to come against a broadshouldered young Russian sentry who shouts 'Hallo' and impas-
sively pokes a tommygun in your middle, staring at you the
while with a cowlike stare off the great steppes.

Our Ukrainian Schoolteacher

Although you see plenty of Russians on the streets and
waiting in line at the ticket offices of theaters and concerts,
it's remarkably hard to get hold of a Russian to talk to. The
obvious hindrance is that very few Russians of the present
generation speak any foreign language but German and that
virtually no Americans speak Russian. A higher hurdle than
the language difficulty is the fact that for nearly thirty years
now the only view of the world outside the Soviet Union its
citizens have had has been through the distorting prism of
Marxist propaganda. Every Soviet citizen feels that a bitter
two-way hostility exists between him and the capitalist
world; and added to that is the wellfounded and pressing fear
in the back of his head that any contact with foreigners will
be misinterpreted by the dangerous snoopers of the NKVD.

Among Americans of all ranks I found, on the other hand,
in Vienna particularly, a great deal of friendly curiosity about
what lay behind the impenetrable boundaries of the Soviet

power and an almost pathetic desire to lean over backwards to understand Russian needs and Russian prejudices. After considerable scouting around, I found an American officer who not only knew Russian and Russia but who knew a Russian. He generously invited us both for a drink at his hotel and afterwards several of us had dinner with the Russian in the hotel's little private diningroom that was paneled in shiny dark wood and hung with English hunting prints and prickly with the horns of small deer.

Our friend wore a major's uniform. He was a typical broadfaced Ukrainian, short and deepchested with light crinkly hair. He said he was looking forward to being demobilized soon and sent home to his small home town in the Ukraine where he taught literature in the normal school. He lectured on American literature particularly. He was enthusiastic about the works of Dreiser and Mark Twain and Sinclair Lewis. *Uncle Tom's Cabin* was one of his favorite American novels. He spoke of novels of mine and of his disappointment that I had not written any work saluting the achievements of the Soviet Union in the war. If I did, he said, smiling, I should come to Russia to see how warmly the Russian people would welcome a writer.

American liberals, he said, were all mixed up about the problems of equality. Wages should be graduated according to a man's value to society. If a man had two left hands he certainly shouldn't earn as much as a man who turned out firstclass work. The more valuable a man was to society, the better living quarters he ought to have, the better car, the better trips to watering places. Trying to even up the wages of a ditchdigger with two left hands and an irreplaceable brainworker was capitalist equalitarianism and a great mistake.

That got us onto the slippery slope of the word 'democracy.' He put in a couple of hot shots on the horror he felt that anybody in a capitalist democracy such as America should be so base as to sell his vote. No soviet citizen would do a thing like that. Who would buy it? asked one of the Americans under his breath. The remark was not translated. In the Soviet Union, the schoolteacher was saying, a man's chief pride was his right to vote. Electoral campaigns were going on at home right now. No, in Russian elections they did not vote on policies, only on personalities. Of course, there was only one candidate, but there was discussion before the nominations. The campaign was not about a man's opinions, but about his qualifications. The voter wanted to know which was the most intelligent, most experienced, best educated man for the job. The campaign going on right now for nominations to the various committees and soviets was the liveliest he ever remembered.

He understood, he said, turning to me with a suspicious narrowing of the eyes, that I was Republican. I tried to explain that I sometimes voted Republican and sometimes Democratic or even Socialist, and sometimes split the ticket. We tried to explain what it meant to split the ticket, but we never got anywhere. He felt I was stalling and had some deep motive for getting out of telling him what my politics were. We got to floundering so helplessly between the two languages that the whole thing got to be a joke and we fell to laughing. The little major was as suspicious of his capitalist friends as a Connecticut farmer out with a bunch of bookmakers, but whenever the situation began to get strained, we managed to save it by shooting in a toast or two to our brave allies. Then his enthusiasm for acquiring information about American literature would get the better of his suspicions of the agents of

Wall Street and he'd be quite easy and friendly. The party broke up in great goodhumor.

We both said goodnight to our hosts at the door of the hotel and were on the point of walking off down the dark street together when the little major suddenly bethought himself and drew back into the doorway. I said goodnight and walked off. After a few seconds, he started off in the same direction, taking care to let me keep ahead of him. I have no doubt that the reason he drew back was because he was afraid the wrong person might see him walking down the street with an American.

The Game of Russian Poker

In the office building occupied by the American end of the quadripartite Military Government, I went around asking men on various shelves of the military hierarchy how they got along with the Russians. The question caused consternation. Some men shut up completely at the mere word. Nobody wanted to be quoted.

On the carpet level, as they call it, that is, on the level of the working committees where the details of local affairs are thrashed out, I found several types of American reactions. Officials who had arrived with high idealistic hopes were usually thoroughly discouraged by their experiences with what they called the arrogance and the doubledealing and the lack of regard for the rights of man of the Russians with whom they negotiated, and spoke darkly and bitterly of the dangers ahead. Then there was a type of official who made a sort of personal specialty of getting along with the Russians and who was on the defensive about it and seemed to regard the fact that his soviet opposite number said good morning with a smile when they met as proof that they had reached a basis of give-and-take co-operation. The West Pointers were doing, on the whole I think, the best job. They were most of them ignorant of Russian history and Russian ways as only an American can be ignorant of a foreign country, but they were dealing with the Russian officers on an 'as one military man to another' basis and meeting problems as they came up by rule of thumb. The discipline and the limited frame of reference of the military mind and its instinctive patriotism was on the whole serving them well.

'If we could only treat Austrian questions separately on their own merits we wouldn't get along so badly,' a man who was near the top of the heap told me, 'but you soon learn that every little item that comes up is considered by the Russians as part of their hand in the great international poker game. . . . We're not really qualified to play that game because we don't know the rules. What we've been trying to do is to get them to put their cards on the table and to tell us what they want, but that seems to be against their religion.'

It becomes clearer every day to the men on the ground that the British and Americans began their game in the privacy of the Big Three conclaves at Teheran and Yalta and Potsdam by dealing out all the trumps to the Russians. They tell you that whoever thought up the plan of placing the quadripartite governments of Berlin and Vienna in zones ruled by the Russians certainly deserves a red star from the Kremlin. The fact that their allies were at a military disadvantage has given the Russians a method of applying gentle pressure that they have not been at all shy about using. The more I talked with the men who were actually racking their brains over the details of the problem of setting up a republican government and a going economy in Austria, the more it came out that the surprising thing was not how badly they got along with the Russians, but how well they got along with them. In optimistic mood men would tell you that, even if we failed completely in accomplishing whatever we were trying to accomplish in Europe, we would at least have trained some army officers and some civilian officers in the art of international poker, Russian style. It was a game we could learn as well as we had learned to build airfields or to organize supply. If we were to keep our heads up as a nation in the very peculiar world we had inherited from the political defeats of World War Two, we damn well had to learn it. 'We never could understand why Hitler made the mistake of jumping the Russians,' said one official in an unguarded moment. 'Now we understand. He had them as allies.'

Tales of the Vienna Woods

Our Missouri driver came in and stood silently beside the table where we were eating breakfast, with his inimitable 'Now you ask me one' expression on his face.

'Is the car running?' we asked.

He shook his head. 'Valves,' he said gently.

'When will they get it fixed?'

'Two days,' he said, in the tone of man breaking the news of a death in the family.

'Well, you wanted to see Vienna.'

'I'm seein' it,' he answered mysteriously. As he started to drift out of the diningroom, he let drop a trailing remark. 'Pretty near got held up last night.'

'When? How? Tell us about it.'

'Well, I got a buddy here I knew in camp back in the States. We got hold of a jeep and was cruisin' around to look

over the town when we picks us up a couple fräuleins. Mine
was a real nice girl. No, she said, she never stepped out with
no Yanks nor nobody, but she said she'd just as soon go ridin'
with us. . . . She took me out to see her grandmother. Well,
we were walkin' around last night. They don't live so far
away . . . Over that way' — he pointed with his thumb over
his shoulder — 'when up comes this Russian an' tries to grab
my wristwatch. I pulled my gun an' started shootin'. You'd
oughta seen him run.'

'Did you hit him?' we asked, but Missouri was already
striding out of the diningroom. 'See you tomorrer,' he said.

So we toured the town in a jeep instead of in the comfortable
civilian car that had brought us from Munich. As we drove
past the Russian headquarters building, where an American
soldier on the tip of the tall extensible ladder of one of the big
red municipal fire engines was busy tinkering with the strings
of electric lights that festooned the oversized countenances of
Lenin and Stalin that decorated its façade, we heard a military
band playing. British troops were drawn up in front of the
Allied Kommandatura around the corner. We got out of the
jeep and joined a scattered group of Viennese who stood
watching the proceedings from the bushes of a little park in
the square opposite. A column of chasseurs led by a band and
a tricolor came swinging into sight. There were military
evolutions, present arms, parade rest, and all the civilians
took their hats off reverently while the *Marseillaise* and *God
Save the King* were played. This changing of the guard at the
Kommandatura meant that the British brasshat who had finished his month's command of the inner city of Vienna was
giving way to his French opposite number. The illdressed
illfed civilians around me, some of them with briefcases under
their arms, were obviously most of them waiting for the

pageantry to clear away before going to wait in line at one of
the Allied offices in the Kommandatura. Their faces betrayed
no impatience. Some seemed to be looking at the military
show with a certain rapture.

I asked my friend who spoke German please to ask the grayfaced man in a green Tyrolean hat on my left how he liked it.
'Schoen,' he answered smartly. 'It makes gay.'
'It's glass I'm thinking about, window-glass. The British
promised us window-glass. Now will we get it under the
French?' was what a small yellowtoothed man with a scraggly
mustache said. 'What else is there to think about?'

My friend wanted to show me the famous deep airraid
shelter Baldur von Schirach built for himself out on the edge
of the city where the famous Vienna woods begin. On the
way we stopped at a school. This school was on the street of
workers' apartments where the Austrian ex-taxidriver who
was driving our jeep lived. It was a very good school, he said,
because it had glass in the windows. Very few schools had
glass. We asked him whether he had any children. No, he
said, his brother-in-law with whom he'd doubled up when his
apartment was wrecked had children. He and his wife had no
children. In these times that was something to thank God for.

The principal of the school was a stubby man with gray
hair clipped very short on his gray head and a shortclipped
mustache. He wore a gray alpaca jacket. He had been forty
years in this school he told us with some pride. He had studied in it as a pupil, he had taught in it as a teacher, and now he
directed it as a principal. I asked my friend to ask him as tactfully as possible how he had managed to weather all the political changes that had taken place in Vienna during these
years. 'Politics is alien to pedagogy,' he answered stiffly, and
made a little washing motion with his hands.

Wouldn't the American officers like to see the classes in English? he asked with an obsequious smile.

In the first classroom we went into, the teacher, a tall dark-browed woman who obviously was wearing all the clothes she possessed, was shivering so from the cold her teeth chattered as she spoke. The children — this happened to be a class of little boys around eight or nine — didn't look exactly starving, but they certainly didn't look well nourished. They looked definitely worse off than the children we'd seen in Nuremberg a few days before. 'Of course, we have always taught English,' said the principal in his ingratiating whisper, 'but now we are intensifying the study of English and in the higher grades Russian.' The shivering teacher made a redeyed little wretch get up and recite a rhyme in English about a pussycat being cozy and warm, and I felt like crying.

'The trouble is,' said the principal as he escorted us down the hall, 'that we shall have to close soon on account of the cold, and then where will the children go? Already they come here early to do their lessons because the school is warmer than their homes. At home they have nothing. You see' — he rubbed his hands with selfsatisfaction — 'we have windows.'

By the time we got out to the police station where a police inspector was to give us the key to Baldur von Schirach's airraid shelter, it had come on to rain again. This police station was in the French zone. When we got into the big inside room divided by a wide counter, we found ourselves in the midst of a confused scene of some kind.

A stocky young man in civilian clothes with a heavy stony countenance was being held up against the counter by two young towheaded Austrian policemen. Roundabout there

milled a crowd of Viennese bystanders and of local plainclothes men with faces out of an oldfashioned Punch and Judy
show, all talking German at once. Behind the counter a number of Frenchmen in various French military uniforms gesticu-
lated and talked French around a stocky youth with light
curly hair in the uniform of a Soviet private who was making
a speech presumably in Russian. He was so much in earnest
that his eyes kept filling with tears. He kept saying the same
thing over and over again and making the same gestures,
starting with his index finger held high as in the statues of
Lenin and bringing it down sharply to his waist. In his
other hand he held somebody's identification card that he
occasionally shook in the faces of the Austrian police.

Meanwhile from the open door of an inner office came in
loud counterpoint the rattle of an altercation in French. The
stonyfaced prisoner wasn't saying a word. The inspector was
desolated, came a message from one of the Austrian plainclothes men, but would we come back in half an hour. He
was very busy.

As we started out the door, I found myself in conversation
with a Frenchman in a big blue béret. 'Qu'ils nous emmer-
dent ces russes,' he cried out. 'Every day every hour it is the
same . . . The Russians are committing a rape. The Russians
have knocked down an old woman in the street and are steal-
ing her clothes. The Russians are pillaging a house . . . Two
of our own detectives were seized in a doorway and stripped
to their drawers. A man walks home with his wife and sees
her raped before his eyes. A little child of nine shoots it out
with the cops with a revolver comme le Wild West. A man
buys a bag of beans and they break into his apartment and
steal it . . . Monsieur, it is fatiguing . . . The life in Vienna
is fatiguing.'

We went to a local café to wait until the police inspector had a moment of leisure. The café was operating, but it had the look of having been closed up for years. The floors were unswept. The springs were bursting through the upholstery on the benches. The marble tables were cracked and grimed. It seemed even colder inside than in the icy downpour on the street. The waiter was very polite and kept up a pathetic mummery of service, bringing us our ersatz coffee with glasses of water on a neat tray with fittings that in the old days had held sugar and cream. In the cream pitcher there was a little extra hot water.

We had hardly started talking about the miserable weather with the waiter when a friend of the man who was interpreting for me came up to the table and was introduced to me as a journalist. He was a thin middleaged man with a long wrinkled diamondshaped face and colorless lips. He wore his hair parted in the middle and oldfashioned blackrimmed pincenez. We asked him to have a cup of the ersatz coffee with us.

'What is it made of?' I asked.

'That is our secret,' he said, smiling.

I asked him which of their liberators the Viennese liked the best.

The French, he answered pat, because there were so few of them. I must forgive him, he went on, but he had to speak of the bitter disillusionment of the Viennese. They had expected too much of their liberators. They had expected the Americans to bring food and businesslike vigor in the management of affairs. They had expected the Russians to bring new ideas, new things, perhaps terrible things but new things. But neither had brought anything new or vigorous. There was nothing new in starvation and looting and murder and rape. There was nothing new in bureaucratic stagnation.

Now things were improving. General Konev had given a great reception and appeared arm in arm with General Clark under the floodlight like in Hollywood at the head of a great stairway in the Hofburg. Now perhaps the liberators would get together enough to let something be done . . . General Clark was a very handsome man. The Viennese liked handsome men. There was a story that he walked around the city a great deal with only a soldier interpreter, talking to people he met on the street and asking how they were faring.

That was true, I said.

'When we think of Konev we think of tommyguns and spotlights,' said the Viennese journalist, 'but when we think of Clark we think of a friend . . . Naturally we like our friends . . . But suppose our friend is unable to accomplish anything for us. And we can't wait. We are sinking. Always he is saying to General Konev, "Let's help the poor Viennese, let's get to work and start up Austria," and Konev he steps into the spotlight and smiles and says, "Yes, let's get things started," but it turns out that Konev is not alone. There is the man who says no. There is Herr Djeltov, the big bullnecked man from the Kremlin, and when he says no it stays no.'

The waiter stood by listening with a frown on his face.

The journalist gave a high cackling laugh. 'You mustn't pay too much attention to what we Viennese say,' he said in a different tone of voice. My interpreter sounded relieved. The waiter's forehead cleared. 'We are a little weak in the head because we have not much in the stomach.'

'People in Vienna,' said my interpreter apologetically as we left the café, 'have started to talk again. After all these years it goes to our heads.'

When we got back to the police station after three quarters

of an hour, we found the same characters still grouped on either side of the counter. Everybody was quieter. The center of the stage was held by two Russian Military Police officers who were listening gravely with white impassive faces to a long explanation in German by one of the plainclothes men.

The police inspector, a youngish man with tousled curly hair who had the distracted air of an elocution teacher trying to rehearse a highschool play when the cast is getting out of hand, rushed up to us full of apologies and explained breathlessly to my interpreter that the truth was coming out. The stonyfaced young man was a Russian who had been arrested for pillaging, but nobody knew if he was a deserter from the Red Army or from Vlassov's pro-German army or whether he had been brought to Vienna for labor by the Germans. 'The documents are conflicting. The translation is difficult.' The young Russian soldier had seen the arrest going on and had intervened. The man was a Soviet citizen, he had said, and the Austrians had no right to lay hands on him. Now the Russian officers were trying to find out what he was.

By the time my friend had explained this to me in English, the police inspector had started addressing me in French. If we didn't mind we would see the shelter in the Wienerwald another day. He himself was desolated, but he couldn't leave. He must explain it all in French to the French commander who was waiting in the office, but he couldn't explain it yet because the Russians hadn't made up their minds whether the young man was a deserter or a prisoner of war or a displaced person.

Didn't he have papers? I asked.

Papers, yes, but there were so many different kinds of papers. The Russian didn't read itself easily.

Threatening voices in French came from the inner office.

The police inspector ran off in the direction with his fists tightly clenched in his curly hair.

Meanwhile the prisoner, who had sat down on a bench by this time, had started to croak something in a kind of German. He wants to go to the latrine my interpreter whispered in my ear in the tone of a man translating the action of a play. When the young Russian soldier saw the Soviet citizen led out by two policemen, he burst into his speech again, this time directing it at the Russian Military Police officers. Everybody started trying to explain to him that he wasn't going far. But he refused to be consoled. Tears spurted out of his eyes. The last we saw of him as we left the police station, he was shouting 'Soviet Citizen' and standing with his right hand with index finger outstretched high above his head in the attitude of the statues of Lenin.

Vienna, November 10, 1945

3

Nuremberg Diary

Nuremberg, November 19

THE DAY is bright and cold. A sharp sun searches out every detail of the heaped ruins of the old city of toymakers and meistersingers, points up the tall slender arches of smashed churches, rounds out the curves of broken bits of renaissance carving. In an open space in the rubbish near the nineteenth-century bronze statue of Albrecht Dürer, German women in coats and sweaters, surrounded by a pack of towheaded children, are putting potatoes to boil in a stove made out of a torn sheet of galvanized roofing. We ask them where they live. They point to the concrete entrance of an airraid shelter that opens beside the chipped pedestal of the statue. A man we talk to has just arrived from Breslau. He is a farmer dispossessed by the Poles. As we turn to leave, a little shower of stones comes our way from some bigger children who are playing on top of a mountain of bricks and ground-up stone. When we look up, they dash out of sight behind tottering walls. On a wall down the street a freshly chalked swastika stares us in the face.

Out at the great battered building in fake medieval style of the old Bavarian Palace of Justice there is a great bustle of jeeps, command cars, and converted German busses. Military Police scrutinize your pass. A tank with a star on it nestles nonchalantly against the wall beside the entrance. Inside, a sound of sawing echoes through the long vaulted corridors. German prisoners of war on stepladders are applying a fresh coat of waterpaint to the walls. Battalions of German scrubwomen in clean dresses and heavy knitted stockings rammed into big boots are swabbing the marble floors. Thronging the corridors are Americans in uniform and out of uniform with a familiar Washington look about their faces.

The vaults resound with the cheerful clack of the heels of American girl secretaries. There are French lady reporters in highpiled Paris turbans. There are Russians and whispering Britishers. There are all the uniforms of the four nations. There's a Post Exchange and a snackbar and a Washington-style cafeteria. In the offices the furnishings have quite an American look, but out of the thick stone walls of the echoing corridors of the old German courthouse and jail, there oozes a sweat of misery Teutonic and alien.

It's the day before the trial. People are a little edgy. They wag their heads and tell you the trial won't start on time. The French are peevish. The Russians have asked for a delay. Press conferences are inconclusive. In the freshly redecorated courtroom with its sage-green curtains and crimson chairs, it's like the dress rehearsal of an amateur play. Interpreters sit behind their glass screen practicing with the earphones. The electricians are testing out the great clusters of floodlights that hang from the ceiling. An American sergeant, with the concerned look of a propertyman, is smoothing out the folds of the four flags that stand behind the judges' dais. Guards with white helmet linings on their heads and white batons

and white pistol-holsters are being shown their stations. The
cast is jumpy. How are we ever going to be able to get the
curtain up tomorrow?

Down the long hall there's a deserted office from which you
can look down through a broken window into a little exercise
yard planted with skinny trees and patches of grass cut into
picture-puzzle shapes by crisscrossing cement paths. Several
men in American fieldjackets, each an equal distance from the
other, are walking briskly about. American guards stride
watchfully among them. We can see the rifle of the guard on
the parapet below pass and repass under the window. We
look at them for a while in silence, keeping back from the
window to be out of sight of the guard. 'Funny to think
those guys may hang in a couple of months,' blurts out somebody. 'They look like anybody.'

'In spite of everything I could do,' said Colonel Andrus at his
afternoon press conference, 'one of my prisoners got sick.' The
colonel looked heartbroken. Colonel Andrus — he hated to be
called the jailor, but that was what he was — was a worried-
looking man with a round face and glasses and a closeclipped
mustache. He had a timid smile. His hairbrush haircut gave
him an incongruously boyish look. He spoke of his prisoners
as if they were a set of dangerous but valuable zoological
specimens that had to be kept in good health at whatever cost.
Intense preoccupation with the importance of his task seemed
to have sharpened the military punctilio of originally mild
and disarming manners. The prisoner he was speaking of was
Kaltenbrunner. He added:

'There has occurred a spontaneous hemorrhage of a small
blood vessel in the back of the cranium. I'll read you the
Latin name. It is not really dangerous . . . More severe it

would have been fatal. It will be impossible for him to appear in court tomorrow. This li'l' hemorrhage is being stopped, but he will have to be kept completely quiet for some time.'

'Did he say anything?' asked a reporter.

The colonel picked up a paper off his desk. He read it off slowly and carefully: '"I am very sorry I cannot be in court tomorrow" was what the prisoner remarked.'

'What caused him to take sick?' asked another reporter.

'His illness was caused by stress of emotion. He has been hysterical for the last three weeks. He has had crying fits in his cell. He is the bully type, strong and hard when on top, cringing and crying when not,'answered the colonel. 'He's much influenced by the period of excitement and worry lately.'

No, Colonel Andrus could not tell which hospital he had been taken to. He was receiving suitable care in a United States Army hospital, that was all he could say. Otherwise the behavior of the prisoners had been uniformly correct. Hess had gained slightly in health, weight, and appearance since his arrival. He complained of abdominal cramps. . . . Frank arrived with a partial paralysis of the left wrist due to selfinflicted wounds . . . improved under heat treatment. . . . Frick's condition was essentially negative, not ill but not very vigorous. . . . Funk had complained of a variety of pains and aches largely imaginary. . . . Goering now admitted that he was in better health than he had been in twenty years. His drug habit had been eliminated. His nervous heart palpitation had disappeared. He had reduced to two hundred and twenty pounds. He had no organic heart ailment of any kind. . . . Jodl's lumbago had been cured by heat treatment. . . . Keitel had a little difficulty with flat feet due to insufficient exercise, now eliminated by exercise. . . . Von Ribbentrop

had suffered some neuralgia which had been relieved by heat
treatment. . . .

'Where was this heat treatment given?'

'It was all given in their cells.'

'Colonel, what are the prisoners going to wear?'

'That has been a problem. I have had to scrounge clothes
for them. Those who have presentable uniforms will wear
them, but without badges or insignia. Those who have no
clothes of their own have been issued conservative irongray
civilian suits and conservative pinstriped shirts.'

'What is their state of mind, Colonel?'

'The prisoners show no sign of emotion. Their attitude is
thoughtful. . . . At seven o'clock they get up and clean their
cells with a broom and a mop. They have cereal for breakfast. . . . For dinner today they had soup, hash, spaghetti,
and coffee. Tonight they will have bean stew, bread, and tea.
They are fed U.S. rations. At first we tried feeding them the
corresponding German rations, but they didn't thrive. . . .
No, the prisoners have no knives or forks. They eat with a
spoon which is taken away from them immediately after each
meal.'

'Thank you, Colonel Andrus.'

The colonel smiled his timid smile.

Nuremberg, November 20

Coming in from the raw air of a gray day, the courtroom
seems warm, luxurious, radiant with silky white light. The
prisoners are already there, sitting in two rows under a rank
of young freshfaced American guards in white helmetcasings.
The guards stand stiff with the serious faces of a highschool
basketball team waiting to be photographed.

There, crumpled and worn by defeat, are the faces that glared for years from the frontpages of the world. There's Goering in a pearlgray doublebreasted uniform with brass buttons and the weazening, leaky-balloon look of a fat man who has lost a great deal of weight. Hess's putty face has fallen away till it's nothing but a pinched nose and hollow eyes. Ribbentrop, in dark glasses, has the uneasy trapped expression of a defaulting bank cashier. Streicher's a horrible cartoon of a foxy grandpa. Funk is a little round man with pendulous greyhound jowls and frightened dog's eyes. Schacht glares like an angry walrus. The military men sit up straight and quiet. Except for Hess, who slumps as if in a coma, the accused have an easy expectant look as if they had come to see the play rather than to act in it. Goering is very much the master of ceremonies. He looks around with appreciative interest at every detail of the courtroom. Sometimes his face wears the naughty-boy expression of a repentant drunkard. He is determined to be himself. He bows to an American lady he knows in the press seats. It's a spoiled, genial, outgoing, shrewdly selfsatisfied kind of a face, an actor's face. Not without charm. Nero must have had a face like that. While the courtroom waits for the judges, a plump American sailor with a shock of red hair and the manners of a window-dresser, moves cheerfully and carefully among the accused, checking on their earphones.

'Attenshun!' calls a tall man in a frock coat. The judges are filing in with a closed nutcracker look about their mouths. First come two Frenchmen, one with bushy Clemenceau mustaches. Then come the two Americans. The light gleams on Francis Biddle's tall forehead above his long sanctimonious face with its thin nose. Then come two Britishers with that indescribable Hogarthian look of the Inns of Court. And last the two Russians in uniform, looking much younger than the rest.

There's not a sound in the courtroom. The two British judges bow slightly in the direction of the motley collection of German lawyers for the defense, who sit on long benches in front of the accused, some in black robes and purple hats, some in dress civilian clothes; one man wears the purple robes of a doctor of law. Lord Justice Lawrence starts to talk in a low precise casual voice.

The earphones resound hollowly. At first the voices seem to clatter and ramble from far away down some echoing prison corridor. Then they clear. The acoustics are so good in the courtroom, you only need the earphones for translation.

Sidney Alderman has started to read the indictment. An Englishman takes his place, then a Frenchman, then a Russian. All day the reading goes on. Out of the voices of the prosecutors, out of the tense out-of-breath voices of the interpreters, a refrain is built up in our ears '. . . Shooting, starvation and torture . . . tortured and killed . . . shooting, beating and hanging . . . shooting, starvation and torture . . .'

Goering shakes his head with an air of martyrdom. Streicher develops a tic in the corners of his mouth. Keitel, looking more like a buck sergeant than ever, is woodenly munching on a piece of bread. Rosenberg sits up suddenly when his name is mentioned, pulls at the neck of his blue shirt and straightens his tie. Occasionally he strips his lips off his teeth with a nervous doglike movement.

'. . . and crimes against humanity and on the high seas . . .'

Nuremberg, November 21

Justice Lawrence has overruled a defense motion that called into question the jurisdiction of the Court and has granted a recess for the defendants to consult with their lawyers before pleading. In varying tones — defiant, outraged, deprecatory — the defendants plead *nicht schultig.*

Robert Jackson steps to the microphone to open the case for the prosecution. He has a broad forehead and an expression of good humor about his mouth. He wears round spectacles. The brown hair clipped close to his round head has a look of youth. He seems completely absorbed in the day's work. He talks slowly in an even explanatory tone without betraying a trace of selfimportance in his voice.

'The privilege of opening the first trial in history for crimes against the peace of the world imposes a grave responsibility.'

The prisoners at the bar, deceived perhaps by his mild unassuming manner, listen at first quite cheerfully. Being able to hear their own voices in court when they plead seems to have bucked them up. At least they are still public characters. Goering's broad countenance has lost the peevish spoiltchild look it took on when Justice Lawrence refused to allow him to make a statement. Now he sits back listening with almost indulgent attention.

'In the prisoners' dock sit twenty broken men. Reproached by the humiliation of those they have led almost as bitterly as by the desolation of those they have attacked, their personal capacity for evil is forever past. . . .'

As the day wears on and Jackson, reasonably, dispassionately, and with magnificent clarity, unfolds the case against them, taking the evidence out of their own mouths, out of

their own written orders, a change comes over accused. They
stir uneasily in their seats. They give strange starts and shud-
ders when they hear their own words quoted out of their own
secret diaries against them. When the prosecutor reaches the
crimes against the Jews, they freeze into an agony of attention.

The voice of the German translator follows the prosecutor's
voice, a shrill vengeful echo. Through the glass partition
beside the prisoners' box you can see the taut face between
gleaming earphones of the darkhaired woman who is making
the translation. There's a look of horror on her face. Sometimes her throat seems to stiffen so that she can hardly speak
the terrible words.

They are cringing now. Frank's dark eyes seem bulging
out of his head. Rosenberg draws the stiff fingers of one hand
down his face. Schacht's countenance is drawn into deep
creases of nightmare. Streicher's head leans far over on his
shoulder as if it were about to fall off his body.

Jackson goes on quietly and rationally to describe the ac-
tions of madmen. Sometimes there is a touch of puzzlement
in his voice as if he could hardly believe the documents he is
reading from. It is the voice of a reasonable man appalled by
the crimes he has discovered. Echoing it the choked shrill
voice of the interpreter hovers over the prisoners' box like a
gadfly.

The Nazi leaders stare with twisted mouths out into the
white light of the courtroom. For the first time, perhaps,
they have seen themselves as the world sees them.

'. . .. You will say I have robbed you of your sleep . . .
These are the things that have turned the stomach of the
world . . .'

Jackson turns a page on his manuscript. As the tension

relaxes, people stir a little in the courtroom. Behind the glass windows under the ceiling you can see the screwed-up faces of the photographers. From somewhere comes the gentle whirr of a movingpicture camera. A pale young soldier, who might be a pupil in a highschool class who has stepped up to help the teacher, is rolling up the white screen on the side wall to uncover a map that shows with colored bands the progressive stages of Nazi aggression, With the calm explanatory voice of a man delivering a lecture in a history course, Jackson begins his exposition of the assault on Europe. Occasionally he points to the map.

The defendants are sitting up attentively. To look at the map is a relief. Some of their faces show something like a glow of pride at the thought of how near they came to winning. They have managed to pull their features together. Ribbentrop has taken off his glasses and is stroking his heavy eyes with the tips of his fingers. When Goering stumbles out to the latrine between two guards, it is with faltering steps as if his eyesight had suddenly grown dim, but when he comes back, walking with a jaunty selfimportant stride, there is almost a smile on his great fatty face. Only Hess is still slumped in his seat with his thin blue jowl dropped on his chest, paying no attention to anything.

Austria, Czechoslovakia, Poland, the history of the early years of the war unfolds. The defendants sit up with squared shoulders during the recitation of their victories.

Gradually as the afternoon slips by, we forget to look in the ranked faces of the prisoners. Robert Jackson, his voice firmer and louder, has launched into the theory he is laying down that aggressive war is in itself a crime under the law of nations.

'To apply the sanctions of the law to those whose conduct

is found criminal by the standards I have outlined is the responsibility committed to this tribunal. It is the first court ever to undertake the difficult task of overcoming the confusion of many tongues and the conflicting concepts of just procedure among diverse systems of law so as to reach a common judgment. . . . The real complaining party at your bar is civilization. . . . It points to the weariness of flesh, the exhaustion of resources, and the destruction of what was beautiful or useful in so much of the world. . . . Civilization asks whether law is so laggard as to be utterly helpless to deal with crimes of this magnitude by criminals of this order of importance. . . .'

Robert Jackson has finished speaking. The Court rises. People move slowly and thoughtfully from their seats. I doubt if there is a man or woman in the courtroom who does not feel that great and courageous words have been spoken. We Americans get a little proudly to our feet because it was a countryman of ours who spoke them.

Nuremberg, November 22

Last night, out at the impossible schloss that the Eberhard Faber family built for themselves in Stein, out of pencil profits and vainglory, and that the occupying authorities took over to house the correspondents covering the Nuremberg trials, I was walking up the huge awkward marble staircase, looking at the red carpets, and the garish mosaics, and the chandeliers, and the statues that had an air of having been carved out of soap. I had been talking to some of the French journalists who had been so skeptical of the Anglo-American plans for the trial before it started. They were full of admiration for Robert Jackson's opening of the case for the prosecution.

They had agreed with me that he had done a magnificent job. A renewed respect for Americans had crept into their manner. In their minds Jackson's speech had re-established the American ethical viewpoint as the basis for an international law. It was a pleasure to hear intelligent Europeans speak of America in terms other than of thinly disguised ridicule and scorn. It was all very cheering. The feeling of pride in your country is one of the best feelings in the world.

I was walking up the stairs to the bar in search of a crony to have a drink of Scotch with when, on the landing in front of the library, a man I did not know addressed me in French. He was not a Frenchman, as he spoke the language with an accent. He might have been a Pole or a South Slav. He certainly came from eastern Europe. He was a mediumsized man with dark brows and a square illshaven jaw. He looked in my face, out of sharp black eyes, and asked me a question in a deferential tone of voice: 'Pardon, Monsieur, is it true that you were much impressed by the proceedings?'

From his manner of speaking I should have imagined him to be a lawyer or a college professor. He was evidently a man who had done considerable reading and considerable talking in public.

If I had a moment, he added politely, he would like to ask me some further questions. I suggested that he have a drink with me, but he refused. We walked back down the stairway, and went out-of-doors and sauntered back and forth in the clammy mist out in the flagged courtyard where the jeeps were parked. He lit a cigarette as we walked up and down. It was too dark to see his face.

'I am not saying that these men should not die,' he said. 'If it depended on me, I should order them shot tomorrow, but I just want to ask you, as a representative of a certain type of opinion in your country, if you think there is anything to be gained by piling new hypocrisy on the monstrous hypocrisies of the world. Justice is something we crave in Europe as much as we crave food, more perhaps. Is this trial helping in the re-establishment of real justice?'

I said I thought it was. Naturally I admitted we didn't come into court with entirely clean hands. No nation could. But if it were possible to establish the legal principle that aggressive war is a crime, wouldn't it arm and implement the principles of the United Nations?

'You mean that every war should be followed by a bloody proscription, not only of the leaders of the losing side, but of their helpless followers. If you establish the principle that the Nazi organizations are criminal in themselves, will you condemn every member of them to death?'

I tried to tell him that fortunately we Anglo-Saxons were not a logical people. I admitted that it was hard to tell where our justice ended and our frameups began. I did insist that sometimes by our great state frameups we established valuable historical precedents. Charles Stuart did not get a fair trial, but his execution established the principle of royal responsibility in England.

We took a couple of turns in silence. Suddenly he asked me sharply:

'Pardon me if I inquire what crimes against humanity the Nazi leaders are accused of that the Allied leaders have not committed or condoned. What did the Nazis do in effect as cruel as your wholesale bombings of civilian centers?'

'They started it, didn't they?'

'Justice, Monsieur, deals with the facts. The slaughter in the German cities was much greater than in England. How can you justify the massacre of the helpless refugees in Dres-

den? Let us turn for a moment to the betrayal of peaceful
states. What have the Nazis done that compares with your
handing-over of Poland, your own ally, into the hands of the
darkest totalitarian tyranny in history? I need not mention
Estonia, Latvia, Lithuania. Perhaps you have not visited
Jugoslavia?'

He paused, but he started talking again before I could find
an answer.

'Crimes against humanity,' he said bitterly . . . 'Isn't it a
crime against humanity to allow fifteen million people to be
driven out of their homes merely because they are accused of
being Germans? In Austria you are doing it yourselves. Why
do you Americans feel this desire for vengeance? I can understand it in the Russians who suffered fearful injuries, but your
cities were not laid waste, your wives and children were not
starved and murdered. Monsieur, do not misunderstand me; I
hate the crimes of the Nazis, but what I fear is that with your
plausible oratory you are putting the seal of respectability on
crimes more hideous than those these men committed. How
would it be if it turned out that out of these dreadful men you
were making martyrs instead of condemned criminals? In a
civilized community, the fact that a man tries to burn your
house down does not justify you in burning his. Can you be
sure that if you legalize these methods of vengeance on the
vanquished in Europe, they will not cross over the ocean to
America? Instead of establishing the rule of the law in Europe, isn't everything you are doing helping to make certain
the rule of violence?'

'That's not our intention . . . I am sure that is not Justice
Jackson's intention,' I stammered.

'The Nazis did not intend to bring ruin on Germany . . .
you must pardon me, Monsieur. Intentions aren't enough.'

I could not answer him. I said goodnight, and went back into the schloss and went gloomily to bed.

Nuremberg, Bavaria, November 23, 1945

4

Retreat from Europe

Sleeper from Berlin

THE TRAIN of scaling Mitropa sleepers stood dingy among the pine trees at the suburban station, the tired old engine sending up an occasional cottony blob of steam into the cold slate sky of an afternoon of whistling east wind. It turned out that we had arrived an hour too soon. Of course, Public Relations hadn't managed to reserve berths. Our names weren't on any of the passenger lists. Don't worry, he'd get us on, the sleepyeyed sergeant drawled soothingly. Meanwhile, we had to wait while colonels and majors and captains filed by into the sleepers. At traintime it transpired that there were some extra berths. I lost the first one on the flip of a coin to a lieutenant. The next one turned out to be occupied by three Wacs. The third one stuck.

The man who had the other berth in the compartment was an American college professor who had been in Germany several months on a mission. He was a large grayhaired man with a large nose set in a large tired wrinkled face and a confiding manner. Immediately we started talking about the Russians. In Berlin there is little else to talk about. Wherever you go the Russians are the positive force. What did I think, he asked me, about the attitude of our people in Berlin toward the Russians? I said it was puzzling.

'Puzzling!' he said. 'It's stark raving crazy.'

'We ought to get to know a little more about the kind of people we are dealing with,' said the redhaired captain who was standing in the vestibule. We invited him in and he sat on the edge of the lower berth with his hands on his knees.

'If the Russians were a choir of angels,' said the professor, 'it wouldn't be safe to make the concessions we make. Of course in fairness to the men we have in charge for us, we have to admit that they inherited from the Big Three an unworkable proposition.'

He added that he thought it had been pretty well proved to everybody's satisfaction that appeasement was a dangerous business. He could understand how Americans should lose interest in Europe and want to go home, but he couldn't understand how a whole nation could take on the psychology of the victim so quickly. . . . We were collectively just like Chamberlain with his umbrella: 'Peace in our time.'

What did he suppose the Russians thought of us? I asked him.

He said he had an idea. He spoke German, he explained, pretty fluently. Talking to Germans who were impregnated with Russian ideas he had discovered that the Communists thought of us in the same terms the Nazis did. That was one of the things that made it so easy for ex-Nazis and Communists to work together. They spoke of Americans as barbarous children. They admitted that we had been able to build up an effective industrial organization and that our industrial organization had won the war for us. But now we were done, they said. War production had been American capitalism's last great effort. Our way of life and our prattle about liberty were obsolete hypocrisies, the reflection of an age that was past. Capitalism would split on its own contradictions. As a nation we were already dead and didn't know it.

'Well, they seem to be a wee mite barbarous themselves, according to our way of thinking,' said the redhaired captain. 'Some of our boys act pretty tough, but if it came to a contest in barbarism, the Russians would win hands down.'

'They don't mean what you mean,' said the professor. 'They mean that we are behind the times . . . still living in the nineteenth century. That we don't understand the world of manipulated political power. . . . They think we have no notion but profits. . . . Money profits as the aim of life seem childish to men brought up in a system where direct power over the life and death of other men is the stakes. . . . Social engineering. That's much stronger meat.'

The train was moving slowly through Potsdam. We crossed a canal choked with a tangle of broken bridges. Along the gray horizon moved long mansarded buildings pitted with shellholes, eighteenth-century façades torn and scaled like discarded stage scenery, smashed cupolas and belfries, pushed in pediments, snapped-off chimneypots at the gable ends of shattered slate roofs.

'What's happened to San Souci?' I asked the professor.

'I don't know,' he answered. 'Some people say the Russians are taking it down and moving it stone by stone into the Soviet Union. . . . That's the trouble with censorship. Beyond the curtain there's only rumor, most of it ugly. . . . I did get into the Russian zone back of Potsdam. A colleague had asked me to find out what had happened to a brother of his and his family. I found out all right. With a couple of other men I got hold of a jeep. We took along some cigarettes.

Whenever we met a Russian sentry, I gave him a pack of cigarettes and he let us by. We found the address. It was in a small semisuburban town. The wife told us the story. When the Russians came she was in her house with her sister and her husband. She wanted to take blankets and hide in the woods. He said what was the use, you could only die once. A group of drunken soldiers broke in. They raped the wife and her sister and made the husband stand on a chair and watch it. Then they shot him in the head.'

The train was passing slowly through a railroad station crowded with Russian soldiers in long greatcoats. Their massed faces passed by the window, a pale blur in the dusk. They were watching the American train go past. There was every type of face, but not a smile.

'Aw, hell,' said the captain. 'I can't make 'em out.' He moved out into the vestibule again.

'They aren't so different from other people,' said the professor in his quiet throaty voice as the station buildings gave place to wide plains sowed in wheat, fading off into the evening murk. 'Of course not,' he went on in a louder voice as if answering a question in his own mind. 'Except for their tremendous indoctrination. . . . After all, we know what the Nazis could do to the German mind in twelve years. The Communists have had a quarter of a century to work on the Slavs.' He paused. 'We should never underestimate the Russians,' he said again. We sat listening to the loudening beat of the wheels over the rails.

'They are one of the most talented peoples on earth. There's a great breadth to the Russian mind, but between them and us there stands the Kremlin and the Kremlin propaganda. . . . Hitler was right about the power of the lie.'

The train had speeded up now. Bright raindrops slanted

across the windows. It was quite dark. We made an effort to talk of other things.

After supper I lay in my berth trying to piece together my few days in Berlin. Berlin had left me with a feeling of nightmare that was hard to define. The drive up from Frankfurt had been fun. The car of the correspondent who had given me a lift had broken down in the little half-timbered town of Northeim on the edge of the Hartz Mountains. We had been put up at the British Military Government hostel by the Town Major, a redfaced and sardonic Scot somewhat gone in liquor, and had taken our meals in a pub across the street run by an American railroad detachment. The sergeant was cheerful and friendly. He came from New Jersey. He seemed to have an endless supply of beer. It was like being in a German restaurant in Newark. The local United Nations Relief representative, a Washingtonian who was on the point of resigning because he could find no good in that organization, drove us over to the British officers' club in Goettigen that evening. Both Goettigen and Northeim, though crowded with refugees, seemed more normal and better organized than towns I'd seen in the American zone. There were more stores open. There seemed to be more lights. There were even strings of sausages hanging in the windows of the delicatessens.

At the officers' club we met a group of bright young Britishers. One young man obviously knew Russian well and had daily contest with the Russian delegation on exchange of populations. Goettigen was one of the spots where Germans coming west into the British zone were exchanged on a count-of-heads basis for Germans traveling east into the Russian zone. The exchange was working fairly well, but the real mobs crossed through the woods, taking a chance on being potted by a sentry. That was what the Germans called the green frontier. We talked about how Germany had become a fluid mass of homeless people, displaced Germans, Poles, Balts, Ukrainians, Serbs, Russian deserters, members of Vlassov's army that had fought on the side of Hitler, even French and Belgians who for some reason didn't want to go home. The authorities in the various zones could not really keep track of them. Shoals of people appeared and disappeared in one place and another as mysteriously as herring in the North Sea.

'You ought to meet my Sergeant Pavlov,' he'd said. 'He's here looking for what the Russians call war criminals. Most of them are merely political opponents of the régime. We let him have a few when he can prove his case, but he's greedy. He's particularly savage after the Estonians and Latvians. At the sight of a Baltic intellectual his teeth chatter like a birddog's. You know the way their teeth chatter when you show them a chicken they can't get at. "No, Pavlov, you can't have that one," we say.'

Our British friends were bright, they were wellinformed, they were the nicest kind of young college men, but after they'd had a few drinks they couldn't disguise the scorn they felt toward us as Americans. They were our hosts and they were making a real effort to be polite and friendly, but when the Scotch mounted in their heads their feelings began to get the better of them. It was quite different from the heavy-handed but basically goodnatured banter that went on whenever the Americans and Australians came together in the Pacific. They couldn't help thinking of us as the usurpers of the Empire that was their birthright. This evening their remarks began to get so personally disagreeable it was a relief to break away from them and to drive back through the icy fog to Northeim.

The next day, when I hitchhiked on British lorries to Berlin, the attitude of the drivers and noncoms toward me as an American was surprisingly different from that of the officers. They were friendly and hospitable and, though the great barrier of British reticence kept them from saying much about it, seemed full of not at all hostile curiosity about the United States and about American ways. They seemed more like Australians.

Aboard the first truck that took me to Brunswick rode two young Danish soldiers. After the war-embittered Europeans I had been seeing, they seemed like creatures off another planet. They were tall and wellfed and goodlooking instead of being ratfaced and puny. They carried immense ham sandwiches with them which they shared with all and sundry. They seemed to have very little bitterness towards even the Germans. In somewhat insufficient English they told me about the struggles of the resistance in Denmark, the blowing-up of war plants, the fury of the German Gestapo when they couldn't get information. The younger Dane showed me his hands. He'd been arrested on account of an explosion. Gestapo agents had torn out one of his fingernails trying to get him to tell on his friends. The nail was just beginning to grow back. He made very little of it. He shrugged his shoulders, smiling, and hurriedly pulled his mitten back on when I made grimaces of sympathy.

At Brunswick I got aboard a three-tonner loaded with materials going up for the Royal Flying Corps. The driver, a lanky young man who spoke some kind of broad North of England dialect, was a sergeant. A pale young naval warrant officer sat on the seat beside him. They cheerfully made room for me between them. As we neared the Russian zone, they took on the attitude of African explorers going into the terri-

tory of an unfriendly but not too dangerous tribe. To be on
the safe side they got the rifle out of its case and looked to see
if there was a clip in the automatic pistol.

'Can't never tell what these Russians'll do. . . . We 'ave
orders never to make the trip after dark. If a lorry breaks
down, we are to remain with it and defend it. They know our
ETA in Berlin and if we don't turn up, they send after us.
They never let anybody spend a night in the road any more.'

'What would the trouble be?'

'Roving bands, deserters. Either they have very little discipline or else they don't want us to be too comfy on the road
into Berlin.'

It was dark when we reached Berlin. My friends left me at
British Headquarters. Everybody in the offices had disappeared for the night except for a lady major who had been left
in charge of transportation. She had just arrived from England. She was very nice and quite pretty, but she didn't have
an idea in the world as to how I could get out to the American
press camp. Her replacement should be there. She really
wasn't on duty any more. She was very sorry she couldn't
order me a car because she wasn't on duty. Finally I set off
with a pinkfaced English schoolboy in an officer's uniform
who was going out for the evening at one of the American
clubs. His German driver had said he could find my address
for me. 'I suppose it's very wrong of me,' the boy said as we
drove out along a wide dimlylit street bordered by stumps of
houses and great oblong piles of salvaged building stone, 'but
I'm having a very good time here. I find Berlin just topping.'

Zehlendorf, where I woke up next morning in a cot in a
chilly room that had the skin of somebody's pet shepherd dog
on the floor as a *déscente de lit* and very little other furniture,
was a dreary suburb of newish rich men's houses that weirdly

resembled Scarsdale. About every fifth house had been bombed out. The others were in various stages of war-weary disrepair. Mines or possibly unexploded bombs were being blown up somewhere in the vicinity because every little while a dull explosion shook the raw air and sent the last autumn leaves on the beeches spinning down onto the ice of the pond back of the house. I remembered how glumly I had roamed around the suburban streets that morning, meeting bundled-up Germans bringing home their bunches of sticks and splintered laths for firewood, and wondering how I could ever get any notion of what was going on in that immense centerless pile of ruins that stretched for so many miles in every direction.

Remembering Berlin, I lay in the berth on the Frankfurt train that was joggling steadily, thank God, away from it, listening to the rumblebump of the square wheels of the decrepit Mitropa sleepingcar. The ruin of the city was so immense it took on the grandeur of a natural phenomenon like the Garden of the Gods or the Painted Desert . . . you drove in past the shattered university and the heaps that had been Friedrichstrasse and the empty spaces where a little of the shell of the Adlon still stood. The Brandenburg Gate was oddly intact. Through it you looked out over the waste, punctuated by a few stumps of trees and a few statues, that used to be the Tiergarten. At the further end of the Tiergarten were crowds of furtive people with bundles under their arms scattered in groups over a wide area that looked like an American city dump. That was the black market. Walking among them I couldn't help thinking of the black markets in Moscow in the old days. Here were the same harassed faces, the same satchels and briefcases stuffed with the miserable débris of a lost way of life. People kept looking over their shoulders as they went about their bargaining and bartering with the same expression of timid puzzlement I used to see in Moscow. They had been brought up to consider trade an honorable and respected way of life. Suddenly it had become illegal and underground. A year ago they were respectable German burghers. Today they were criminals.

Further on into the city, across the one intact bridge over the Spee, I remembered a residential quarter of great ugly square houses tolerably intact where, dim and washed-out, flags fluttered from every window. At the time of the Allied entry, the Russians had ordered the people to put out flags. They hadn't been able to buy flags, so, as the orders of the Russians tended to be obeyed, women sat up all night sewing them together out of odds and ends of cloth. Each housewife had assembled red, white, and blue strips, according to her particular notion of some national flag. There were surprisingly few hammers and sickles on red, but weird renditions of the Union Jack and the Stars and Stripes were everywhere. The Russians hadn't said what flags, they had just said flags.

Further on workmen with cables were pulling down broken brick walls. Everywhere among the ruins you passed groups of German women, old women, young women, women who looked as if they were accustomed to labor and women who had never wielded any tool heavier than a needle in their lives, carrying buckets full of bricks out of the crumbling heaps. Others stood at the brickpiles in the street rubbing the bricks together to clean them. They were frowsty and their faces gray with dust and the skin under their eyes was blue with fatigue. The weather was raw and cold with that drizzling mixture of sleet and rain that is a specialty of Berlin. The women had bundled themselves up with all the clothes they had to keep warm. Long strings of them passing the heavy buckets from hand to hand toiled over the rubbish heaps.

'Oh, they like to do it,' one young American had assured me cheerfully. 'If they do heavy labor they get a heavy labor card . . . more food . . . greedy bitches.'

These realities, I was thinking, as I lay squirming in the lumpy berth, were all very far away when you dined with American officials in comfortable wellheated requisitioned houses, or went with them to visit their Russian opposite numbers in handsome offices in the imperial old building the Quadripartite Council had taken over in Schoenberg. Talking to the officials, you got the feeling that there was reason and sense to everything that was being done. Foundations were being laid, problems examined, reports prepared. The men living in that official dreamworld of international conferences, diplomatic secrets, commitments among bigshots, I was telling myself, had no more idea than their equivalents years ago at Versailles that what they were probably laying the foundations for with so much selfimportance was the slaughter of their own children. No matter what it is, a man has to justify his job to himself.

It wasn't that we didn't have some firstrate men representing us. . . . General Lucius D. Clay, with his aquiline nose and bright brown eyes, had sat at his polished desk talking easily and succinctly in his soft Deep South voice about how we were going to start up democracy in our zone in Germany. Democracy didn't mean anything, he had said, unless it started from the lowest level in the village and county. We were starting from scratch. Germany had never known elections for local officials. In his opinion that was why the Weimar Republic failed. He had added with a smile that we weren't necessarily trying to produce an efficient Germany, we were trying to produce a democratic Germany. . . . The trouble was — he had looked down with a thoughtful smile into the cuffs of his wellpressed khaki trousers — that we didn't know what kind of Germany we were going to have to work with, four separate Germanies or a unified Germany. That decision couldn't seem to get past the Council. It must be said, he had added, as they all did, that there was the greatest personal cordiality between the delegates in the Quadripartite Council. But in spite of these splendid personal relations, they had been marking time.

'Marking time.' General Robertson, Lucius Clay's opposite number for the British, had used the same expression at his press conference. Robertson was a youngish general, very Sandhurst, with a sandy mustache and reddish tortoiseshell spectacles. He talked well, too, though perhaps a little more cautiously than our General Clay. The difficulties in the Control Council, he explained, were not yet removed, though the Russians showed a certain measure of satisfaction on the subject of deliveries of industrial plants in advance of reparations. We must remember, he added, almost slyly, that international negotiations did not go well all the time. They went in waves, at times well and favorably, and at other times they rolled backwards. . . . Of course, he had hastened to add, personal relationships between the Big Four had been happier and more intimate than ever before.

I had been going around asking everybody I met in Berlin how they got along with the Russians. People were very much on the defensive in their answers. Some dreaded them like cholera and some insisted stubbornly on their attitude that the Russians were just like anybody. A newspaperman tended to want to keep his Russian acquaintances, if he had any, to himself. I got to know a young Berliner who had lived in Connecticut and served in the U.S. Army. He said he met the Russians in nightclubs. The Russian officers seemed to feel that the only place it was safe for them to be seen exchanging a few words with foreigners was a nightclub. So one snowy night we'd gone rumbling around town in a command car looking for the Femina. It took us so long to find it that we got there just at nine-thirty closing time. When we drove up a German in a belted raincoat with his felt hat pulled down over his face came out of the shadows and offered us a hundred marks — that was ten dollars — for a pack of American cigarettes. As we'd been warned about the immense cost of drinks at the Femina, one of the officers in the car sold a pack. 'Look at the girls,' he whispered as we were climbing out of the car. 'They consider four cigarettes good pay for all night. . . . A can of corned beef means true love.'

A blast of stale dank air hit us in the face as we walked in up broad stairs covered by a red carpet grimed with dirt. Halfway up the stairs a pretty goldenhaired German girl, quite drunk, teetered and snatched at every uniform that passed. Inside, the place looked like any nightclub anywhere, only indescribably warworn. As the electric light had failed, the tables were lit by candles stuck on plates. The musicians were packing up their instruments. There were a few slightly drunk American officers, a sprinkling of grimfaced Russians, and a lot of welldressed German women and moderately welldressed men. Nobody was laughing. Except for the Americans who were obviously sightseers there was a look of business on every face. Not woman business. Under every arm were the dreary satchels and briefcases I'd seen in the Tiergarten. A man sidled up to us, whispering, 'Cigarettes?' From the other side a Russian approached saying, 'Uhr . . . Uhr.'

'Anybody want to sell a watch?' someone whispered.

None of us wanted to sell anything or buy anything. We didn't even want to try an expensive ersatz drink. The place was too cold and dreary. There was a furtive, awkward, embarrassed look on every face as chilling as the icy damp of the rooms. This was a place where trade was the vice, not liquor or cardgames or sex. We walked out with a feeling of disgust and pity stiffening our throats and drove out to the American Press Club, where there were comfortable chairs and it was warm and people still looked like human beings.

As I lay in that jiggling berth in the military train out of Berlin, I was trying to define the feeling of nightmare I was carrying away with me. Berlin was not just one more beaten-up city. There, that point in a ruined people's misery had been reached where the victims were degraded beneath the reach of human sympathy. After that point no amount of suffering affects the spectator who is out of it. Maybe it was such a mechanism that enabled the Germans to look with complacency on the extermination of their Jewish neighbors, and that enabled the Russian Communists to see without tears the results on the lives of other men of the Kremlin's various feats of social engineering, and that today enables perfectly decent Americans, brought up in the habits of democracy, to remain indifferent to the plight of the tortured peoples of eastern Europe. Once war has broken the fabric of human society, a chain reaction seems to set in which keeps on after the fighting has stopped tearing down the decencies and the inhibitions that hold together the framework of civilization.

In Berlin I had thought of these things whenever I passed the Stettiner Station. That was the station where displaced Germans and prisoners of war arrived from the Russian zone. I never actually saw one of those trains come in, but always around the outskirts of that station and huddled under its drafty scorched shell was a crowd of dazedlooking people with bundles and knapsacks, men, women, and children, with staring frightened eyes. The skin hung on their bones like candledrippings. There was something weird and wraithlike about their shambling gait, their restless, purposeless shuffling, about the Gothic length of their faces, that brought to my mind the look our starved and imprisoned Americans had in the concentration camp at Santo Tomas when our troops first entered Manila.

Praying to whatever forces of good there are in the world that no fate like the Germans' would ever come to the people of my country, I finally fell asleep.

Waiting for breakfast in the morning in the corridor of the diner, I fell to talking to the redheaded captain again. He was from San Francisco. He had practiced law there. He was now in Military Government and he was fed up to the ears.

'I get a feeling,' he said in a low bitter voice, 'that there is a sort of competition among our politicians as to who shall sell the United States further down the river. If the American people want to commit suicide, I suppose in a democratic country it's the politician's business to tie the noose for us so that we can slip it comfortably around our necks. . . . It's all this apologizing that makes me sick. With all our faults we have invented a social system by which the majority of men for the first time in human history get a break, and instead of being cocky about it we apologize about it. . . . We built up the greatest army in the world and won the war with it, and now we're letting everything go to pieces because we don't know what to do next. . . . We apologized to the French for saving their country and we apologize to the British and we apologize to the Russians. . . . First thing you know we'll be apologizing to the Germans for licking them. . . . And they all hate our guts and it damn well serves us right.'

Paris Promenade

Paris, cold and hungry and diminished in spirit, is still the capital if only of the rump of Europe. There is still the Eiffel Tower and the bridges across the Seine and the sky above the Place de la Concorde. The weatherbeaten old Institut de France is still the most beautiful building in the world. The autumn salon is open, the great old pictures are on show at the Louvre. Men still sit out in the ruddy metropolitan sunlight on the terrace of the Café de la Paix. Pigalle rages and the slippery vicious streets that climb Montmartre. Welldressed crowds still turn out on the Champs Elysées these fine winter afternoons. The women wear full dresses and great spiraled turbans and towering stiff hats. Their hair is piled in blond or black billows on their heads like the topsails of a fullrigged ship. They have no stockings, and their legs are chapped from the cold, but they still walk with elegance on the solid wooden soles they have to wear instead of leather. You see girls riding bicycles balancing a superstructure of perfectly arranged curls on their heads. The wooden soles look stylish. The girls sit attractively on their bicycles.

A man of fifty and a man of twenty-five, both wearing the same khaki, are walking down the quai Voltaire past the bookstalls. They walk out onto the bridge in front of the Institut to look at the delicately poised dome and the jade-green river and the sky full of fluffy clouds touched with rose and faint citrus colors arching over the great slate roofs of the Louvre. The younger man has a sharp brown face behind his shellrimmed glasses. He is a reporter for *The Stars and Stripes*.

He is trying to get an interview out of the older man. They stand leaning against the rail.

'Now what would you say is the difference, sir, between Europe after World War One and Europe after World War Two?'

'Well, for one thing World War One cut a path of devastation across the continent, but it didn't destroy the whole fabric of society. . . . I'd say that the moral and social destruction just about matched the physical destruction.'

'We've made some progress in the art of destruction. This time we really did a job,' said the younger man, briskly bringing out his notebook. 'What other differences do you note, sir?'

'The level of European civilization sank after the first war. This time it has sunk very much more. After World War One we felt hopeful about the human race. The Russian Revolution seemed to open great vistas for the workingclass, the possibility of a society without exploitation of man by man. Everything seemed easy in those days.'

'The Soviet Union's certainly been a success. You wouldn't deny that, would you, sir?'

'I certainly would. It's produced a different social setup, but instead of wage slavery you've got real slavery to the State. We used to hope the revolution would produce more freedom and more selfgovernment instead of less. The untrammeled power of the ruling class in the Soviet Union makes you wonder whether the profit motive is as bad as it has been painted.'

'A man who's out of a job hasn't got much of a profit motive, has he, sir?'

'He's a hell of a lot freer on relief in the United States than he is with a job in the Soviet Union, and somewhat better fed.'

'Food isn't the only thing in life . . . there's human dignity . . . security . . . sometimes I think instead of taking a newspaper job over here, I ought to go home and join the picketline.'

'What do you think they'd do to you if you went on the picketline in the Soviet Union?'

'The workers don't need to strike in the Soviet Union. They own the means of production.'

'You'd better go and see for yourself how much of the means of production they own,' says the older man wearily.

'Now,' insists the young man, poising his pencil over his notebook, 'tell me a little about the Peace of Versailles.'

'At the time it seemed to us cruel and unworkable. But looking back on it, it seems like the New Jerusalem compared with what's going on now. There was some effort to secure democratic liberties and selfdetermination of peoples.'

'The Soviet Union is assuring the democratic liberties of the countries in the east of Europe.'

'Young man, you're talking doubletalk and you know it.'

He smiles condescendingly. In the brown eyes behind the glasses the older man can see the young man's mind closing up like a clam.

'In a word, sir,' he insists politely, 'what would you say were the results of the Peace of Versailles?'

'Fascism.'

'And what do you think the results of this present peace will be?'

'Fascism multiplied by Fascism, I suppose.'

'Then aren't the Russians right in insisting that we stamp out Fascism in Europe?'

'The only cure for Fascism is liberty. The Englishspeaking peoples at least have developed a system that assures the indi-

vidual a certain amount of liberty and that carries within it
the machinery for peaceable adaptation to change. . . . It's
one of the ironies of history that you young fellows should be
losing faith in it just at the moment when the world needs it
most.'

'Don't forget, sir, that we were products of the Depression.
How can you have faith in Congress and the lynching politicians and the greedy monopoly of big business? Better make a
clean sweep like the Russians did.'

'The trouble is we would find out as the Russians did that
we had made a clean sweep of civilization, too. There are no
short cuts to democracy. You've just got to go home and
work it out little by little.'

'Have you ever thought, sir, what you'd think of yourself?
I mean what your old self that was in Paris while they were
making the Peace of Versailles would think of your new self
that is here writing for the monopoly interests?'

'You mean I'd think I was an old reactionary. . . . No, I
don't think so . . . I have changed and so have the times.
After all, we've got the sample of Communism to look at. In
those days the Soviet Union was a dream. Now it's a reality.'

'They don't pretend to have Communism yet. The standard
of life there will improve as the effects of the war wear off.'

'How do you know it will? . . . I think you young fellows
are the reactionaries. . . . You can't build a free society from
the Kremlin down. It's got to come up from selfgovernment.
The individual man has got to be strong enough socially and
economically to stand on his own hindlegs and to talk back
to his Government if he has to. No man has ever lived who
can be trusted with absolute power.'

'This talk about freedom is mostly eyewash put out by the
National Association of Manufacturers. Security is what

people really want,' says the younger man, biting off his words.

'It's only in a free society that life is secure. I don't understand why you boys won't see that. . . . It seems so axiomatic.'

The dusk is closing in around them. The Institut is a blue silhouette against the west. The rare streetlights along the river are opening like crocuses. It's chilly. Both of them have begun to shiver.

'Better move along, I guess. . . . Thank you very much, sir,' the young man says. They start to walk briskly across the bridge.

'We are not making much headway toward reconciling two points of view, are we?' says the older man.

'We're not making much headway, sir, period.'

Leave Train for Home

Drunk and dusty and sweating and holloweyed and sleepless, the soldiers shuffle bowed under heavy barracksbags down the dimlylit platform onto the train. A slow dense stream of khaki bodies fills the platform. The train is made up of incredibly ancient French coaches. The cushions are gone from some of the seats. The glass in the windows has been broken and replaced by plyboard. The doors are boarded up. There are no lights. The men and their gear are packed tight into the compartments. They hunch on their bags in the corridor. We huddle in the dark with our knees grinding into the knees of the men opposite. There are elbows in our ribs, heads on our shoulders. The train starts to move with an almost imperceptible jiggling motion and is drawn out of the station into the foggy night. It is only when a man strikes a match to light a cigarette that you can see his face. The faces are young and flushed under the grime. The voices are hoarse from long trainrides and too many drinks and too many cigarettes and too many women.

'Christ, I've never had so much of it in my life,' says a voice out of the dark.

'I didn't know there was so much of it in the world,' answers another.

'You ought to been in Germany, boy, you just lift your finger and they spread their legs.'

'There was plenty in North Africa, but I didn't know what the word meant till I got to Italy. It was all right in the South of France, but when I got to Germany I got so much of it, I about blew my top. Now I'm going home. I got a wife and two kids at home.'

'How old are you, bud?' drawls a voice in a maturer tone.

'Nineteen.'

'At nineteen there's no limit. A man sure can go to town at nineteen. Damn! You got busy early, bud. . . . I'm twenty-seven . . . I'm sick of all this stuff. I'm going home and settle down. I don't want no more women.'

'Back home it's different.'

'The English girls are crazy for it.'

'Nothing to those fräuleins.'

'The French girls are all right, but it costs you money in France. The French are too damned stingy.'

'Me and my bud comin' up through France we had plenty. Didn't cost us no money either. We was always after it. He got his, poor kid. Up in them mountains. Vosges. We were comin' up through an orchard. There was fruit on the trees. God, we were thirsty. We all got sick eatin' that fruit. There was some ripe pears on a table in front of a kinder little house.

I stopped a second to pick up a ripe pear and he went on ahead. We were cleanin' out those trees at the top of the hill. He was just a little way ahead. Two krauts with a burp gun were hidin' behind a big ole apple tree an' they gave it to him. Must have been the last shot fired that day. I was scared up in that orchard. He had it right there. God, I felt bad . . . I feel bad right now. He was a swell kid.'

The voices were quiet.

'Don't talk to me about no burp guns,' said somebody savagely from a corner.

The train rumbled. Crowded together into the clattering dark they went on talking until one by one the voices grew slow with sleep and stopped.

New York, December 15, 1945

5

Two Wrongs Don't . . .

THE SHIP is bucking into the teeth of a heavy westerly gale. Gusts of snowy wind screech in the steel ladders that lead to the bridge. After every lunge of the bow into the toppling spumestreaked seas pillars of spray move across the wet flight-deck and rattle against the plates of the superstructure. The wind indicator on the bridge reads fifty-five knots. Below on the hangar deck there's a smell of stuffy bodies and sour wool and vomit. All the central part of the great long hollow space like a floating garage is filled with a structure of bunks and baggageracks five tiers high. Soldiers with sallow faces and rumpled hair crawl in and out of it like wasps in a wasps' nest. Through a single door open onto a sponson continually swashed with seawater to leeward, a group of us are looking out at the marbled green and gray slopes of ocean that tower over our heads and break and seethe and drop away. As we look, black fins cut the waves and a school of porpoises flashes out into the light. They arch and skid down the inclines of spinning water and are gone.

Further aft grouped round the small rubbertired tractors that tow the planes, under a movie screen that hangs against a complicated tangle of gear and whitepainted steampipes, a few soldiers are trying to keep their footing in the line waiting for mess. Through the muffled sounds of wind and waves and the heavy regular breathing of the engines and the hubbub of voices comes the shrill piping of the boatswain's whistle and a voice over the public address system: 'All men whose cards read that they should eat at eleven hundred fall into the designated chowlines.'

Down in our cabin in the officers' country belowdecks there's a crowd of men talking. The bulkheads creak from the pitching and straining of the ship. Men have wedged themselves in corners to hold themselves steady against the punishing motion. There's a man in every chair. There is a man in every bunk. The air is dense with cigarette smoke and with the allpervading staleness of packed troops.

'Don't think I'm sticking up for the Germans,' the lanky young captain in the upper berth says for the third time. 'But . . .'

'To hell with the Germans,' interrupts the broadshouldered dark lieutenant who is balancing himself in the doorway. 'It's what our boys have been doing that worries me.'

The lieutenant who's speaking comes from the packinghouse district of Chicago's South Side. He served nineteen years as a Regular Army sergeant. His old man runs a tavern. He's led a rough-and-tumble life. He's made five landings on European beaches, and won his commission in the field. He hasn't seen his wife and children in three years. He has a slow seasoned well-pondered way of saying things. He has been talking about the melting morale of the Army, the sale of Army property, gasoline leaking away into the black market even while the fighting was going on, the way we kick around the civilians, the looting . . . 'If I didn't want to stay on in the Army, I could tell some tales. By God, I could write a book.'

'Lust, liquor, and loot are the soldier's pay,' interrupts a redfaced major in a challenging tone.

'I can't help it,' drawls the lieutenant, 'two wrongs don't . . .'

'Aw, you said that before,' interrupts the captain and lets himself sink back into his pillow again. 'At every goddam bullsession on this ship, I hear the same thing.'

'Well, it's true. It's time we got wise to ourselves. We're making a mess of this business. It's all right to arrest the Nazis we've got something criminal on, but why can't we try to help out the decent people more? We ought to be helping all Europe — I don't mean just Germany — get on its feet. The time may come when we'll need some friends in this world.'

A lighthaired young man in a navy gray shirt who has just come off watch is so in earnest when he speaks, he almost pitches forward out of his chair.

'I'd like to see us show the cockeyed world,' he says with a blue glare of enthusiasm in his eyes. 'If we do the right thing it will be more profitable in the long run, too. Look here . . . The only way the United States can remain prosperous and keep up a high standard of living is by full employment and full production. Isn't that true? Well, the only way we can do that after we've saturated the domestic market is to play for foreign markets. To keep going we've got to have a high standard of life in the rest of the world. We have got to have democracy and high wages in the rest of the world. Instead of giving in to the Russians at every step, we ought to compete with the Russians. I don't mean fight 'em, I mean do our kind of social engineering. We've got more to give the world than they have.'

'If we go easy on the krauts, it'll be just like last time,' growled the captain from his bunk. 'They'll get on their feet again and start another war.'

'If people are prosperous and happy, they won't want to fight a war. Wars and dictatorships come out of depressions, don't they?'

Everybody is quiet. Nobody seems to want to answer that one.

'I don't know about that, but one thing I do know,' says the lieutenant from Chicago slowly. 'We got to get wise to ourselves. What we are doing since the fighting stopped in Europe is wrong. Two wrongs don't make a right.'

THE END